American Diplomacy During the Second World War, 1941-1945

Second Edition

AMERICA IN CRISIS ❧

A series of books on American Diplomatic History

Editor: ROBERT A. DIVINE

American Diplomacy During the Second World War, 1941-1945

Second Edition

Gaddis Smith
Yale University

Alfred A. Knopf

New York

Second Edition
987654

Library of Congress Cataloging in Publication Data

Smith, Gaddis.
    American diplomacy during the Second World War, 1941–1945.
        Bibliography: p.
        Includes index.
        1. World War, 1939–1945 — Diplomatic history.
    2. United States — Foreign relations — 1933–1945.
    I. Title.
    D753.S54   1985   940.532   84-17103
    ISBN 0-394-34202-X

Manufactured in the United States of America

Cover Photographs: The outcome of World War II was determined by both military and diplomatic efforts. Diplomacy was shaped in large measure by the relationships between (from left) Marshal Joseph Stalin, Premier of the Soviet Union, President Franklin D. Roosevelt of the United States, and British Prime Minister Winston Churchill, here shown at the Teheran conference in November 1943. (Photo courtesy of the National Archives) The culmination of the Allied military operations was the D-Day invasion of France. During the days following the initial landing, enormous quantities of supplies and reinforcements continued to flow onto the French beaches. (Photo courtesy of the U.S. Coast Guard)

Foreword

"The United States always wins the war and loses the peace," runs a persistent popular complaint. Neither part of the statement is accurate. The United States barely escaped the War of 1812 with its territory intact, and in Korea in the 1950s the nation was forced to settle for a stalemate on the battlefield. At Paris in 1782, and again in 1898, American negotiators drove hard bargains to win notable diplomatic victories. Yet the myth persists, along with the equally erroneous American belief that we are a peaceful people. Our history is studded with conflict and violence. From the Revolution to the Cold War, Americans have been willing to fight for their interests, their beliefs, and their ambitions. The United States has gone to war for many objectives — for independence in 1775, for honor and trade in 1812, for territory in 1846, for humanity and empire in 1898, for neutral rights in 1917, and for national security in 1941. Since 1945 the nation has been engaged in the continuing Cold War with the Soviet Union.

The purpose of the series is to examine in detail critical periods relating to American involvement in foreign war, from the war with Mexico down through the Cold War. Each author has set out to recount anew the breakdown of diplomacy that led to war and the subsequent quest for peace. The emphasis is on foreign policy, and no effort is made to chronicle the military participation of the United States in these years. Instead the authors focus on the day-by-day conduct of diplomacy to explain why the nation went to war and to show how peace was restored. Each volume is a synthesis combining the research of other historians with new insights to provide a fresh interpretation of a critical period in American diplomatic history. It is hoped that this series will help dispel the illusion of national innocence and give Americans a better appreciation of their country's role in war and peace.

ROBERT A. DIVINE

Preface to the 1985 Edition

The first edition of this book was written twenty years ago. It sought to present the issues of American diplomacy during the Second World War as they were perceived at the time by President Franklin D. Roosevelt and his associates rather than as they appeared subsequently through the lens of the Cold War. The revised edition holds to this same objective, but I am now more strongly aware than I was in the 1960s of the inevitable influence of the present on every historian's view of the past.

The first edition was written at the end of the Kennedy and very beginning of the Johnson administrations, before the depth and tragedy of American involvement in the Vietnam war were evident. I shared the optimism of that time and, as a consequence, was too harsh in my judgment of Roosevelt's failures. I was insufficiently appreciative of the limits of American power and of the intractable obstacles facing even the most conscientious, competent, and well-intentioned leader. The last two decades have taught the country and this particular historian some hard lessons in that regard. Thus, the first difference between the first and present editions is a matter of tone—less stridency in condemnation, a greater effort to understand what Roosevelt sought and why he failed.

The second difference is the result of the vast amount of documentation and—even more important—the innumerable outstanding works of scholarship which have appeared since the first edition was written. I am deeply in debt to the historians who have written between 1965 and the present, just as I continue in debt to those who wrote before 1965. Without that work this book could not have been written. My debt is indicated in the footnotes.

I have not changed my basic interpretation of events. New documents and scholarship on the American side have made me more aware of disagreements within the American government with Roosevelt's approach to the Soviet Union. I have given those disagreements more attention. New scholarship has also confirmed my original attention (almost unique in the early 1960s) to areas we now call "the Third World." I have expanded that material — especially in regard to Latin America, the Middle East, Korea, and Indochina. I also have commented at greater length on American policy toward the development and use of the atomic bomb.

It is a pleasure to thank hundreds of students and colleagues with whom, over the years, I have discussed the Second World War. Lack of space prevents mentioning them all; however, let me single out John M. Blum, John Coogan, Wilton B. Fowler, Gregg Herkin, Michael H. Hunt, John D. Langer, and Martin J. Sherwin. I owe a special debt to Warren F. Kimball and Mark Lytle for their careful readings of a draft of this edition and for the many constructive suggestions which I have adopted. Above all I want to thank Robert A. Divine, general editor of this series, Katie Vignery of John Wiley & Sons, and David Follmer of Alfred A. Knopf for their gracious persistence and patience.

GADDIS SMITH

New Haven, Connecticut
September 1984

Contents

MAPS

American Diplomacy During the Second World War, 1941-1945

Second Edition

CHAPTER 1

The Nature of
Wartime Diplomacy

In the first half of the twentieth century, the human population approximately doubled, industrial production quadrupled, forms of government over most of the earth were altered, and humanity's power to kill increased a thousandfold. Chronic, dangerous instability was the result. World stability depended as never before on international cooperation, but suspicion and hostility between states were the rule. Some nations longed for peace but prepared fearfully for war. Others denied the validity of accepted norms of international behavior and gloried in the use of force.

At first the United States considered itself blessedly immune from the world's violence. In 1914 President Woodrow Wilson urged neutrality as the right course, one that would keep the nation out of war and protect its rights. Neutrality proved impossible; the United States joined the war and tipped the military balance sufficiently to bring about the defeat of Germany and the armistice of November 1918. Wilson then said that the acceptance by all nations of the ideals of self-determination, democracy, and collective security through the League of Nations was the only way to secure lasting peace. Wilson also believed that these ideals would fulfill real national interests by opening the world economy to American enterprise and preventing wasteful military expenditures.

The American people, however, rejected membership in the League, and that organization proved weak and ineffective from the beginning. Its failure to turn back Japanese aggression against China in 1931 and Italian aggression against Ethiopia in 1935 were mortal blows. Even more ominous was the rise of Adolf Hitler in Germany. By 1936—having repudiated the restrictions,

3

placed by the Treaty of Versailles in 1919, on Germany's right to have an unlimited military establishment — he was poised for conquest. In 1938 Germany annexed Austria. In September of that year the British and French, fearing themselves too weak to resist Hitler's demands, acquiesced at the Munich conference in Germany's annexation of part of Czechoslovakia (the remaining portion was gobbled up in early 1939). The Munich conference was the high point of British and French "appeasement" — a word that soon became synonymous with craven, immoral surrender to a ruthless totalitarian regime. President Franklin D. Roosevelt was an unhappy bystander in these events, restrained by an isolationist public and Congress from doing more than condemn international lawlessness. Congress, in the meanwhile, was busy passing laws designed to preserve neutrality and noninvolvement in the event of the next war, now ominously visible on the horizon.

Hitler had acquired Austria and Czechoslovakia without firing a shot. But in September he invaded Poland. Great Britain and France finally abandoned appeasement and declared war on Germany, although there was nothing they could do for Poland. Germany and the Soviet Union, in cynical collusion, divided Poland and the Baltic states. Hitler soon struck to the west, conquering Denmark, Norway, the Netherlands, and Belgium in quick succession. Italy, stabbing France in the back, joined its Nazi ally. In June 1940 the French government surrendered to Germany. Hitler, now dominating western Europe, was planning to invade Great Britain. War was also raging in Asia, where Japan, having wrested Manchuria from China in 1931–32, resumed its aggression in 1937. In September 1940 Japan joined Germany and Italy in a military alliance known as the Axis. Its purpose from the Japanese point of view was to frighten the United States into accepting Japan's domination of China and conquest of southeast Asia. From Roosevelt's point of view, the Axis alliance confirmed that Japan, Germany, and Italy were a united threat. The American government's response was to impose economic sanctions against Japan, first cutting off the export of high-octane fuel, then metals, and finally, in July 1941, all trade.

Both the American public and Congress were bitterly divided before the spectacle of unchecked aggression in Europe and Asia. Vociferous and well-organized groups argued that the United States must remain isolated from the world conflict. Equally vociferous and well-organized groups proclaimed that American security demanded the fullest possible support for the victims of aggression, and President Roosevelt agreed. He moved cautiously during 1940, lest too much boldness cost him the presidential election and put an isolationist in the White House. The Republicans, however, nominated Wendell Willkie, a foe of isolationism, with general views on foreign policy close to Roosevelt's. Willkie's nomination freed Roosevelt to give fifty destroyers to Great Britain and to receive in return American leases on a string of British bases in the Western Hemisphere.

After his victory in the 1940 presidential election, Roosevelt won increased congressional support for rearmament and aid to the countries fighting Germany and Japan. American industry turned increasingly to war production, making the United States the "arsenal of democracy." Congress put aside the neutrality laws and passed the Lend-Lease Act in March 1941. It permitted the United States to give military aid to any nation whose defense the president deemed vital to American security. Isolationists bitterly opposed lend-lease and warned that Roosevelt, in arrogating powers never contemplated in the Constitution, was dragging the country toward war. We should, they said, build a "fortress America" and let the benighted nations of Europe and Asia solve their own problems.

In June 1941 Hitler attacked the Soviet Union. Some Americans believed that the United States should stand aside and let two totalitarian nations destroy each other, but the majority supported Roosevelt's decision to extend lend-lease aid to Russia. Roosevelt claimed repeatedly that his aim was to keep the United States out of war, but by late 1941 many Americans realized that the higher aim of checking aggression might soon make war inevitable. In the autumn of 1941 the American navy and German U-boats began an undeclared war on the Atlantic sea lanes over which supplies were flowing to Britain and Russia.

Japanese leaders, in the meanwhile, concluded that American economic sanctions and general refusal during diplomatic negotiations to accept Japan's supposed right to control China left no alternative but war. Any reader of newspapers in the autumn of 1941 knew that Japan was likely to strike. But where? Against the Soviet Union? Against British and Dutch colonies in southeast Asia? American cryptographers were able to read many of Japan's secret radio and cable communications. They picked up thousands of clues that something drastic was about to happen but not enough unequivocal clues pointing to the actual target. The blow came at Pearl Harbor, on December 7, 1941. Now that the United States was at war with Japan, Germany and Italy immediately declared war on the United States. The period of equivocal undeclared war was over.[1]

Repeatedly and without success the United States had tried various unconditional approaches to peace and security: neutrality in 1914, fighting for an idealistic world vision in 1917–18, isolation in the 1930s. Now the nation sought security by the unconditional defeat of the enemy and through a determination to avoid the mistakes that had blighted the years between 1919 and 1939 and brought on World War II. In undertaking this task, Americans assumed that the enemy's existence was the principal cause of insecurity. When all nations were freed from enslavement and fear of Axis aggression, they would embrace American ideals of democracy and peaceful conduct. Win the war, and all else would be easy. Other nations — Great Britain, for example — might stray from a proper course, but a little friendly diplomatic persuasion would be sufficient to return them to the paths of righteousness.

Absolute military victory was achieved in less than four years. But at the moment of victory in 1945 American leaders were on the verge of the realization that there were no unconditional solutions and that final, complete security in the twentieth century was unattainable.

ᏨᏉ

The first diplomatic objective on the road to unconditional victory was coordination of the American, British, and Russian efforts. This was a task for the three heads of government: President Roosevelt, Prime Minister Winston S. Churchill, and Premier Josef V. Stalin. The Big Three at the summit decided grand strategy and papered over potentially disruptive disagreements. Their subordinates bargained to allocate materials, provide shipping, assign troops, arrange for control of occupied

---

[1] These events are surveyed in Robert A. Divine, *The Reluctant Belligerent: American Entry into World War II*, 2nd ed. (New York: Wiley, 1979).

areas, design postwar international organizations, and secure postwar political and economic assets. Diplomacy, instead of retiring to the sidelines until the fighting was over, became indispensable to every aspect of the war and thus to the future shape of the world. The small corps of career diplomats in the U.S. State Department was soon submerged and often pushed aside by military negotiators and the staffs of special wartime agencies dealing with military and economic aid, propaganda, intelligence gathering, civil government for liberated or occupied areas, and covert activities. President Roosevelt, at the top, presided serenely over bureaucratic chaos. He made no effort to impose order and thereby left many of his subordinates filled with frustration.[2]

In December 1941 the potential power of the United States was enormous, but the immediate outlook was disastrous. The navy was crippled by the Japanese blow at Pearl Harbor; the army was an expanding swarm of civilians without sufficient equipment, training, or experienced officers; and industry was only partially converted from peacetime production. Germany controlled western Europe and its armies were wintering deep in Russia. Who dared predict that Russia would be able to withstand the onslaught through another summer? Another German force seemed on the verge of driving the British from Egypt and taking the vital Suez Canal. At any moment Franco, in Spain, might snatch Gibraltar. Hitler could then close the Mediterranean and dominate the Middle East and North Africa while choking off the British Isles with a cordon of U-boats. The Western Hemisphere would be directly threatened. In Asia and the Pacific, there seemed no limit to Japan's wave of conquest. Half of China, the Philippines, Indochina, Burma, Malaya, the Netherlands East Indies, and scores of smaller island groups were within the Japanese grasp. Would they seize India, Australia, Siberia, Hawaii? Who could stop them? Anything was conceivable.

Fortunately, the United States was not paralyzed by immediate military peril. Leaders and people responded to an optimistic view of the nation's historical experience and to the buoy-

---

[2] Herbert Feis, *Churchill, Roosevelt, Stalin: The War They Waged and the Peace They Sought* (Princeton, N.J.: Princeton University Press, 1957), remains the classic survey of the main lines of wartime diplomacy. See also Warren F. Kimball, "Churchill and Roosevelt: The Personal Equation," *Prologue* 6 (Fall 1974): 169–182.

ant personality of the commander in chief, President Roosevelt. Americans were later to be led astray by too much optimism; but on the dark morrow of Pearl Harbor, optimism enabled them to begin planning and working for victory. Notwithstanding the pain and humiliation of retreat in the Pacific, they turned first to developing a strategy for the defeat of Germany. This priority was maintained on the sound assumption that Germany without Japan would be as strong as ever, while Japan without Germany could not long stand.

The remembered experience of the First World War exercised a profound effect on American strategic thinking. Americans had misleading and exhilarating memories. In the summer of 1918 large numbers of American troops faced the enemy for the first time. By November the war was over. Admittedly, circumstances were now radically different, but the experience of 1918, combining with a long tradition favoring concentration in force against the enemy's strongest point, led Americans to favor a direct attack as soon as possible (preferably 1942 but certainly 1943) across the English Channel against the center of German power.

The favored strategy of Great Britain, also based in large measure on experience of the First World War but also on the reality of limited manpower, was different. From the autumn of 1914 until the summer of 1918, while the United States remained neutral or in a state of preparation, Great Britain and France had seen an entire generation of young men die in the stinking trenches of the western front. For four years gains and losses were measured in yards, casualties in millions. Now, twenty-five years later, France had collapsed and Britain, having narrowly evacuated its small army from the French port of Dunkirk in 1940, stood alone in western Europe. What Englishman could advocate a deliberate return to the horrors of land war on the Continent before the enemy had been weakened to the edge of defeat by all other means? Certainly not Churchill, who had in the First World War been a leading, if unsuccessful, critic of the stationary slaughter in the trenches. Churchill now argued tirelessly against a premature frontal attack, both in a desire to limit British casualties and out of a determination to maintain British influence in the peripheral areas vital to the British Empire. Not all his alternative proposals were adopted, but he did succeed in postponing the main attack until Anglo-American strength was overwhelming.

Until that attack came, in June 1944, the competition between two strategies—a massive direct assault vs. shifting operations on the periphery—was a central theme in Anglo-American diplomacy, to which all other issues were in some way related.

Russia, the third great ally, had only one possible strategy: maximum defensive pressure against Germany while urging the United States and Great Britain to open the second front in Europe without delay and simultaneously hoping that Japan, a neutral in the Russo-German war, would not attack in Siberia. The keynote of Russian diplomacy was surly suspicion—a compound of Marxist-Leninist-Stalinist theories, Russia's interpretation of events since 1917, and anticapitalist propaganda (which Soviet leaders no doubt had come themselves to believe). The Soviet view of the past was highly colored but not inaccurate. The capitalist nations—especially Britain and France—had hoped to see the Soviet Union die in infancy, and between 1917 and 1920 they did make some desultory and ill-coordinated efforts to promote that outcome. And in the 1930s they did try to save their own necks by turning Hitler against Russia. Such was one of the meanings of the Munich concessions to Hitler in 1938. Stalin scarcely concealed his suspicion that Anglo-American friendliness was the product of fear and the mask to a continuing hope that Russia would bleed to death; postponement of the second front in Europe, while millions of Russians died in battle, was simply an expression of this hope. Stalin was right about the fear although not about the supposed hostile hope.[3]

British and American leaders were angered and hurt by the Soviet suspicions, but they differed in their opinions of how to deal with them. The British were relatively unruffled: Russian suspicions were a fact of life; Russian demands for an immediate second front were understandable but must be firmly refused until the time was ripe. The British doubted that Russia would make a separate peace with Germany if it did not receive full and immediate satisfaction. Similarly, the British argued that Russian cooperation in the postwar world would depend on the balance of power at the time and not on fanciful Russian gratitude for favors that the West could not afford to grant.

[3] An outstanding analysis of Soviet wartime policy is Vojtech Mastny, *Russia's Road to the Cold War* (New York: Columbia University Press, 1979). See also Albert Resis, "Spheres of Influence in Soviet Wartime Diplomacy," *Journal of Modern History* 53 (September 1981): 417–439.

The American attitude toward Russia was not monolithic, but the dominant view was that of Roosevelt himself — conciliatory, indulgent, and tinged with fear that an angry Russia might make a separate peace. Roosevelt and his closest advisers were far readier than the British to meet Russian military demands, to see some truth in Russian distortion of the past, to make every allowance for Russian unpleasantness, and to declare that the way to win Russian trust was to begin by trusting. Furthermore, Americans proclaimed that the future peace of the world depended on friendship, not on balance of power. In short, Americans were pessimistic concerning what Russia might do if its wishes were not met but optimistic in their belief that Western attitudes and actions could shape Russian behavior both during and after the war. The ramifications of this Anglo-American-Soviet interplay appear everywhere in the diplomacy of the war. They affected the debate over grand strategy and they touched such questions as shipping and the allocation of supplies. They lay behind the formulation of war aims for Europe and Asia and for the nature of the United Nations. They also produced suppressed disagreement and frustration among American officials who did not share Roosevelt's perceptions or enjoy his confidence. In this tension among the three nations and among Americans can be found some of the origins of the Cold War.

American optimism extended to the war against Japan. This segment of the conflict remained a matter of second priority until the day of victory in Europe, but it absorbed an increasing amount of diplomatic energy and military resources. The ocean war in the Pacific was an American show and required few diplomatic arrangements, but on the mainland of Asia diplomacy encountered its most complicated, difficult, and frustrating task: the support and reform of China. Of all the allies of the United States, China excited the highest, least realistic hopes and ultimately provided the greatest disappointment. The reasons are embedded in both Chinese and American history as well as in the hard realities of geography and military power during the war. Had the China of Chiang Kai-shek conformed to the romantic image cherished widely in the United States, all would have been well. According to this image, which had flourished since the early nineteenth century, China was yearning and able to follow in the ways of its great benefactor and friend, the United States. If

China could only be freed from foreign oppression, an efficient, modern democracy would emerge. The Japanese occupation was a serious obstacle on this road to freedom, but, according to American illusion, the full moral support of the United States plus whatever equipment could be spared would bring ultimate triumph and a united, independent, pro-American China — one of the four great powers upon whose permanent friendship the peace of the world would depend.

Such was the dream. Before long it became a nightmare, and even Roosevelt's inveterate optimism was shaken. Before his death he reached the conclusion that it would take China a generation to become a stable, reliable great power. In China the United States confronted another immediate conflict of basic strategies. Chiang Kai-shek considered himself China's indispensable leader and China the most important theater of the war. He sought massive American military aid in order, first, to preserve his position against the Chinese Communists and other domestic foes and, second, to defeat the Japanese. But American world strategy placed China fourth in line as a recipient of supplies: behind Anglo-American operations in Europe, behind Russia, and behind the naval war in the Pacific; and at no time was the United States willing to see its limited aid to China used for any purpose except the waging of war against Japan. Geography and logistics influenced American priorities. Because Japan controlled the land and water routes into China, every ton of supplies had first to be transported to northeastern India and then flown "over the hump" of the Himalayas at astronomical expense. For equal expenditure, the United States could deliver hundreds of tons of supplies to England for every ton delivered to China. The irreconcilable conflict between Chiang and the Chinese Communists exacerbated all other problems. Few Americans could comprehend the murderous bitterness of this antagonism or why the Chinese could not forget their differences, like good Democrats and Republicans in the United States, in the patriotic struggle against Japan. Throughout the war and for more than a year afterward, the United States sought to unify the Chinese factions. It was a futile effort, for neither side would accept a settlement that denied ultimate power to itself.[4]

[4] A recent overview is Michael Schaller, *The U.S. Crusade in China, 1938–1945* (New York: Columbia University Press, 1979).

༆

Diplomatic historians are sometimes criticized for writing "palace history" — for concentrating too much on great figures at the expense of the thousands who shaped and implemented policies from below. But in the case of the American diplomatic experience during the Second World War, "palace history" is necessary and an understanding of President Roosevelt's attitudes and personality is essential. No president before or since has taken crucial diplomatic negotiations and decisions more completely into his own hands.

A good way to assess Roosevelt is to compare him with Woodrow Wilson. There was nothing cheerful about Wilson's solemn crusade of Christian good against the forces of evil. Roosevelt, in contrast, always gave the appearance of a happy man, sometimes to the point of inappropriate frivolity. Wilson found it hard to like many people with whom he was forced to deal; Roosevelt seemed to like almost everybody. Wilson was solitary; Roosevelt loved a crowd and the feeling of presiding over a numerous family. Wilson put millions of words on paper; Roosevelt thought by talking and listening and wrote comparatively little.[5]

Associates found both Wilson and Roosevelt difficult to work with, for different reasons. Wilson would concentrate for long periods on a single issue and ignore others of equal importance. Roosevelt would dabble with a dozen issues simultaneously, acquiring a superficial acquaintance with thousands of details. He loved to ramble and he seldom studied deeply.

Wilson was stubborn and opinionated; his dislike for advice that did not conform to his own conclusions often became dislike for the adviser. Roosevelt, on the other hand, would feign agreement with an opinion rather than produce argument and disappointment. In domestic politics this habit of trying to please everyone caused confusion but no lasting harm. When Roosevelt's final views on an issue emerged, the person misled could resign. A few did.

But this Rooseveltian technique had doleful results when applied to international affairs, where all the favorable conditions that Roosevelt enjoyed at home were missing. Disagreements in

[5] A full and sympathetic study is Robert Dallek, *Franklin D. Roosevelt and American Foreign Policy, 1932–1945* (New York: Oxford University Press, 1979).

domestic affairs were over means, not basic objectives. All Americans desired a healthy economy, an end to unemployment, and a broadening of security among the whole population. There were no disagreements that could not be faced and thrashed out by men of goodwill. But how different the conduct of international affairs, especially in the emergency conditions of a world war. The nations in uneasy coalition against the Axis disagreed not only on the means of winning the war but also on fundamental objectives for the future. Differences were too profound to be dissolved by geniality. Disgruntled allies, unlike domestic subordinates, could not be ignored. Roosevelt either forgot these truths or else believed that his power to make friends was so irresistible that opposition could be charmed away. But in his defense, one must ask whether the American and Allied cause would have been better served had Roosevelt insisted on making every difference explicit and forcing every potential argument into the open and to a conclusion. His cavalier and casual ways may well have concealed a deeper realism.

As the most successful American politician of the century, Roosevelt had a superb sense of how much support he could command for domestic programs. But he had a timid grasp of what the people would accept in foreign affairs. This reinforced his tendency to shy away from problems lest publicity cause political damage at home. In general, he overestimated the strength of isolationism and underestimated the ability of the American people to absorb bad news and undertake new responsibility. As a result, Roosevelt sometimes gave the public a falsely optimistic picture, especially in regard to Russia and China. He also gave the Russians the impression that the United States would probably withdraw into partial isolation after victory and that Russia, therefore, need not worry about American opposition to its postwar ambitions.

Two further traits of Roosevelt's character should be noted. The president had a boy's delight in military and naval affairs. Under the Constitution he was commander in chief of the armed forces, and he gave practical as well as theoretical meaning to the title. He consulted closely with military and naval authorities. Usually he took the advice of the chiefs of staff, but on occasion he made important military decisions independently.

Finally, Roosevelt, unlike Wilson, was a practical man who knew that good and bad were always mixed together. He had no qualms about further blending the two or about settling by way of compromise for the best that seemed available. He was no metaphysician, losing sleep by wondering whether evil means could contaminate a worthy end. He was more inclined to act and let the historians worry about the philosophical problems involved. Such practicality often served the nation and world well, but on occasion Roosevelt's means were questionable and the results worse.

Roosevelt's character produced the worst results in his diplomacy with Stalin; with Churchill, the best. Churchill and Roosevelt enjoyed the closest personal and official relationship that has ever existed between an American president and the head of another government. It was not, however, a relationship of equality. Churchill, acutely aware of the British Empire's dependence on the United States, kept Roosevelt informed with an almost daily stream of incomparably lucid and persuasive letters and telegrams. Frequently, he traveled to meet Roosevelt in Washington, at Hyde Park, in Canada, and in the Mediterranean. Roosevelt never met with Churchill in Great Britain, although both Roosevelt and Churchill did meet Stalin on or near his home ground. No other man could have won Roosevelt's approval of such a large measure of British policy. But sometimes Roosevelt and his advisers did refuse Churchill's requests. On those occasions Churchill gave way with a grace both uncharacteristic and serviceable to the preservation of good Anglo-American relations.

Roosevelt's personal relations with Stalin were the least effective aspect of his diplomacy. The president met Stalin's displays of temper, suspicion, and churlish obstructionism with redoubled efforts at conciliation. Early in the war he tried to please Stalin by an implied promise of an immediate second front in Europe (a promise that was not and could not be kept), and later he remained almost silent in the face of barbarous Soviet conduct in Poland. Sometimes he tried to win Stalin's confidence by ridiculing Churchill and hinting at a Soviet-American alignment against British colonialism. In personal relations and in diplomacy it is unwise and dangerous to pretend to denounce a proven friend in order to ingratiate oneself with a third party. Churchill bore the humiliation manfully; Stalin was not fooled. He listened to Roosevelt's chatter, said little himself, and coolly pushed the Soviet advantage in Europe and Asia without regard to the idealistic principles of self-determination. Stalin acted on the assumption, which Roosevelt's words and behavior amply confirmed, that neither the United States nor Great Britain would or could raise any effective opposition to Russian expansion. Late in the war Churchill began to warn of ominous consequences and Roosevelt, too, had moments of uneasiness over Soviet behavior. But by that time, the Russian position had been consolidated. Short of an immediate and unthinkable transition from war with Germany to war with the Soviet Union, the outcome was inevitable.

The results of Roosevelt's contact with Chiang Kai-shek of China and Charles de Gaulle of France—the proud and haughty leaders who ranked just below the triumvirate—were poor. Chiang and de Gaulle each claimed to represent a great power suffering temporary eclipse; each was quick to resent the slightest reflection on his personal prestige or the prerogatives of his nation. Roosevelt treated them in opposite fashions—more in terms of his preconceived notions about France and China than on the basis of the actual situation. The president seemed an infatuated captive of the myth that China under Chiang was one of the world's four great powers and deserved to be treated as such. No amount of evidence concerning Chiang's maladministration, the disunity of the country, the strength of the opposition, or the inefficiency of his armies shook Roosevelt from his public maintenance of the illusion—although in private he had doubts. But again in Roosevelt's defense, one must ask whether public comment on Chiang Kai-shek's inadequacies would have served a useful purpose—except, perhaps, to have mitigated some of the subsequent American disillusionment.

For modern France, in contrast, Roosevelt had acquired an attitude of contempt as extreme as his admiration for China. He considered France a morally decadent nation which, by laying down before Hitler and giving way to Japan in Indochina, had forfeited the right to be respected. Roosevelt saw de Gaulle as a pompous adventurer who represented only a small clique and who aimed at dictatorial power.[6] Ultimately, Roosevelt's attitudes led to severe friction with France and to bitter misunderstandings

[6]See Milton Viorst, *Hostile Allies: FDR and Charles de Gaulle* (New York: Macmillan, 1965).

on the part of the American people when Chiang's regime collapsed so ignominiously in the civil war with the Communists.

ᝍ

Although wartime diplomacy dealt most frequently with military operations, one overriding question was always present: What kind of postwar world did the major allies desire? Each sought, first of all, a victory that would prevent yet another war while protecting its own interests. American leaders, in and out of government, gradually developed some broad ideas on how this might be done, but Roosevelt himself was loath to make commitments. Thus, despite a great deal of talk and writing during the war about the future, many decisions were postponed or left indefinite.

There were several ways the goal of American postwar security might be sought. Isolation had failed and was now discredited, more thoroughly than Roosevelt realized. A unilateral pax Americana in which every threat to security would be met by superior force was technically worth considering but not politically feasible. A pax Anglo-Americana in which the United States and Great Britain would run the world together had appeal for some Americans and briefly for President Roosevelt, but it, too, was not feasible. Roosevelt until 1944 favored a peace secured by the armed cooperation of the "four policemen": the United States, Great Britain, Russia, and China. Little countries would be required to keep quiet and take orders. This concept had numerous flaws. A vacuum would appear in western Europe where, according to Roosevelt's conception, neither Germany nor France would be allowed power or influence. This would be dangerous if Roosevelt's assumption of cooperation between Russia and the West proved unfounded.

In Asia there was considerable doubt whether the Chiang Kaishek regime in China could survive, much less serve as a policeman for others. In addition, the outcry of small nations at being herded about by the great powers would be too loud to ignore in the United States and Great Britain, countries that prided themselves on respecting the rights of others. There was also an incompatibility between the concept of four policemen preserving the status quo and the evolution of colonial regions to independent nationhood, an idea much favored by Roosevelt and many Americans.

Since the largest colonial regions in the world were British, Churchill feared that the United States was aiming at the dissolution of the British Empire.[7] The prime minister's own program for securing the peace was equally objectionable to most Americans. Churchill's guiding star was the preservation of a traditional balance of power. He assumed that the fate of Europe would determine the fate of the world; that there was a fundamental conflict of interest between Russia and the West; that these differences should be faced openly and realistically; that western Europe had to be rehabilitated as quickly as possible, with France and eventually Germany forming a counterweight to Russia; and that the United States ought to join in checking Russian expansion. Churchill somewhat grudgingly accepted the inevitability of granting colonial peoples increased internal self-government, but he believed that imperial powers should continue to exercise responsibility for their colonies.

Roosevelt abandoned the concept of the four policemen not in favor of Churchill's balance-of-power program but in response to rising enthusiasm in the United States for a universal collective security organization, the United Nations. Secretary of State Cordell Hull, for example, argued that great-power cooperation must be embedded in a world organization which would, in effect, be a resurrection of the Wilsonian League of Nations. The alternative was a third world war. Hull's views were shared by thousands of opinion leaders: writers, teachers, clergy, labor leaders, senators, and congressmen. As Americans became fully committed to the idea of the United Nations, they became increasingly suspicious of Churchill's ideas. Some even believed that British colonialism and continued adherence to the idea of a balance of power were greater threats to security than anything the Soviet Union might do.

This does not mean that Americans were hostile to Great Britain; rather, they looked upon that nation as a misguided friend unfortunately wedded to dangerous and outmoded behavior. It was the duty of the United States to set the British right for their own good and the good of the world. The Americans who were most critical of Britain tended to be those most sympathetic to Russia — in their view, a maligned giant yearning inwardly to be

[7] The most detailed study of this subject is Wm. Roger Louis, *Imperialism at Bay: The United States and the Decolonization of the British Empire, 1941–1945* (New York: Oxford University Press, 1978).

friendly but too scarred by unhappy memories to take the initiative. Russia's enormous loss of life—the final figure is generally estimated to be 20 million—strongly reinforced a sympathetic attitude. Those Americans who disputed this rosy picture were often denounced in internal debate as callous reactionaries.

While Roosevelt, Churchill, and their advisers privately wrestled with different theories for the maintenance of future security, the official public declaration of Anglo-American war aims remained the Atlantic Charter, a generalized statement drafted by the two leaders in August 1941 and subsequently accepted by all countries joining the war against the Axis. The Atlantic Charter denied that its adherents sought self-aggrandizement, condemned territorial changes against the will of the peoples concerned, favored the right of all people to choose their own form of government, advocated liberal international trading arrangements, called for the disarmament of aggressor nations, and glanced cautiously at a possible "permanent system of general security." The Soviet Union adhered to the charter—with the capacious qualification that "the practical application of these principles will necessarily adapt itself to the circumstances, needs, and historic peculiarities of particular countries."[8] In other words, Russia would not be deflected in the slightest by the Atlantic Charter from the pursuit of its own aims in its own way. Churchill also had reservations concerning the applicability of self-determination to the parts of the British Empire.

Roosevelt thought that Russia wanted nothing but security from attack and that this could easily be granted. Personally uninterested in Communist or any other kind of theory, and president of a country where ideological passion was out of style, Roosevelt tended to assume that national security meant approximately the same thing in Moscow as it did in Washington. Russia's territorial objectives in Europe were clearly stated. They included restoration of the June 1941 boundary, which meant that Russia would enjoy the fruits of the 1939 Nazi-Soviet pact—specifically the annexation of the three Baltic states (Latvia, Lithuania, and Estonia), pieces of Finland and Rumania, and nearly half of prewar Poland. The Baltic states, it should be

[8]Statement of September 24, 1941, by Soviet Ambassador to Great Britain Ivan Maisky, quoted by Feis, *Churchill, Roosevelt, Stalin*, p. 24.

noted, had been Russian provinces from the eighteenth century until the end of the First World War. Germany was to be dismembered into a cluster of weak separate states, and hunks of territory were to be given to Poland and Russia. Russia insisted on "friendly" governments along its European borders. In practice this meant Communist regimes imposed by totalitarian means and the ruthless suppression of political liberty and democracy as it was understood in the United States. In Asia the Soviets sought the expulsion of Japan from the mainland and the restoration of Russia's position as it existed at the height of czarist imperial power in 1904. This would entail serious limitations on China's sovereignty in Manchuria.

Roosevelt shared these aims as far as they applied directly to Germany and Japan, but everything beyond that was in actual or potential conflict with the Atlantic Charter. By postponing decisions on these conflicts, Roosevelt convinced himself that he was preventing discord with Russia without making final concessions in violation of the Atlantic Charter. But postponement seemed to indicate a willingness to condone all Russian objectives on the assumption that once they were attained, Russia would feel secure and would cooperate without reservations in the new world organization.

In retrospect it seems clear that Roosevelt's assumptions were wrong. Russia could assign no limits to the requirements of security; expansion and security were sides of the same coin; ideology taught that communism and capitalism would forever be in conflict. Roosevelt also misjudged the willingness of Americans to accept Soviet violations of democratic ideals and the ways in which disillusionment would inflame American domestic politics.

∽

Historically, most wars have been accompanied by considerable diplomatic contact between enemies; the two sides test each other's determination and bargain, often in secret, over terms while the guns are still firing. In the Second World War, the war of unconditional surrender, the United States refused such contact with the enemy. Germany and Japan, thus, were denied the opportunity to split the coalition arrayed against them. But within their spheres, they carried on negotiations that significantly influenced the outcome of the war. To generalize, the Axis lost through blundering many of the advantages it had gained by arms. Had Germany and Japan been as skilled at dealing with each other, with neutrals, and with conquered peoples as they were in launching military offensives, the plight of the Allies would have been far more drastic than it was. Instead, Axis diplomacy was one of the greatest assets enjoyed by the Allies.

Hitler and the militarists of Japan came to power because the German and Japanese people were dissatisfied with the conditions that prevailed after the First World War and found an expansionist, totalitarian new order appealing. In like manner, Germany and Japan scored great initial military success because the populations of the areas invaded lacked a commitment to defend a status quo that had not brought security and prosperity. In order to exploit this advantage, it was necessary for Germany and Japan to coordinate their activities and to convince neutrals and the conquered that, as their propaganda claimed, the new orders for Europe and Asia offered genuine benefits for those willing to cooperate. They failed utterly on both counts.

It was not necessary for the Allies to seek to separate Germany and Japan because they were never together, notwithstanding the alliance signed in September 1940. The two countries were profoundly suspicious of each other and withheld information with a fervent secrecy more appropriate to enemies. The major decisions of each — Germany's invasion of Russia and Japan's attack on the United States — were made without the other's advance knowledge. Ultimately, these decisions meant defeat; perhaps it could not have been otherwise, given the inferiority of the Axis in population and resources. But coordination might have placed the outcome in doubt.

Geographical separation was, of course, a huge obstacle to coordination, but military action might have brought the two into contact. That was a nightmare of the Allies. But ideological antipathy was more divisive than geography. Japanese propaganda stressed opposition to European imperialism and appealed to the idea of Asia for the Asians. It was thus difficult to sympathize with the boundless growth of German power. Would Germany insist on acquiring new imperial status in the Far East? The Japanese could not be sure. Hitler's ideological dislike for the Japanese was even stronger. He was a believer in the "yellow peril" and found the spectacle of Japanese victories over white people disturbing even when the whites were his enemies. In short, there was "a fundamental inconsistency in the alliance between Nazi Germany, the champion of the concept of Nordic racial superiority, and Japan, the self-appointed defender of Asia against Western imperialism."[9] In March 1942, to illustrate the point, Hitler is reported to have indulged in the thought that it would be satisfying to send England twenty divisions to throw back the yellow horde in Asia.

Few nations have ever been as brutal and selfish as Germany and Japan during the Second World War. They went to war to indulge nationalism of the most aggravated sort and lost partly because that nationalism prevented their cooperation. Still less could they cooperate with smaller countries and colonial peoples who had no love for the Allies and who might have been made into effective collaborators had the Nazis tried seduction instead of rape. In Europe Hitler had an opportunity to win support from anti-Russian nationalists in the Balkans, Poland, and the Ukraine. He imposed slavery instead. He could have had greater support from Vichy France and Franco's Spain if he had offered them advantages in the new Europe. Different diplomacy and military strategy could have brought Hitler control of the Mediterranean and North Africa. He then could have exploited anti-British sentiment in the Middle East and brought that crucial area into his orbit. India was also susceptible to anti-British appeals, and if India fell, Germany and Japan would be linked along the southern rim of Asia.

Similarly, in Asia, Japan had great opportunities as it conquered colonies whose populations longed to be rid of European rule. By acting sincerely in tune with their propaganda and granting some scope to the national aspirations of these peoples, the Japanese might have forged a chain of allies across southeast Asia. In many places they did receive an initial tentative welcome, but soon their arrogance and brutality as conquerors produced bitter hatred. The colonial peoples knew that European imperialism was bad, but Japanese imperialism was worse.

[9]F. C. Jones et al., *The Far East, 1942–1946* (London: Oxford University Press, 1955), p. 102.

CHAPTER 2

The Diplomacy of Counterattack

In the months after Pearl Harbor the Axis held the military initiative. Defense and then counterattack were first orders of the day for the United States. "We had to attack to win," wrote the general who was eventually to command all Allied troops in western Europe.[1] The diplomat was servant to the soldier, and the soldier dealing with Allied counterparts served as diplomat.

The news of Pearl Harbor filled Prime Minister Churchill with exhilaration and somber thanksgiving: now eventual victory was assured. He departed almost immediately, with an entourage of high military officers and economic planners, on a battleship for the United States. The conference in Washington that followed (December 1941 and January 1942 — code name, Arcadia) reflected Churchill's high spirits and American optimism. On the economic level, for example, goals were announced for the production of ships — on which all else depended — and armaments. The figures were so incredibly high that many observers scoffed in disbelief. The goals were subsequently met and surpassed thanks in part to the successful operation of a variety of Anglo-American and Canadian combined boards for the production and allocation of resources.

The Arcadia conference also succeeded on the level of personal relations. The president and the prime minister deepened their rapport in formal daytime discussion and in private conversation over cocktails and late into the night at the White House,

---

[1] Dwight D. Eisenhower, *Crusade in Europe* (Garden City, N.Y.: Doubleday, 1948), p. 26. See also Stephen E. Ambrose, *The Supreme Commander: The War Years of General Dwight D. Eisenhower* (Garden City, N.Y.: Doubleday, 1969).

where Churchill stayed as a guest. Harry Hopkins — Roosevelt's closest adviser and a man of energy, loyalty, ingenuity, and frail health — was always present to smooth over incipient disagreement. Hopkins was idea man, expediter, and legman extraordinary. Since the president often bypassed his secretary of state and rarely used ambassadors for important discussions, Hopkins's importance in diplomacy can scarcely be exaggerated. It was second only to that of the president, whose views and instincts he always faithfully represented.[2]

At the same time American and British generals and admirals — instructed by Roosevelt and Churchill to cooperate fully — were weighing each other's talents and personalities and creating an institution for unified command. The resulting Combined Chiefs of Staff functioned successfully in Washington throughout the war. Some of the British resented the loss of status symbolized by the selection of Washington as headquarters for the overall direction of the war, but the tact of leaders on both sides prevented serious friction. Of particular importance was the mutual confidence and good sense of General George C. Marshall, the American chief of staff, and Field Marshall Sir John Dill, who remained in Washington as representative of the British chiefs of staff.[3] The work of the Combined Chiefs was made easier by the decision of March 1942 to divide the world into spheres of primary military responsibility corresponding roughly to each country's political interests. Responsibility for Europe was shared; the American sphere covered the Western Hemisphere and the Pacific, including Australia and China; Britain had primary responsibility for Africa, the Middle East, India, and southeast Asia. Later the United States felt impelled to encroach on the British sphere. The results, as we shall see, were always interesting and sometimes acrimonious.

The most publicized result of the Arcadia conference was the Declaration of the United Nations, dated January 1, 1942, a reaffirmation of the ideals of the Atlantic Charter and a mutual pledge not to make a separate peace. Drafted by the British and Americans, the declaration was signed by all nations at war against the

[2] Robert E. Sherwood, *Roosevelt and Hopkins: An Intimate History* (New York: Harper, 1948), was the first book to give details of secret wartime negotiations on the American side; it remains fascinating.

[3] General Marshall's achievements are described meticulously in volumes 2 and 3 of Forrest C. Pogue, *George C. Marshall* (New York: Viking, 1966 and 1973).

Axis powers. Roosevelt chose the phrase "United Nations" in preference to the flat term "Associated Powers," which evoked unpleasant memories of disunity in the First World War, when President Wilson had insisted in a cold and correct manner that the United States was an "associated power" and not an ally. In 1945 the phrase "United Nations" was officially applied to the new world organization, but the two uses should not be confused. During the war it meant the nations at war, not the UN of the future.

The conference decided that there should be no swerving from the informal 1941 Anglo-American agreement to make the defeat of Germany the first priority. The British had good reason to fear that after Pearl Harbor the United States might turn exclusively to fighting Japan, leaving an exhausted Britain and Russia to stagger on alone against Hitler. Japan was a more psychologically satisfying enemy to many Americans. Dramatic voices like that of General Douglas MacArthur from the Philippines and stern ones like that of Admiral Ernest J. King were heard urging that more resources be allocated to the war against Japan. But the president remained fully committed to the strategy of Germany first, and so did General Marshall and his military planners. The temptation to make the defeat of Japan the first priority never disappeared, but it never prevailed.

Misfortunes of war soon overturned the specific decisions of the conference. In order to stop the Japanese in southeast Asia and the Pacific, the United States suggested and the British accepted the formation of a unified American-British-Dutch-Australian command under British General Sir Archibald Wavell. In weeks the Japanese overran much of the area the command was to have protected: Burma, Malaya, Borneo, and the Netherlands East Indies (Indonesia after 1948). It became necessary, in sheer desperation, to rush far more men, ships, and supplies to the Pacific than had originally been intended.

The Japanese onslaught and the sickening success of German U-boats in the Atlantic so depleted the number of available ships that no timetable for carrying the war to Hitler could be followed. Churchill agreed with his military advisers that an attack on the continent of Europe in the foreseeable future was out of the question. He persuaded Roosevelt to favor Anglo-American landings in French North Africa, designed to link up with British forces that were driving the Germans westward away from the borders of Egypt. This operation was approved in January but discarded in February for lack of ships and enough trained men.

North African operations, however, remained one of Churchill's first priorities. His worst fears were that German forces under General Erwin Rommel, "the desert fox," would move out of Libya, capture Egypt and the Suez Canal, and gain control over all the Middle East. Such a German success might then bring Spain into the war on Germany's side, lead to the loss of Gibraltar and the British, and convert the Mediterranean into a German-controlled lake. His hopes were that Anglo-American success would not only protect a lifeline of the British Empire but also ensure Spanish neutrality, demoralize Italy, and encourage French resistance to Germany.

The euphoria of Arcadia faded quickly. War news through the first months of 1942 was uniformly terrible. The area of Japanese conquest spread like spilled ink across a map. Britain's supposedly impregnable base at Singapore, essential for the projection of naval power throughout southeast Asia, fell in February, and 60,000 British were taken prisoner. China grew more feeble. The Japanese overran Burma and the Netherlands East Indies. India felt threatened. Australia feared invasion. The Philippines fell. U-boats were sinking more ships than the Allies could replace. As spring came on, German armies resumed their advance into Russia and the British defense of Egypt weakened.

In Washington military planning, which had to be developed almost from scratch, moved constructively ahead. Dwight D. Eisenhower, assistant chief of staff under Marshall, prepared a grand strategic plan for concentrating on the British Isles as the launching platform for a direct invasion of Europe. Marshall and Secretary of War Henry L. Stimson agreed with the plan's assumption that peripheral operations, like Churchill's project for French North Africa, would waste resources to little avail — and meanwhile Russia might go under. The army planners argued that a cross-Channel invasion must be launched no later than the spring of 1943 but that a smaller emergency operation should be readied for September 1942 in case Russia was on the brink of defeat. Great risks would be justified to prevent such a catastrophe.

Roosevelt accepted the army plan and sent Hopkins and Marshall to England to win British approval. "Dear Winston," Roosevelt wrote to Churchill,

What Harry and Geo. Marshall will tell you about has my heart and mind in it. Your people and mine demand the establishment of a front to draw off pressure on the Russians, and these peoples are wise enough to see that the Russians are killing more Germans and destroying more equipment than you and I put together. Even if full success is not attained, the big objective will be.[4]

After a week of arduous discussion, the British seemed to accept the American strategy. Hopkins, who placed great emphasis on the necessity of helping Russia, was overjoyed. Marshall, with more restraint, noted that British approval was carefully hedged with conditions. Colonel Albert C. Wedemeyer, soon to rise to high command, suspected the British of duplicity, of accepting in principle what they never intended to carry out. British generals, in turn, privately belittled the military intellect of the Americans. Marshall was a gentleman, wrote the chief of the Imperial General Staff, "but did not impress me with the ability of his brain."[5] The British were convinced that an invasion of Europe before 1944 would lead to disaster. An emergency operation to take the pressure off Russia was even more absurd. If Russia was about to go down, they reasoned, it would be all the easier for Hitler to devour a landing in France.

In the weeks that followed, American planners became increasingly irritated with what they considered British procrastination and obstruction. Eisenhower went to England to build a fire under them, but he returned discouraged. "It is necessary to get a punch behind the job or we'll never be ready by spring, 1943, to attack," Eisenhower noted. "We must get going."[6] At the same time Russia's apparently worsening plight convinced many Americans that the emergency landing in France had to be attempted, no matter how great the risk. The British, however, were less supportive by the week. Their battle to defend Egypt was going badly. U-boats were preventing a buildup of force in the United Kingdom. Nothing could be done.

[4]Winston S. Churchill, *The Hinge of Fate* (Boston: Houghton Mifflin, 1950), p. 314.

[5]Arthur Bryant, *The Turn of the Tide: A History of the War Years Based on the Diaries of Field-Marshall Lord Alanbrooke, Chief of the Imperial General Staff* (Garden City, N.Y.: Doubleday, 1957), p. 290.

[6]Ray S. Cline, *Washington Command Post: The Operations Division* (Washington, D.C.: U.S. Government Printing Office, 1951), p. 163. This is a volume in the official history of the United States Army in World War II.

By June 1942 a disgusted General Marshall was contemplating a radical reversal of American strategy, a turning away from Europe and a full effort against Japan. This would have pleased the American navy but might have meant disaster for Britain and Russia. At this moment of crisis Churchill's thoughts ranged back to French North Africa and on to adventurous possibilities throughout southern Europe. He returned to the United States to work on Roosevelt and Hopkins. The three men conferred first at Roosevelt's country home in Hyde Park, New York. Roosevelt was convinced by Churchill's persuasive unfolding of the advantages of landings in North Africa.

But Marshall and his military planners believed that the operation (code name, Torch) would mean an indefinite postponement of the main invasion of Europe (Roundup, later called Overlord). The military were overruled by the commander in chief. Roosevelt decreed that American troops had to engage German troops somewhere in 1942. He was afraid that without action the American public might lose interest in the German war and he hoped to prevent any Soviet thoughts about negotiating with the Germans. Since Europe was out, North Africa was the only alternative. The American chiefs reluctantly accepted the order of the president. General Eisenhower was named commander of the operation. Planning for the landings, which took place on November 8, 1942, began immediately.

❦

Thus, the basic decision of where and when to counterattack was made by two men at the top. But in order to ensure the immediate and long-range success of the invasion, many tasks had to be completed or continued by diplomats at all levels on several continents.

Let us begin with the Western Hemisphere. Here it was necessary to organize the twenty republics of Latin America for defense. Unless the security of the home hemisphere was maintained, the United States could not safely devote the required men and resources to Europe and the Pacific. This security could not be taken for granted. At worst the Latin American republics might split into pro- and anti-Axis blocs; their territory might become an open field of operations for spies, saboteurs, and political subversives; German U-boats might find comfort in Latin

American ports and receive directions from Latin American radios; the United States might be cut off from vital raw materials; and, finally, all hope of postwar hemispheric stability might be shattered. At best all the American republics might join the struggle against the Axis, take effective action to eradicate Axis influence from the hemisphere, and maintain an abundant flow of strategic materials to the United States. The outcome was closer to the best than the worst possibility, but in the process the United States made its share of mistakes. This is not to suggest that Latin America was at the center of United States concern. It represented not an immediate problem but a potential difficulty that could be avoided with forethought.

When the Japanese attacked at Pearl Harbor, the United States enjoyed strong assets but labored under some liabilities in its relations with Latin America. The first asset was the Good Neighbor Policy which, since 1933, had convinced many Latin Americans that the United States had abandoned the "right" of intervention in the internal affairs of its neighbors. The administration's recent peaceable acceptance of Mexico's nationalization of the oil industry — despite outcries from American oil interests and the Catholic church — illustrated the point. A second asset was the record of inter-American cooperation during the neutrality period of 1939–41. The United States military, after years of disdaining the Latin Americans, had begun programs of aid and training, especially for those nations closest to the United States. Nine of these countries declared war on the Axis immediately after Pearl Harbor and three others broke diplomatic relations. Another asset, or source of leverage, was the American ability to buy Latin American raw materials at high wartime prices and to serve as virtually the only source of needed industrial imports.

The greatest liability of the United States was the cultural and political resentment felt by many Latin Americans against the "colossus of the north." Pious pronouncements in favor of "good neighborhood" could never completely wash away that resentment and sensitivity to American power and economic influence. If the United States tried to persuade with too much vigor, the cry of "Yankee imperialism" was likely to be heard. The larger the Latin American nation and the further its location from the United States, the greater its resentment was likely to be. In Washington this resentment was sometimes confused with Nazi influence. Some North Americans developed an obsession with the specter of Nazi penetration—spies, sinister control over Latin American governments (possibly abetted by pro-Axis immigrants), and long-range plans for taking over the Western Hemisphere. These fears had some basis in fact but were much exaggerated in Washington. A final liability was American naval weakness at the beginning of the war. Chile, with thousands of miles of Pacific coastline, and Argentina on the Atlantic doubted that the United States could protect them should Japan and Germany attack.[7]

President Roosevelt exercised general supervision over Latin American policy but did not participate personally in negotiations, which for this region, unlike the rest of the world, were left in the hands of the State Department. The chief negotiator was Undersecretary of State Sumner Welles—suave, experienced diplomat, personal friend of Roosevelt, and critic of Secretary of State Cordell Hull, whom he considered "devoid not only of any knowledge of Latin-American history, but also of the language and culture of our American neighbors."[8] In January 1942 Welles headed the United States delegation to a conference of American states held at Rio de Janeiro, Brazil, in order to consider the emergency created by Pearl Harbor. The United States hoped to obtain a declaration by all American republics that diplomatic relations with the Axis were severed. Before the conference opened, Welles received assurances of support from all countries except Argentina and Chile.[9]

The exceptions were crucial. Argentina and Chile ranked second and fourth in population among South American states and equally high in strategic and economic importance. If they

[7]For an overview see Irwin F. Gellman, *Good Neighbor Diplomacy: United States Policies in Latin America, 1933–1945* (Baltimore, Md.: Johns Hopkins University Press, 1979). Also see Stetson Conn and Byron Fairchild, *The Framework of Hemispheric Defense* (Washington, D.C.: U.S. Government Printing Office, 1960). Bryce Wood praises Roosevelt's approach to Latin America in his *The Making of the Good Neighbor Policy* (New York: Columbia University Press, 1961); for a contrary view, see David Green, *The Containment of Latin America: A History of the Myths and Realities of the Good Neighbor Policy* (Chicago: Quadrangle, 1971).

[8]Sumner Welles, *Seven Decisions That Shaped History* (New York: Harper, 1951), p. 119.

[9]For a full discussion, see Michael J. Francis, *The Limits of Hegemony: United States Relations with Argentina and Chile during World War II* (Notre Dame, Ind.: University of Notre Dame Press, 1977).

adopted a strong anti-American line, Bolivia, Paraguay, and Uruguay might swing into their orbit. At the conference Welles confronted the alternative of winning universal approval of a weak resolution recommending that each country break relations with the Axis when circumstances permitted or forcing through a strong resolution that Argentina and Chile would reject. He chose the first alternative as the only way to preserve unity. Back in Washington, Secretary Hull noted press reports that the United States had suffered a diplomatic defeat. In anger he ordered Welles by telephone to withdraw American approval of the resolution even though it had been passed by the conference. Welles believed such a move would destroy the conference, encourage the formation of an anti-American bloc, and play directly into the hands of the Axis. He appealed over a three-way telephone hookup to President Roosevelt, who listened and then countermanded Hull's instructions. This, wrote Welles later, was "the decision which saved New World unity." Hull, however, remained convinced that it would have been better to defy rather than conciliate Argentina and Chile. Similar incidents widened the breach between the two men, and in August 1943 Hull forced Welles to resign.[10]

Reasonable progress was made during the remainder of 1942 in organizing Latin America for war, especially in supplying military aid to Brazil as a means of ensuring against a German thrust across the south Atlantic from Africa and as a counterbalance to Argentina. Brazil received 75 percent of the relatively small amount of United States aid to Latin America.[11] Mexico received the next largest amount, much of it directed at rebuilding its railroads. Brazil and Mexico were the only two Latin American countries to send combat units into action in Europe. Chile, moaning about the Japanese naval threat to its coast, finally declared war in January 1943.

[10]Hull gives his side of the Rio conference controversy in *The Memoirs of Cordell Hull*, vol. 2 (New York: Macmillan, 1948), pp. 1143–1150. See also the documents in U.S. Department of State, *Foreign Relations of the United States, 1942*, vol. 5 (Washington, D.C.: U.S. Government Printing Office, 1962), pp. 6–47. Hereafter this important serial publication of diplomatic papers will be cited as *Foreign Relations*, with appropriate year, volume, and special designation where necessary.

[11]For details, with emphasis on the bearing of internal Brazilian politics, see Frank D. McCann, Jr., *The Brazilian-American Alliance, 1937–1945* (Princeton, N.J.: Princeton University Press, 1977).

Argentina remained a problem far longer. The United States charged that German agents were operating in Argentina with government approval and that Argentina was doing Germany's work by fomenting unrest in neighboring countries. Secretary Hull blamed Argentina for an allegedly pro-Nazi coup in Bolivia in late 1943 and tried to bring down the Bolivian regime through diplomatic and economic sanctions. The effort failed and made the United States look ridiculous.

The situation seemed to be improving when the Argentine government broke diplomatic relations with the Axis in January 1944. But the government was shortly overthrown by a military coup engineered by officers sympathetic to Germany. The new government, nominally headed by General Edelmiro Farrell but with Colonel Juan Perón as the dominant power, proceeded to establish the trappings of fascism in Argentina while defying the United States and giving comfort to Germany. To Hull this was intolerable. He began a campaign to smash the regime. Diplomatic recognition was withheld, punitive economic sanctions were imposed, more arms were sent to Brazil in preparation for war with Argentina, and Great Britain was pressured into reducing its ties with Buenos Aires. Hull's heavy-handed tactics served only to strengthen the Farrell regime and antagonize the British, who depended on Argentina for nearly half their meat imports and believed that Hull was exaggerating the extent of Argentine aid to the Axis. Until the end of his days Hull blamed sinister, commercial, reactionary, and British influences for thwarting him. In December 1944 he resigned, a physically and mentally exhausted man.

After Hull's resignation, American policy toward Argentina became somewhat more conciliatory, in part because of the new assistant secretary of state for Latin American affairs, Nelson Rockefeller. In March 1945 Argentina declared war on the Axis in order to be on the bandwagon of victory. In April 1945 the United States extended diplomatic relations and proceeded, although without enthusiasm, to override Soviet objections and secure for Argentina a seat at the San Francisco conference for the formation of the United Nations organization.[12] Wartime diplomacy in Latin

[12]See Randall B. Woods, *The Roosevelt Foreign-Policy Establishment and the "Good Neighbor": The United States and Argentina, 1941–1945* (Lawrence, Kans.: Regents Press of Kansas, 1979).

America had achieved its immediate purpose: defense and security in the hemisphere in order to free American resources for war in Europe and Asia. Subsequent events revealed flaws in that achievement. By concentrating on and exaggerating the Nazi threat, American officials had failed to understand Latin American conditions and had neglected the region's vast internal problems, particularly nationalism and underdevelopment. Furthermore, the emphasis on military relationships, understandable in wartime, began a pattern in which weapons from the United States were used by despotic governments to keep themselves in power.

☙

This excursion into Latin American relations has moved us ahead of the story. Now let us return to 1942 and the diplomatic preparations for the North African invasion—specifically to the role of Spain. Francisco Franco, the Spanish dictator, had seized power through the bloody civil war of 1936–39, waged with military assistance from Germany and Italy. When the Second World War broke out, Franco sympathized with the Axis but was determined to keep his exhausted country out of the fighting unless Hitler could guarantee victory and enormous material advantages. Hitler's inability to make this guarantee led Spain to remain neutral. But a neutral Spain was still dangerous; thus, the need for careful diplomacy on the part of the United States and Great Britain.

Allied objectives were to prevent Spain from (1) joining the Axis as a belligerent, (2) giving military assistance short of going to war, (3) supplying the Axis with strategic materials, and (4) withholding strategic materials from the Allies. The first objective was fully achieved thanks to Hitler's failure, the second almost fully, and the last two partially. The principal method was economic coercion and concession—the stick and the carrot. The United States preferred to inflict harsh treatment in the belief that Spain would behave if sufficiently injured by embargoes. This was similar to the American approach to Argentina. The British placed a higher value on Spain's goodwill and argued that punishment should be infrequent and rewards generous. The actual treatment of Spain was a compromise: harsh at first but moving toward gentleness as the date of the North African invasion approached.

Had Spain joined the Axis, it could have seized Gibraltar and closed the Mediterranean. The entry of the United States into the war placed a Nazi victory sufficiently in doubt to deter Spain from joining the Nazi side. But it was conceivable that Franco would allow a German army to cross Spanish soil. Spain was important to both sides as a source of tungsten, a mineral essential to the manufacture of weapons-grade steel. Here the advantage lay with the Allies because of Spain's dependence on imports for petroleum, much food, and other essential commodities. The United States could supply Spain's needs. Germany could not.

Immediately after Pearl Harbor, the United States applied heavy pressure by suspending all shipments to Spain (oil being the most important) on the double grounds of scarcity in the United States and Spanish ties with the Axis. The British and American representatives in Spain argued that this harsh policy was folly, for it was paralyzing the economy and making the Spaniards bitter. Resumption of shipments, on the other hand, would make it easier for Franco to resist German pressure and would increase Allied prestige. From Madrid the American embassy warned of dire political, social, and military complications. A crisis was averted by Welles, acting during March 1942 as secretary of state in Hull's absence. Welles persuaded Roosevelt to order immediate oil shipments and also to appoint as ambassador to Spain the distinguished historian and eminent Roman Catholic Carleton J. H. Hayes.

Hayes and the oil arrived in Spain in the spring of 1942; by summer there were signs of a Spanish shift toward greater cooperation. The tone of the press became less hostile, more favorable arrangements were reached in regard to strategic materials, and Serrano Suner, Franco's brother-in-law and a violent Axis supporter, was replaced as foreign minister by General Gomez Jordana. "This means," wrote Ambassador Hayes to Roosevelt in September,

> the replacement of a petty, intriguing, and very slippery politician, troubled with stomach-ulcers and delusions of grandeur, by a gentleman who is. . . honest, dependable, hard working, and endowed with good health and a sense of humor. To us, it means more — the replacement of a military pro-Axis man by a man who is pro-Spanish first and then more sympathetic with the Allies than with the Axis.[13]

[13]*Foreign Relations, 1942*, vol. 3 (1961), pp. 296–297. For details, see James W. Cortada, "Spain and the Second World War," *Journal of Contemporary History* 5 (1970): 65–75.

Conciliation had succeeded. Three months later American troops landed in French North Africa and Spain watched in benevolent inaction. Thereafter, the United States and Great Britain had less to complain about in Madrid as Hitler's star went down. By late 1944 the Spanish government was making overtures to the United States for special economic, political, and military understandings. Franco was ever on the side of the big battalions. The first diplomatic result of this new alignment came immediately after the defeat of Hitler. At the Potsdam conference in July 1945, Stalin said that Franco should be destroyed in order to make a clean sweep of the Fascist dictators. Churchill defended Franco and cited Spain's helpfulness in the war. President Harry S. Truman agreed, although with less enthusiasm. Stalin's proposal was rejected, although the Big Three did agree to block Spain's admission to the United Nations.

Spain's smaller neighbor Portugal was also neutral and of great strategic and some economic importance. Portugal, like Spain, was a producer of tungsten, vital for the manufacture of weapons. More important was its ownership of the Azores, mid-Atlantic islands that Britain and the United States considered essential as bases for combating U-boats and as way stations for wartime and postwar transatlantic air flights. Conversely, use of the Azores as bases for German submarines, rather than for their hunters, would result in injury to Allied shipping too great to contemplate. In 1940 Hitler had been on the verge of seizing the islands but had changed his mind when his naval advisers argued that the risks were too great.

Antonio Salazar, the Portuguese dictator with an extraordinary talent for survival, performed as shrewdly as Franco in calculating his country's interests. Fearing that the United States and Britain might take the Azores by force (such an operation was under consideration in Washington and even in London from time to time), he used his bargaining power well. Roosevelt and Churchill agreed that Britain, whose treaty relations with Portugal dated from 1373, would take the initiative in dealing with Portugal, although Washington did try the tactic of having Brazil bring diplomatic pressure on its mother country. In the opinion of many Americans, the British were too mild, but with the improving military position of the Allies, Salazar began to do as he was asked. In 1943 he granted facilities in the Azores to Great Britain and in 1944 also to the United States. Meanwhile, the Allies were paying high prices for Portuguese tungsten and threatening economic sanctions if Portugal did not cut off its exports of the mineral to Germany. In 1944 Salazar complied. Portugal thus moved, like Spain, steadily toward the Allies. Subtle British persuasion, instead of the bludgeon instinctive to some American policymakers, contributed significantly to this satisfactory result.

∽

The most difficult and controversial diplomatic preparations for the North African invasion involved American relations with Vichy France and Vichyite Frenchmen in North Africa. In the summer of 1940, Hitler, choosing to occupy only the north of France, allowed a nominally independent French government at Vichy to administer the rest of the country and the French colonies. The Vichy regime was obnoxious to the American people, but the United States maintained diplomatic relations with it for several reasons. Hitler did not yet control the French fleet, French North Africa (Morocco, Algeria, and Tunisia), or other strategic colonies, including those in the Western Hemisphere. An American diplomatic presence and a few driblets of economic aid might, it was reasoned, encourage the Vichy regime to resist further concessions. Also, diplomats in France and North Africa might gather valuable information.

The British disapproved of American Vichy policy and could not see the benefits imagined in Washington. They looked on the Vichy regime as a contemptible satellite of Germany. Vichy leaders, in turn, despised the British because in July 1940 the British had attacked Vichy French warships in Oran, North Africa, in order to prevent them from falling into German hands. The British had also given asylum and a political base to General Charles de Gaulle and his resistance movement, the Free French. The Vichy government considered de Gaulle a traitor and had him under sentence of death.

After Pearl Harbor, the Vichy policy came under increasingly strong attack in the United States. Liberals charged that the ideological purity of the American cause was befouled by contact with this Fascist, puppet regime. They could find no evidence that American recognition had inhibited the subserviency of Vichy to

Germany or provided vital information. Equally reprehensible, said the critics, was Washington's stubborn refusal to recognize Charles de Gaulle—head of the "Free French" government-in-exile in London—as a genuine representative of democratic France and symbol of resistance to Nazi tyranny.

Any possibility that the American government might become more receptive to de Gaulle was destroyed in December 1941 by an affair of trivial proportions but with lasting and bitter repercussions: the St. Pierre and Miquelon incident. St. Pierre and Miquelon are tiny islands off the south coast of Newfoundland, anomalous remnants of France's original North American empire. In 1941 the islands were under the jurisdiction of a Vichy official, Admiral Georges Robert, stationed at Martinique in the Caribbean. The United States had made an agreement with Robert that there would be no change in the political status of French possessions in the Western Hemisphere. This agreement was designed to exclude Germany; it also excluded de Gaulle. When German U-boats began to operate off North America, St. Pierre and Miquelon acquired sudden importance because of their powerful wireless station, which could communicate with submarines. In the midst of negotiations among the British, Canadian, and American governments for placing the wireless station under special controls, a small Gaullist naval force suddenly seized the islands. The American public cheered this swashbuckling and bloodless operation, but Secretary of State Hull was apoplectic. His view was that the agreement with Robert had been violated by an irresponsible and dangerous man. Hull issued a strong public denunciation of the seizure and received, in turn, an even stronger onslaught of criticism for his own anti-Gaullist prejudices. Having long enjoyed immunity from public attack, he was deeply hurt. His antipathy to de Gaulle became an obsession and continued to influence his behavior as long as he remained in office. Of greater importance was the fact that President Roosevelt developed his own intense dislike for de Gaulle.[14]

The information received in Washington from American diplomats in Vichy France and French North Africa contributed to an underestimation of de Gaulle and an exaggerated belief in the

[14] The full story is presented by Douglas G. Anglin, *The St. Pierre and Miquelon Affair of 1941: A Study in Diplomacy in the North Atlantic Quadrangle* (Toronto: University of Toronto Press, 1966).

utility of continued relations with Vichy. Admiral William D. Leahy, American ambassador to Vichy until July 1942 and thereafter President Roosevelt's personal chief of staff, was familiar only with members of the Vichy government and had learned nothing of the undercurrents of resistance to Hitler that flowed so strongly through France and ultimately rallied to de Gaulle. Similarly Robert D. Murphy, the chief American agent in North Africa, was in contact almost exclusively with conservatives who despised de Gaulle; thus he was incapable of judging what strength de Gaulle might be able to command. As the date for the North African invasion approached, American planners believed that the only safe course was continued cultivation of Vichyite elements in the hope that they might be persuaded to join the fight against Hitler.

In the autumn of 1942 American agents tried to arrange with Vichyites for the peaceful reception of American troops in North Africa. The effort failed. American troops landing on Morocco's Atlantic coast and British troops coming ashore in Algeria on November 8 met sharp fire from local French forces. It appeared that thousands of American and French lives were going to be lost. In haste a deal was arranged between Admiral Jean Francois Darlan, a high-ranking Vichy cabinet member who happened to be in North Africa at the time, and General Eisenhower, commander of the American forces. Darlan ordered a cease-fire and was obeyed by French troops. In return he was granted political authority over French North Africa.

Darlan sympathized with some aspects of nazism, was a violent Anglophobe, and once would have been pleased with a German victory. Now he saw a chance to save his skin. To the American and British public it appeared that the United States had installed a reptile who symbolized all that the democracies were fighting against. Roosevelt, forced on the defensive, called the Darlan deal "only a temporary expedient, justified only by the stress of battle." The public was not convinced. As a historian who was then an official in the State Department recalled, the episode "shook hard the faith of many in the durability of the principles for which we professed to be fighting, or in our devotion to them."[15]

[15] Herbert Feis, *Churchill, Roosevelt, Stalin: The War They Waged and the Peace They Sought* (Princeton, N.J.: Princeton University Press, 1957), p. 91. For a detailed discussion, see Arthur L. Funk, *The Politics of TORCH: The Allied Landings and the Algiers Putsch, 1942* (Lawrence, Kans.: University Press of Kansas, 1974). For a semiofficial justification of American policy toward the Vichy regime, see William L. Langer, *Our Vichy Gamble* (New York: Knopf, 1947).

Darlan's day was short. He was assassinated on Christmas Eve, 1942, by another Frenchman (there is no evidence of American involvement, although the deed was certainly convenient). General Henri Giraud, previously selected by the United States to lead French troops in North Africa, was elevated to Darlan's place while retaining his military command. Giraud, though not a Vichyite, was a poor choice. An enthusiastic field commander with a romantic record of having escaped from German prisons in two wars, he was also an incompetent administrator and politically naive. Throughout 1943 and into 1944 Giraud remained the American candidate to lead the French and resist the growing influence of de Gaulle. But Giraud failed and eventually slipped into oblivion.

ᥫ᭡

At the time the decision to invade North Africa was made, nearly every American military planner believed that the operation would provide inadequate relief for Russia and was an unwarranted diversion from the main purpose of striking Hitler where he was strongest. They feared that the true second front might be indefinitely postponed because of Mediterranean entanglements. Distant allies were even more disappointed and bitter. In Chungking, Generalissimo Chiang Kai-shek was demanding that China be treated as an equal to Britain and Russia and it be sent the same amounts of weapons and supplies. Ominously, he hinted at making a deal with the Japanese to withdraw from the war. And Stalin, beset by Hitler's full offensive power, demanded massive help from the Western Allies. When the United States and Britain were unable to oblige, he charged treachery and caused Americans to worry about the possibility of a separate Russian peace with Germany. The North Africa decision, in short, placed a heavy burden on diplomats whose duty it was to propitiate the disaffected and prevent the threatened disintegration of the coalition against the Axis.

CHAPTER 3

Unconditional Surrender

Josef Stalin demanded three things of his allies during 1942: formal recognition of Russia's territorial demands, enormous deliveries of military supplies, and a second front in western Europe. He was thrice refused. Chiang Kai-shek longed to see China become a major theater, with his armies superbly equipped by the United States. He received far less than Stalin. These denials were unavoidable because of German and Japanese strength, limited resources, the decision to undertake the North African invasion as the primary Anglo-American operation of 1942, and American adherence to the moral principles of the Atlantic Charter. Americans could not accept the unavoidable easily. They were haunted by visions of the catastrophes that would occur if Russia and China were not satisfied and left the war through defeat or a negotiated separate peace. President Roosevelt sought to relieve this anxiety by explanations, promises, and then, in January 1943, by the fateful announcement that the United States would accept nothing less than the "unconditional surrender" of Germany, Italy, and Japan.

Russia, before the German invasion of June 22, 1941, was not seen as a friend by America and Britain. But Russia's valiant resistance to the full weight of Hitler's power transformed aversion to admiration by the time of Pearl Harbor. In the summer of 1941 Harry Hopkins, as Roosevelt's personal envoy, made a successful visit to Stalin in Moscow. Ever after, Hopkins and Roosevelt believed that personal contact with the Soviet premier could melt discord. As a material expression of the new American attitude, a lend-lease credit of $1 billion was granted in the autumn and supplies were delivered as fast as ships could be found.[1]

As the winter of 1941–42 froze the German advance 30 miles from Moscow, the American and British governments became convinced that victory over the Axis would be in doubt if Russia left the war. This must not be allowed to happen. Beyond that one conviction, however, Washington and London mingled hopes, fears, and guesses to reach separate conclusions concerning what Russia might do in various circumstances. Separate conclusions led to disagreement over the proper response to Stalin's three demands for territory, supplies, and an immediate second front.

Anglo-American disagreement over Russia was related to differing expectations concerning the nature of the postwar world. Americans looked for a radical break with the past; the British expected that continuity would be as evident as change and that past experience would be repeated. Thus, Churchill and his advisers remembered that, for centuries, British security had been based partly on the existence of a balance of power in Europe. They reasoned during 1941 and 1942 that acquiescence in Russian territorial demands, even if idealistically suspect, was consistent with the need to use Russian weight against Hitler's attempt to destroy the balance of power. Americans, on the other hand, wishfully thought that the old balance of power had been forever discredited. Of course, Russia should be supported in the war against Hitler, but not by openly condoning its desires to annex people without giving them a chance to determine their own future. There must be no immoral transfer of territory in violation of the Atlantic Charter.

But even while refusing to approve Russian aims, Americans wanted very much to believe that Nazi aggression had somehow reformed and purified Soviet behavior. No longer would Communist Russia contemplate imperial expansion or political subversion in the interests of world revolution, at least not if the West showed the Russians they had nothing to fear. The British were less sanguine. They believed that Russia would continue to expand, that nothing could prevent this expansion in eastern Europe, and that what could not be prevented might as well be

---

[1]An important work is George G. Herring, Jr., *Aid to Russia, 1941–1946: Strategy, Diplomacy, and the Origins of the Cold War* (New York: Columbia University Press, 1977).

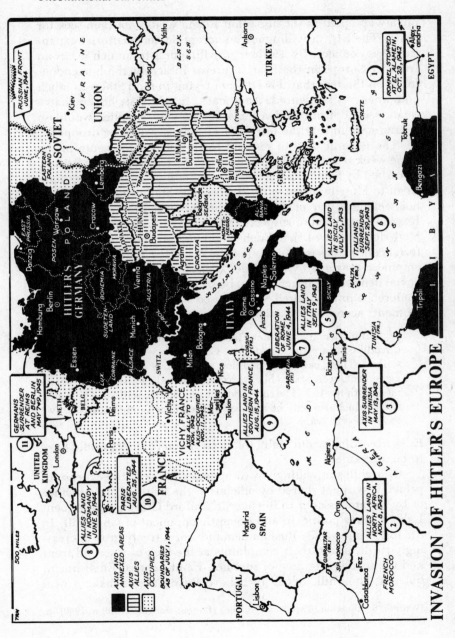

INVASION OF HITLER'S EUROPE

openly accepted in the hope that Russia would not then seek for more. The British willingness to accept Soviet territorial expansion was connected with their unwillingness to launch a second front in Europe in the near future or to accept the horrendous losses on the seas that flowed from trying to send Stalin as much equipment as he desired. Americans, in contrast, hoped that a quick second front and a generous flow of supplies would so reassure Stalin that the territorial demands would be dropped.

The issue of how to respond to Russia became acute in the same week that the Japanese attacked Pearl Harbor. The British, disturbed by Soviet antagonism, sent Foreign Secretary Anthony Eden to Moscow in an effort to convince Stalin that Britain was not seeking a war of mutual German-Soviet exhaustion, as the Russians appeared to suspect. In Washington, Secretary of State Hull rightly feared that Eden might sign a treaty making territorial concessions in violation of the Atlantic Charter. He sent an emphatic warning. When Eden reported on the full extent of Soviet demands, Churchill — on board ship bound for the Arcadia conference in the United States — used strong words that, for the moment, accorded with the American point of view:

> Stalin's demand[s] about Finland, Baltic States, and Rumania are directly contrary to . . . Atlantic Charter, to which Stalin has subscribed. There can be no question whatever of our making such an agreement, secret or public, direct or implied, without prior agreement with the U.S. The time had not yet come to settle frontier questions, which can only be resolved at the Peace Conference when we have won the war.[2]

Eden accordingly told Stalin that a treaty on frontiers would have to be postponed.

Churchill's unwillingness to appease Stalin at the expense of principle was not shared by officials of the British Foreign Office or by the ambassador to Russia, Sir Stafford Cripps, a prominent Labour party politician and domestic opponent of Churchill. In the following weeks, Russian demands for a treaty grew increasingly shrill, as did their complaints at the lack of a second front and the inadequate flow of supplies. Faint-hearted Englishmen, but not Churchill, began to believe Russia might make a deal

[2]Winston S. Churchill, *The Grand Alliance* (Boston: Houghton Mifflin, 1950), p. 630.

with Germany. The British government sought the approval of the United States for territorial concessions.

The State Department reacted with angry indignation. Hull penned a fiery memorandum against a retreat from principle. He then fell ill and left Sumner Welles in charge of the department for two months. On February 18, 1942, Welles had a verbal battle with Lord Halifax, the British ambassador in Washington. "Could it be conceivable that any healthy and lasting world order could be created," said Welles,

> on a foundation which implied the utter ignoring of all of the principles of independence, liberty, and self-determination . . . in the Atlantic Charter? If that was the kind of world which we had to look forward to, I did not believe that the people of the United States would wish to be parties thereto.

Halifax replied with a patient disquisition on the necessity of using Russia as a counterweight to Germany after the war. Welles said such an idea showed "the worst phase of the spirit of Munich."[3]

President Roosevelt tried to postpone the issue by saying he would discuss the matter directly with Stalin, but the British would not be put off. The Foreign Office believed that Roosevelt was naive in thinking that Stalin would accept anything less than the annexation of the three Baltic provinces—Latvia, Estonia, and Lithuania—on which the question of a treaty had come to focus. Sir Stafford Cripps, no longer ambassador to Russia, argued that Stalin considered the acceptance of his demands "the acid test." If they were met, said Cripps, Stalin would have no further desires; if they were refused, there might result "a complete reversal of Stalin's attitude toward the war."[4] The British cabinet was frightened. Washington was told on March 30 that the British government would negotiate a treaty with or without American approval.

Here was the first major crisis of wartime diplomacy. Roosevelt weakened. He suggested that if a treaty must be signed there should be a provision allowing people "who desired not to be returned to Soviet domination to have the right to leave" their homelands. The president did not indicate where they might go.

[3]U.S. Department of State, *Foreign Relations of the United States, 1942*, vol. 3 (Washington, D.C.: U.S. Government Printing Office, 1961), p. 520.

[4]Ibid., p. 531.

This, said Welles unconvincingly to Halifax, was "more nearly in accord with the spirit of the Atlantic Charter."[5] No one was happy with the concession. Assistant Secretary of State Adolf A. Berle, for example, touched the quick when he wrote to Welles:

> I should have preferred and I believe the Soviet Government would have preferred a blunt and frank statement of our views, namely, full willingness to assure the satisfaction of every Russian interest consistent with the maintenance of the cultural and racial existence in their homelands of three free, decent, unambitious and hard-working peoples who are now apparently to be eliminated from the earth.[6]

Secretary Hull, when he later reviewed Roosevelt's suggestion, reacted in a similar fashion.

While the British prepared to negotiate a treaty with Russia, the Polish government-in-exile in London raised a loud and disturbing protest. Although the British did not intend at this time to make any concessions directly at Poland's expense, the Poles felt that a vital principle was at stake. Prime Minister Wladyslaw Sikorski said there would be incalculable consequences from the proposed abandonment of "a considerable part of Europe to Soviet Russia, whose final object is to provoke a World Revolution rather than subdue Germany."[7] The plight of the Poles was later to become the major issue between Russia and the West, but in 1942 Polish protests were regarded as an inconvenient nuisance. Many times the Poles were told to stop accentuating differences among the Allies and concentrate on the primary objective of winning the war. Sikorski and his colleagues, however, continued to mention unpleasant truths about Russian motives.

∾

In April the snow in Russia began to melt. Soon the German offensive would begin again. American planners entertained grave doubts about whether Russia could survive without immediate relief in the form of a second front in Europe. To make matters worse, the Germans launched an air, surface, and submarine

[5]Ibid., p. 538.
[6]Ibid., p. 541.
[7]Ibid., p. 141.

campaign to stop the convoys carrying military supplies through the Arctic to Archangel and Murmansk. At this juncture General Marshall presented the grand strategic plan for a cross-Channel attack in 1943, with provision for opening, in 1942, an emergency second front in France to avert a Russian collapse.

President Roosevelt, as we have seen, approved this plan on April 1, 1942. He saw it as a reassuring signal to the Soviet Union of Anglo-American determination and as a partial solution to the vexing problem of Stalin's territorial demands. If the Russians could be persuaded that a second front would be opened without fail in 1942, perhaps they would desist from their embarrassing drive for a treaty in violation of the Atlantic Charter. With tantalizing enthusiasm Roosevelt sent a message to Stalin:

> I have in mind very important military proposal involving the utilization of our armed forces in a manner to relieve your critical western front. . . . I wish you would consider sending Mr. Molotov [Soviet Foreign Minister] and a General upon whom you rely to Washington in the immediate future.[8]

Stalin cordially agreed, but insisted, against Roosevelt's desire, on having Molotov stop first in London for negotiation of the controversial Anglo-Soviet treaty.

The sequence of visits was crucial. If Molotov got what he wanted in London, Roosevelt's scheme would be foiled. Accordingly, the Russian government was showered with sweet words about secret military plans and imminent improvement of the northern convoy situation. At the same time the British were subjected to more lectures on morality. Secretary Hull, up from his sickbed, cabled to London that if the treaty were signed it would be publicly denounced as immoral. "This would be a sharp break within the United Nations," Hull wrote later, "but there was no other course we could logically pursue."[9] Roosevelt, in giving his approval to this threat, ignored the implicit commitment he had made to acquiesce in the treaty when he suggested the idea of transferring Baltic populations.

Molotov arrived in London on May 20, 1942, and entered into hard negotiations with Eden. The Soviet foreign minister refused

[8] Ibid., p. 543.
[9] Cordell Hull, *The Memoirs of Cordell Hull*, vol. 2 (New York: Macmillan, 1948), p. 1172.

to accept Roosevelt's suggestion about populations and then angered the British by making unacceptable demands concerning the Polish-Russian boundary and secret agreements directed against Finland and Rumania. Suddenly, when the talks were at their bleakest, the Russians retreated. On May 26 they signed an innocuous treaty that made no mention of frontiers but merely pledged the two countries to continue mutual aid in the war and not to enter into or conclude separate peace negotiations. "I was enormously relieved," said Hull.[10] Why did the Russians abandon an objective that they had been pursuing so insistently for nearly a year? Probably Stalin decided that the chance of a second front in 1942 was worth a momentary political retreat.

Three days later Molotov arrived in Washington to collect payment for the concession. For nearly a week Molotov listened while Roosevelt talked. The president said he was glad that frontiers were not mentioned in the recent treaty, although the question could be raised at the proper time. On the second day Molotov came to the point. Was the United States going to establish a second front during the summer? "He requested a straight answer." As the interpreter recorded the conversation,

> The President then put to General Marshall the query whether developments were clear enough so that we could say to Mr. Stalin that we are preparing a second front. "Yes," replied the General. The President then authorized Mr. Molotov to inform Mr. Stalin that we expect the formation of a second front this year.[11]

There was the promise, the implicit quid pro quo for the denial of the treaty on frontiers. After Molotov's return to Moscow, a public communique was issued. "In the course of the conversations full understanding was reached with regard to the urgent tasks of creating a second front in Europe in 1942," it said.[12]

Roosevelt had purchased a few weeks of calm, but he was courting more serious difficulty for the future because the promise could not be kept. Churchill tried to prepare the Russians for disappointment. They pretended not to hear. Inside Russia the press

---

[10]Ibid., p. 1174.

[11]Robert E. Sherwood, *Roosevelt and Hopkins: An Intimate History* (New York: Harper, 1948), p. 563. For additional minutes of the Molotov-Roosevelt-Hopkins conversations, see *Foreign Relations, 1942*, vol. 3 (1961), pp. 566–587.

[12]Ibid., p. 594.

proclaimed that a solemn promise had been given. The Russian people celebrated. On June 22 the American ambassador in Moscow warned "that if such a front does not materialize quickly and on a large scale, these people will be so deluded in their belief in our sincerity of purpose . . . that inestimable harm will be done. . . ."[13]

At that moment Churchill was in the United States persuading Roosevelt that a cross-Channel operation in 1942 was too risky and that the North African invasion ought to be undertaken instead. Next, the Germans sank twenty-three of thirty-four ships that sailed on June 28 from Iceland for Archangel. The British thereupon canceled further sailings for the summer. Within the space of two months Stalin had been denied all three of his demands. Churchill, fearing there would be hell to pay, went to Moscow to explain in person to Stalin why there could be no second front in Europe. The confrontation with Stalin (August 12–16) was tempestuous. Stalin accused the British of cowardice in their attitude toward convoys and the second front. Churchill repulsed Stalin's insults and unfolded the advantages of the North African and subsequent operations in the Mediterranean, which he described as the "soft under-belly" of the Hitlerian crocodile. Churchill assured Stalin that the massive cross-Channel invasion against the beast's hard snout would be launched in 1943. The meeting ended on a somewhat better note.

In October it was Roosevelt's turn to worry. The convoy situation was little improved. German troops were at the outskirts of Stalingrad, on the great bend of the Volga, and the Soviet government was publicly blaming Russia's plight on the lack of support from the United States and Britain. Stalin was relapsing into his normal attitude of distrust and recrimination. Suddenly the president saw "our whole relations with Russia" endangered. Words of reassurance were rushed to Stalin about convoys and possible air support for the beleaguered south Russian front. Then came the British victory at El Alamein in the Libyan desert, followed immediately by the landings in French North Africa.

Roosevelt now decided that he could make a new start with the Russians. He sent a colorful troubleshooter, Patrick J. Hurley, to Moscow without noticeable results. Next the president urged

[13]Ibid., p. 598.

Stalin to come to a meeting with him and Churchill. Stalin said he could not leave Moscow, and Roosevelt settled for a meeting with Churchill and the Combined Chiefs of Staff, scheduled for January 1943 in Casablanca, French Morocco. Thus the year 1942 came to an end. The record contained little cause for encouragement, but Roosevelt, as he looked forward to Casablanca, felt his spirits rising.

༄

By the time the United States entered the war, China had been fighting Japan spasmodically for a decade and continuously for four and a half years. The Japanese had annexed Manchuria in 1931–32 and, since 1937, had occupied the coastline and most of the major cities of central China. That China still resisted was a tribute to the courage of the people and perhaps to the personality of Generalissimo Chiang Kai-shek. But by late 1941 it was doubtful how long this resistance could last without a great infusion of outside aid. Chiang Kai-shek's government and party, the Kuomintang, were losing popular support and becoming increasingly incapable of coping with the rudimentary economy, the political disunity, or the war. The bulk of the government's military resources was being husbanded as protection against internal Communist foes. Little remained to hold back the Japanese. The air was full of rumors of collapse or separate peace or both. Then came Pearl Harbor, a seeming gift from heaven. Chiang Kai-shek thought his problems were solved. Unlimited American aid would pour into China and an offensive under his own masterful command would expel the Japanese.

These unrealistic hopes lasted a matter of days. The Japanese advance mocked the plans of the Western Allies. Hong Kong fell, then Singapore and Malaya, Burma, the Netherlands East Indies, the Philippines. China was cut off except for the perilous air route from India, which itself was threatened. Meanwhile, the United States had received Britain as a full military partner in the Combined Chiefs of Staff. Great quantities of aid were going to Russia, and a master strategy for Europe was being prepared.

It seemed to Chiang that China had been forgotten. His outcries, loud and continuous, were heard in Washington, where diplomats, military men, and economic experts tried to figure out what to do. Their desire was great, their achievements meager.

The situation was complicated by a highly emotional American bias in favor of the Chinese people. It was assumed that the United States had a unique mission to assist China and that the Chinese understood and were grateful. China, many believed, longed for nothing so much as American tutelage and help in expelling the selfish imperialists, among whom the Japanese were the most recent, who had denied China its rightful place. In short, Americans felt an attachment and responsibility for China that transcended the immediate object of victory over the Axis. If Churchill had understood this, he would have been less amazed at "the extraordinary significance of China in American minds, even at the top, strangely out of proportion."

Churchill believed that the United States "accorded China an almost equal fighting power with the British Empire, and rated the Chinese armies . . . in the same breath as the armies of Russia."[14] This was an exaggeration. Americans did pretend to ignore the shabby reality of Chinese weakness. They talked as if China were a great power; action was another matter. It should also be pointed out that Anglo-American differences over China, unlike differences over Russia, had slight influence on events. The British had little voice in Far Eastern affairs. They retained the habit of caustic comment but left the decisions and responsibility to the United States. Diplomacy with China, therefore, depended largely on the interplay of internal American opinion.

Three contrasting attitudes toward China were held by American policymakers. The most extreme opinion, shared by many Far Eastern specialists in the State Department, saw the outcome of the war and the fate of the world depending on the American effort in China. The chief spokesman for this group was Stanley K. Hornbeck, who had devoted a long career to the thankless task of encouraging the Chinese to resist encroachment on their independence and to acquire the strength and skills of a modern, self-reliant nation in friendly partnership with the United States. Hornbeck had been encouraged by China's fight against the Japanese and especially by the personal qualities of Chiang Kai-shek. His heart was so filled with high hopes that he paid slight attention

[14]Winston S. Churchill, *The Hinge of Fate* (Boston: Houghton Mifflin, 1950), p. 133. For a brilliant discussion of the Asian dimensions of Anglo-American relations, see Christopher Thorne, *Allies of a Kind: The United States, Great Britain, and the War Against Japan, 1941–1945* (New York: Oxford University Press, 1978).

to disagreeable evidence concerning China's weakness. Daily he urged that the United States save China, win the war, and safeguard the future; daily he lamented what he considered the misguided strategy of concentrating on defeating Germany. In Hornbeck's opinion China was the most important issue in American foreign policy, and any sacrifice elsewhere in the world was justified to meet China's needs.

The second group, which included President Roosevelt and several of his advisers in the White House, accepted Hornbeck's words about the importance of China and used them in propaganda for the public. Roosevelt's rhetoric did place China on a level with Russia and Britain. But the president's military decisions did not conform to his words. He made promises to Chiang Kai-shek, but he never departed from the Germany-first strategy. Hornbeck, noting the gap between word and deed, thought that subordinates were sabotaging the president's intentions. It was not so.

The third attitude was held by most American diplomatic and military personnel stationed in China. They had to deal with chaos as it was, not comfortable theory. This group believed that China was a minor asset in the war against the Axis. The asset could become a major liability or, with care, its value could be slightly enhanced. The untruthful propaganda in the United States (sheer "rot," Ambassador Clarence E. Gauss called it) that depicted China as a great military power and Chiang Kai-shek as an incomparable leader was dangerous and should be stopped. Those on the scene also considered that the inefficiency and corruption of Chiang's regime were as great an obstacle to progress as were the Japanese. They urged reform.

Immediately after Pearl Harbor, the generalissimo asked for a China-first strategy. In reply he was named commander of Allied forces in China — without the forces except his own poor armies and a token unit of American airmen. Soon he asked for full Chinese representation on the Combined Chiefs of Staff and on the board that allocated available weapons among the Allies. He was refused then and every time he made the same request throughout the war. He asked for more lend-lease equipment. The British took, for the defense of Burma, some material en route to China. He asked for men, planes, trucks, and guns. There were none to spare.

He also asked for money — a $500 million loan from the United States and the same amount from Britain. The British said no, but some Americans, frustrated by their inability to give concrete aid and obsessed by the fear that China would leave the war, eagerly embraced the idea. From Chungking an agent of the U.S. Treasury wrote, "a substantial loan to China, the bigger the better, would be invaluable in keeping China going against the Axis."[15] Others said it would bolster Chiang's regime. The money would be a token of American faith in China and might be used to check inflation, but as long as transportation was lacking there was nothing it could buy. Ambassador Gauss admitted that a small loan might have a useful political impact but, fearing personal profiteering and corruption among the recipients, he said the United States should have some assurance that the money would be put to good use. The Chinese government said it would regard any strings attached to the loan as an insult. The officials in Washington agreed: half a billion and no strings. As Herbert Feis, who participated in the negotiations, wrote:

> The President's compliance was due in part to the compulsion he felt to evade Chinese requests to share in the making of decisions about the distribution of weapons among the Allies. General Marshall urged quick action, since he thought the fall of Singapore and Rangoon might give great force to the Japanese appeal to the races of Asia to stand together. Stimson agreed, believing that we must at any price keep China in the war.[16]

On February 6, 1942, Congress passed the necessary appropriation without a dissenting vote.

The money soon disappeared into obscure places. Inflation continued unchecked, as did talk of "undeclared peace" between China and Japan. So did the generalissimo's complaints. "China is treated not as an equal like Britain and Russia, but as a ward," he said in April.[17] Meanwhile, a hard-nosed American general with experience in China and a knowledge of the language, Joseph W. Stilwell, arrived in China to head the American military effort and to serve as Chiang's chief of staff. Chiang and Stilwell quickly

[15] *Foreign Relations, 1942, China* (1956), p. 419.

[16] Herbert Feis, *The China Tangle* (Princeton, N.J.: Princeton University Press, 1953), p. 22.

[17] *Foreign Relations, 1942, China* (1956), p. 33.

developed a violent personal antipathy which grew stronger as the American's efforts to reform the Chinese armies and infuse some fighting spirit came to naught. Stilwell would have been recalled except that General Marshall considered him the best man for the job of keeping China in the war. This goal was important because of the emotional importance of China to many Americans. It was important militarily because the U.S. War Department planned on eventually building airfields in China from which to bomb Japan.

In June 1942 British setbacks in North Africa led to the diversion to the Middle East of bombers and transport planes intended for China. Cargo deliveries into China suffered. "Now what can I say to the G-mo?" General Stilwell wrote in his diary. "We fail in all our commitments, and blithely tell him just to carry on, old top."[18] Chiang asked Roosevelt to send Harry Hopkins to Chungking, but a lesser White House aide went instead. By midsummer, when the decision to concentrate on the North African invasion was made, American policy toward China was in confusion. The embassy in Chungking believed that little could be done without internal reform. One diplomat reported that the Kuomintang government sought "to insure its own perpetuation and domestic supremacy and to come to the peace table as militarily powerful as possible." The United States, therefore, could not "induce the Chinese to assume the offensive" unless Chiang believed that all equipment used "will be immediately replaced with interest."[19] In the State Department, Hornbeck was crying out,

> China can be kept in this war at comparatively small cost. China can be made a base of operations from which Japan can be greatly damaged, at a comparatively small cost. China and the whole Far East can be lost as effective allies and, if lost, can be turned against the Occident. . . .[20]

At this point Secretary of State Hull, hovering ineffectually on the edges of China policy, decided on a special gesture: the relinquishment by the United States and Great Britain of extraterritorial rights. For a century Western nations had enjoyed special privileges in China, including the right to have their citizens tried

---

[18]Quoted by Feis, *The China Tangle*, p. 43.

[19]Memorandum by John P. Davies, July 31, 1942, *Foreign Relations, 1942, China* (1956), p. 129.

[20]Memorandum by Stanley K. Hornbeck, August 17, 1942, ibid., p. 139.

by Western, not Chinese, courts for crimes committed in China. This was "extraterritoriality." Hull reasoned that a voluntary abandonment of this right and other privileges would encourage the faltering Chinese war effort. The British questioned the timing of the gesture and suggested that it might be received cynically, since the Japanese occupied most of the areas where the privileges had been enjoyed. Ambassador Gauss warned Hull not to expect any gratitude from the Chinese. Hull, however, was enthusiastic; he argued that American public opinion demanded this act of generosity. The British agreed to go along. A treaty abandoning all special rights was negotiated and formally signed on January 11, 1943. This gesture, like the $500 million loan, had no discernible effect.

The months went by and the sense of crisis continued. President Roosevelt tried a little personal charm. On the eve of the Casablanca conference he tempted Chiang with visions of China's future greatness as one of the "four policemen" and as the leader in the abolition of colonialism in Asia. Chiang was unimpressed and resentful that he had not been invited to Casablanca. Roosevelt, however, hoped that a new approach might emerge from that conference with Churchill.

ᕦ

On January 9, 1943, President Roosevelt left Washington on the first of his three momentous overseas missions. He was accompanied by Harry Hopkins and the American chiefs of staff, but he deliberately excluded Secretary of State Hull. (Churchill wanted to bring Foreign Secretary Eden, but Roosevelt said no. He felt that if Eden came it would be hard to exclude Hull.) This attitude reflected the declining importance of the State Department and the president's jaunty confidence in his own ability to make great decisions with little preparation and without systematic advice. From Casablanca until his death the president took diplomacy more and more into his own hands.

The tone of the Casablanca conference was buoyant. The tide of battle was turning. All of Africa would soon be in Allied hands, although not quite as soon as expected. The Russians were winning a great victory at Stalingrad and ever after would grow stronger while the German armies retreated. Soon the island-hopping advance across the Pacific toward Tokyo would begin. Roosevelt and Churchill enjoyed the Moroccan sunshine, good food and drink, and a chance to relax. Only in the China theater was the prospect grimmer than on the day of Pearl Harbor.

The chief military purpose of Casablanca was to decide what to do next. General Eisenhower favored an invasion of Sardinia or Sicily. Churchill argued that only an attack on Sicily and then mainland Italy could keep sufficient pressure on Germany to satisfy the Russians. General Marshall was not happy to see a continuation of "periphery pecking," but he nevertheless concurred in the decision for Sicily. The basic commitment to an eventual frontal attack on Germany, however, was reaffirmed and planning for the cross-Channel invasion (soon to be called Operation Overlord) was accelerated. In May 1942 Roosevelt had promised this second front for the same year; in Moscow, in August, Churchill had promised it for 1943; now 1944 was established as the most likely target date. The Russians would not be happy when they learned. It was also decided to increase the weight of the strategic bombing offensive against Germany, to continue to send supplies to Russia, and to let the Americans step up operations in the Pacific. But China got short shrift. A campaign to recapture Burma in 1943 was tentatively approved (but quickly postponed after the conference) and the air-combat and transport effort in China was to be increased slightly.

The Casablanca conference took place on the eve of the military turning point of the war. In the months ahead defense would give way to advance. The German troops at Stalingrad surrendered on February 2, 1943. The last resistance in North Africa ended in May, and in July Sicily was invaded. The basic strategic decisions had been made. Victory was far off but in sight. The time had come to indicate something of the terms of that victory. What would happen to enemies? Even more important, what would happen to Allies? These were most difficult questions to which Roosevelt preferred to give as little thought as possible. But at Casablanca he realized that there were great dangers in a policy of total silence and great advantages in proclaiming that the United States would fight until the unconditional surrender of the Axis was achieved.

The danger in continued silence was the possibility that Russia and China might become so distrustful of Anglo-American motives that they would break up the coalition on the threshold of victory. What then would happen to the stability of the postwar world? Roosevelt in particular placed great emphasis on the long-term cooperation of the "four policemen." Unfortunately, the course of events during 1942 did not of itself give much cause for optimism. Stalin and Chiang Kai-shek were continually implying treachery or charging the West with bad faith and nefarious motives. The generalissimo asked whether Asians were always to be treated as inferiors. "If we are thus treated during the stress of war, what becomes of our position at the peace conference?"[21] The Soviets, in their turn, seemed wedded to the dark suspicion that Britain and the United States desired them to suffer maximum injury and to emerge from the war as weakened as Germany, thus leaving the world for the capitalists. Although Stalin had endorsed the deal with Darlan as acceptable expediency, inevitably the question arose whether the United States and Britain might not connive in similar fashion with Hitler or Japan at the expense of Russia and China.

Thus, an authoritative guarantee was needed that the United States and Britain would not lay down their arms before victory for all four Allies was achieved. But what were the objectives of victory? Roosevelt could not give a specific description lest it conflict with the Atlantic Charter. Also, many remembered the difficulties Woodrow Wilson had encountered with his Fourteen Points. None of the victors of 1918 had been satisfied and, what was worse, Germany had charged that it had been tricked into an armistice on the basis of conditions that were then violated. Planners in the State Department suggested to Roosevelt that this time the enemy must have no chance to claim that they were not completely defeated. Roosevelt liked the suggestion.

Roosevelt decided before leaving Washington that at Casablanca he would announce the demand for unconditional surrender. At the conference he and Churchill agreed on an announcement. But first there were other matters, including the planning of military operations and a comic opera interlude when Roosevelt and de Gaulle met for the first time and formed mutually unpleasant impressions. Roosevelt hoped that Giraud might yet develop as the American-chosen instrument to lead

---

[21] Ibid., p. 34

French fighting forces and replace de Gaulle. Then, on the last day of the meeting, Roosevelt spoke to a press conference.

> Peace can come to the world only by the total elimination of German and Japanese war power. . . . The elimination of German, Japanese, and Italian war power means the unconditional surrender by Germany, Italy, and Japan. That means a reasonable assurance of future world peace. It does not mean the destruction of the population of Germany, Italy, or Japan, but it does mean the destruction of the philosophies in those countries which are based on conquest and the subjugation of other people.[22]

Churchill associated Great Britain unequivocally with the proclamation. The two leaders sent hearty messages to Stalin and Chiang Kai-shek and the conference came to an end. The future would reveal whether unconditional surrender would have the marvelous effect on Russia and China that Roosevelt hoped.

The proclamation of unconditional surrender has been condemned as one of the great mistakes of the war. Critics argue that the war was unnecessarily prolonged at terrible cost because the German and Japanese people believed that unconditional surrender would mean individual and national annihilation. Therefore, they fought with the fanatical desperation of the doomed. These critics conveniently play down the fact that the original proclamation, supplemented by many public statements of Roosevelt and Churchill, indicated that unconditional surrender did not mean extermination or slavery. Guilty governments were to be eliminated unconditionally, but peoples would be rehabilitated and in time a normal, although disarmed, national life would be resumed. It is true that German and Japanese propagandists distorted the phrase in order to maintain the war spirit, but propagandists can distort anything. It is also true that after Hitler's defeat many German leaders claimed that the Fuhrer would have been overthrown except for the demoralizing impact of the "unconditional surrender" formula on anti-Nazi resistance. Such testimony, however, must be used with caution, for it comes from those who sought, after defeat, to give the impression that

[22]Quoted by Herbert Feis, *Churchill, Roosevelt, Stalin: The War They Waged and the Peace They Sought* (Princeton, N.J.: Princeton University Press, 1957), p. 109. For full documentation on the conference, see U.S. Department of State, *Foreign Relations: The Conferences at Washington, 1941–1942, and Casablanca, 1943* (Washington, D.C.: U.S. Government Printing Office, 1968).

they had always opposed Hitler and thus did not share the guilt for his atrocities. The charge that the goal of unconditional surrender prolonged Japan's will to fight applies primarily to the American refusal to promise that Japan could keep the institution of the emperor.

What then was the harm of "unconditional surrender"? The harm was in the impact of the slogan on the formulation of American policy. Unconditional surrender was in spirit the antithesis of careful long-range planning. It encouraged the delusion that once the Axis was defeated, there would be few obstacles in the way of establishing the peace of the world. Some Americans, nevertheless, did attempt to plan, but their efforts were disconnected, on a small scale, unsustained at the highest level, and never coordinated into a unified policy. The goal of unconditional surrender and the practice of postponing issues not directly connected with defeating the Axis were complementary aspects of the same attitude.

CHAPTER 4

The Road to
Teheran, 1943

This chapter focuses on 1943 — arguably the most satisfying year of the war for President Roosevelt and his diplomatic and military advisers. The tide was running fast toward victory, and the disputes over the shape of the postwar world, although beginning, had not yet reached an acute stage. Italy surrendered; China was recognized in principle as one of the four great powers; and Anglo-American differences over strategy were blended into a firm decision to launch the cross-Channel invasion in the spring of 1944. Stalin berated the British and Americans for not moving sooner, but by the end of the year Soviet-Western relations were much improved. Russia made a public pledge to support a postwar world security organization and indicated secretly that it would enter the war against Japan after Germany's defeat. The year ended in a climax of apparent goodwill and unity at Teheran (Iran) when Roosevelt, Churchill, and Stalin met together for the first time.

Optimism nourished by military success could not have been maintained without hope in Russia's willingness to cooperate in the postwar world. Holding to that hope, American leaders throughout 1943 believed that it was wise to explore the political issues that would have to be solved after the defeat of the Axis while postponing all difficult decisions on the assumption that victory would make the thorniest problem seem easy. They also assumed that the United States would withdraw quickly from direct involvement in European affairs after the war; thus, they believed that military decisions should be designed to defeat the enemy as quickly as possible and to minimize the chance of future political commitments.

ᏻ

After the Casablanca conference in January 1943, General Marshall and his military colleagues worried that the peripheral operations which began with the North African invasion might delay indefinitely the decisive cross-Channel attack. At Casablanca the British prevailed with arguments in favor of an attack on Sicily as the next step. "We came, we listened and we were conquered," General Marshall's chief adviser on strategy commented bitterly.[1] The Americans were now reconciled to the move against Italy. General Eisenhower was even enthusiastic. But now they struggled against British proposals for operations in the eastern Mediterranean. The Aegean islands? The Balkans? Would diversions never end?

The arrival of spring brought a welcome change in outlook. President Roosevelt, who had overruled the military by deciding on the North African invasion in 1942, now became less interested in Churchill's peripheral strategy and started to give more support to his own military advisers. The shift may well have been facilitated by Admiral William D. Leahy, who, as personal chief of staff to Roosevelt and chairman of the Joint Chiefs of Staff, interpreted the military to the president and vice versa. Leahy believed passionately in the cross-Channel operation, was deeply antagonistic to British suggestions, and retained many isolationist assumptions concerning America's future role in European affairs. Leahy did not shape policy directly, but by controlling much of the military information that reached the president's desk, he conditioned the atmosphere in which decisions were made.

The change was evident at Trident, the full-dress diplomatic and military conference held with the British in Washington in May 1943. With the president's support, Marshall won agreement to the principle that further Mediterranean operations would be undertaken only if they did not constitute a drain on the buildup for the main attack in 1944. The Americans, in turn, agreed that the elimination of Italy from the war was a practical objective for 1943, and the British for the first time accepted a precise date for

---

[1]General Albert C. Wedemeyer, quoted by Ray S. Cline, *Washington Command Post: The Operations Division* (Washington, D.C.: U.S. Government Printing Office, 1951), p. 236.

the cross-Channel attack: May 1, 1944. At the same time an increase in the tempo of Pacific operations was sanctioned. The Japanese, having failed to hold naval superiority at the battles of the Coral Sea and Solomon Islands in 1942, were now in retreat, with their vast island perimeter of conquest beginning to shrink back toward the Philippines and the homeland. The war in the Pacific, it should be noted, was almost exclusively an American show and as such required far less diplomatic negotiation than operations in Europe. That explains the relative neglect of the Pacific in this study.

In the summer Americans completed basic plans for the great operation, now known as Overlord, and secured further British commitment at the Quadrant conference in Quebec during August.[2] Meanwhile, Mussolini had been ousted as head of the Italian government (July 25, 1943) and his successor, Marshal Pietro Badoglio, was hinting at Italy's readiness to switch sides. In August Anglo-American forces captured Sicily, and during the first days of September the Italian government surrendered as Allied troops landed on the mainland. By now the tide was running strongly against Germany in Russia. The Red Army, after the crucial victory at Stalingrad in January 1943, gained the permanent initiative. Stalin gradually became convinced that the cross-Channel invasion would, at last, take place as promised. The last vestige of fundamental Anglo-American strategic uncertainty for Europe was removed in December at the Sextant conference in Cairo. An official U.S. military historian has written: "If, in planning for the offensive phase of coalition warfare against Germany, Trident symbolized for American strategists a half-way mark, and Quadrant the start of the final lap, Sextant represented reaching the goal."[3] There were still military disagreements in the months ahead, but they dealt with tactics and political implications rather than with grand strategy.

That, in brief, was the optimistic background to the year's political discussions. The British, convinced of the necessity of

---

[2]The documentation for the 1943 Anglo-American summit conferences appears in U.S. Department of State, *Foreign Relations of the United States: The Conferences at Washington and Quebec, 1943* (Washington, D.C.: U.S. Government Printing Office, 1970).

[3]Maurice Matloff, *Strategic Planning for Coalition Warfare, 1943–1944* (Washington, D.C.: U.S. Government Printing Office, 1959), p. 393.

making political plans, took the initiative by sending Foreign Secretary Anthony Eden to Washington in March 1943. The significant portion of the Eden conversations took place in the White House with Roosevelt and Harry Hopkins, who filled a role equivalent to the national security adviser of a later generation, while unhappy Hull, the secretary of state, was pushed farther into obscurity. The president's habit of excluding Hull from all important conversations meant that the professional officers of the State Department were isolated from the conduct of foreign policy. They worked hard, wrote detailed and often discerning memoranda, and made recommendations, but the president seldom acknowledged their existence.

Russia was the first topic in the White House talks with the British foreign secretary. Roosevelt asked Eden for an opinion on the thesis "that the Soviet Government was determined to dominate all of Europe by force of arms or by force of communist propaganda." Eden replied with an optimistic analysis (which the British later abandoned). Stalin, he said, hoped for cooperation with the United States and Britain but "in any event a wise and expedient thing was to cultivate to the utmost . . . the friendship and confidence of the Soviet Government." Roosevelt agreed wholeheartedly. The conversation turned to Russia's territorial objectives. Eden said Stalin would insist on annexing the three Baltic republics. Roosevelt said that was lamentable but could not be prevented. He hoped for the sake of appearances that Russia would conduct plebiscites to show that the Baltic people wanted to be incorporated into the U.S.S.R.

Next came some discussion of the friction between Russia and the Polish government-in-exile. It was agreed that the London Poles were troublemakers whose complaints and unreasonable demands were endangering relations with Russia. Roosevelt said that a Polish settlement would have to be dictated; "as far as Poland is concerned, the important thing is to set it up in a way that will maintain the peace of the world." The readiness to dictate to a small power reflected Roosevelt's conviction that the "four policemen" would run the world. He said there might be a world organization with general membership, "but . . . the real decisions should be made by the United States, Great Britain, Russia and China, who would have . . . to police the world." The president laid particular emphasis on the importance of strengthening China as the leading power in Asia. Eden disagreed and said he "did not much like the idea of the Chinese running up and down the Pacific." Positions were reversed in regard to France. Roosevelt said France should be disarmed and Eden said it should be restored as a European power. Germany, they both agreed, "must be divided into several states, one of which must, over all circumstances, be Prussia."[4]

The conversations were rambling and inconclusive but of great importance as a revelation of Roosevelt's attitudes. Many of his passing remarks were to broaden into basic themes of policy for the remainder of the war. Later decisions would be based on the hope of cooperation with Russia, on annoyance with the claims of small countries and especially Poland, on a preference for a postwar world ruled by great powers, on support for China's future prominence, on antipathy to France, and on a belief that a power vacuum in the heart of Europe — in place of Germany — was desirable. Eden thought Roosevelt approached the future with "cheerful fecklessness. He seemed to see himself disposing of the fate of many lands, allied no less than enemy. He did all this with so much grace that it was not easy to dissent. Yet it was too like a conjuror, skillfully juggling with balls of dynamite, whose nature he failed to understand."[5]

Roosevelt, who usually avoided bringing discordant topics into any conversation, did not explore with Eden one of the most significant aspects of this thinking: the idea that Britain, rather than Russia, might be the principal disruptive force of the postwar world. First, he feared that the British might return to an old-fashioned scramble for political spheres of influence in Europe, thus frightening the Russians, who were naturally sensitive about their security, and ultimately provoking a third world war. Roosevelt also believed that British imperialism, especially in India, would produce explosive unrest unless the colonial peoples were granted independence or placed under trusteeship in preparation for independence. He did cast a few darts at Eden on this subject during the conversations.

[4] The account of the Eden mission and the quotations are derived from *Foreign Relations, 1943*, vol. 3 (1963), pp. 9–41.

[5] The Earl of Avon [Anthony Eden], *The Eden Memoirs: The Reckoning* (Boston: Houghton Mifflin, 1965), p. 374.

Notwithstanding Eden's insistence on the importance of cultivating Russian friendship, Roosevelt had reason to believe that a
serious Anglo-Soviet rivalry for power in postwar Europe was a
possibility. There were British procrastination over establishing
the second front and reluctance to make sacrifices to maintain the
flow of convoys to north Russia. There were also Churchill's obsession with Mediterranean operations that would contribute little
to the quick defeat of Germany and his eagerness to restore the
military power of France for questionable political reasons.
Above all there was British history: the decades of anti-
Bolshevism and the centuries of reliance on the bankrupt (in the
American view) balance of power. Roosevelt believed he could
prevent this dangerous rivalry by convincing Stalin that the
United States was an unselfish mediator interested only in preserving peace, not an accomplice of Great Britain ready to gang up
against Russia. Accordingly, the president suggested to Stalin that
they meet alone for confidential talks free from the embarrass-
ment of Churchill's presence.

In order to emphasize the urgency of such a meeting, Roosevelt sent Joseph E. Davies, a former ambassador to Russia
(1937–38), on a special mission to Moscow in May 1943. Davies
was an admirer of Stalin and a man who refused to allow contrary evidence to undermine his faith in Soviet good intentions.
Davies flattered Stalin, told American news correspondents in
Moscow that any criticism of Russia bordered on treason because
it played into Hitler's hands, and showed an embarrassingly
propagandistic Hollywood movie based on his previous experience as ambassador. He gained Stalin's tentative agreement to
a one-on-one meeting with Roosevelt, but Stalin later changed his
mind when he learned there would be no second front in western
Europe before 1944.[6] Meanwhile, Churchill learned of Roosevelt's
attempt to arrange a meeting from which he would be excluded.
The prime minister protested:

> I do not underrate the use that enemy propaganda would make of
> meeting between the heads of Soviet Russia and the United States at
> this juncture with the British Commonwealth and Empire excluded.
> It would be serious and vexatious, and many would be bewildered
> and alarmed thereby.

[6]See Elizabeth Kimball MacLean, "Joseph E. Davies and Soviet-American Relations, 1941–43," *Diplomatic History,* 4 (Winter 1980): 73–93.

Roosevelt, who was sometimes careless with the truth, replied, "I did not suggest to U.J. [Uncle Joe; i.e., Stalin] that we meet alone."[7] Churchill let the matter drop and the president now joined him in trying to arrange a three-way meeting with Stalin.

Although denied his meeting alone with Stalin, Roosevelt continued until his death to seek a special personal relationship with the Soviet dictator and to court Russian approval by seeming to belittle his interest in Anglo-American ties. "The President's plan," an American diplomat who worked with Roosevelt has written, "was to make the Russians feel that the Americans trusted them implicitly and valued Soviet-American cooperation in war and peace above any other prospective alliance."[8] Churchill described the same attitude as "a strong current of opinion in American Government circles, which seemed to wish to win Russian confidence even at the expense of coordinating the Anglo-American war effort."[9]

$\sim$

Russian behavior made it difficult for many American officials to accept the president's perspective. For example, the Russians were surly and uncooperative recipients of lend-lease aid. They harassed American lend-lease administrators in Russia with petty indignities and refused to provide the basic information on their resources which the United States considered essential if aid was to be effective. In March 1943 Admiral William H. Standley, the American ambassador in Moscow, cabled to Washington:

> I am becoming convinced that we can only deal with [the Russians] on a bargaining basis for our continuing to accede freely to their requests while agreeing to pay an additional price for every small request we make seems to arouse suspicion of our motives in the Oriental Russian mind rather than to build confidence.[10]

[7]Churchill's telegram of June 25, 1943, and Roosevelt's reply of June 28, *Foreign Relations of the United States, The Conferences at Cairo and Tehran, 1943* (1961), pp. 10–11.

[8]Robert Murphy, *Diplomat Among Warriors* (Garden City, N.Y.: Doubleday, 1964), p. 210.

[9]Winston S. Churchill, *Closing the Ring* (Boston: Houghton Mifflin, 1951), p. 311.

[10]*Foreign Relations, 1943*, vol. 3 (1963), p. 510.

The ambassador was told firmly from Washington that there must be no change of approach. Shortly thereafter Admiral Standley resigned. He was replaced at the end of 1943 by W. Averell Harriman, a man familiar with lend-lease problems and the Soviet Union. George F. Kennan was appointed second in command to Harriman in the Moscow embassy.

Soviet recrimination over the delay in the opening of the second front was a most serious symptom of bad feeling. Stalin, unimpressed by the announcement of the doctrine of unconditional surrender, began the year by complaining of the inadequacy of the military decisions reached at Casablanca. The second front must be launched in the spring or summer of 1943, he said. When Joseph Davies was in Moscow in May, he warned Roosevelt that a failure "to 'deliver' on the western front in Europe this summer" might have a serious impact on Russia's war effort and "participation in the reconstruction of peace."[11] Then Stalin learned of the Trident decisions that the cross-Channel operation would not be undertaken until the spring of 1944. His response to this news was virtually a charge of "deliberate bad faith" by the United States.

> Your decision creates exceptional difficulties for the Soviet Union, which, straining all its resources, for the past two years, has been engaged against the main forces of Germany and her satellites, and leaves the Soviet Army, which is fighting not only for its country, but also for its Allies, to do the job alone, almost single-handed, against an enemy that is still very strong and formidable.
>
> Need I speak of the dishearteningly negative impression that this fresh postponement of the second front and the withholding from our Army, which has sacrificed so much, of the anticipated substantial support by the Anglo-American armies, will produce in the Soviet Union—both among the people and in the Army?
>
> As for the Soviet Government, it cannot align itself with this decision, which, moreover, was adopted without its participation and without any attempt at a joint discussion of this highly important matter and which may gravely affect the subsequent course of the war.[12]

[11] Ibid., p. 658.

[12] *Stalin's Correspondence with Churchill, Attlee, Roosevelt and Truman, 1941–45* (London: Lawrence & Wishart, 1958), Document No. 92.

Soviet suspicions were further heightened by the manner in which the United States and Great Britain conducted the negotiations for Italy's surrender. The Russians resented that they were not consulted in detail and they expressed uneasiness over the lenient treatment accorded to the reactionary regime of Marshal Badoglio. Did that mean, asked the famous Soviet writer Ilya Ehrenburg, that Britain and the United States would someday deal with Hermann Goering in Germany? The question was misleading because Italy was in no way comparable to Germany in Anglo-American thinking.

Mussolini, in power since 1922, did not excite the same loathing as did Hitler. He was viewed as a distasteful windbag who had performed useful services for his country (the cliché was that he made the trains run on time) until, in the 1930s, he became intoxicated by an antique and unfortunately grandiose vision of Italian imperialism, while, at about the same time, coming under the sinister influence of Hitler. The Italian people were regarded with pity and condescending affection. They had been tragically misled, so went the popular wisdom, by Mussolini into committing a series of cowardly deeds; nevertheless they retained an image of being fun-loving and humane, quite different from the cold and deadly Germans. Unconditional surrender specifically applied to Italy, but the American and British governments implied that Italy would be forgiven if it abandoned Germany. For example, as the invasion of Sicily began in July 1943, Italian cities were showered with leaflets in which Roosevelt and Churchill held out the hope that Italy might regain "a respected place in the family of European nations. . . . The time has come for you to decide whether Italians shall die for Mussolini and Hitler — or live for Italy, and for civilisation."[13]

The response from Rome came quickly. Mussolini was removed from office July 25 and his successor, Badoglio, soon sent out peace feelers through agents in Lisbon, Tangier, and then Madrid. Roosevelt and Churchill now found themselves subjected to the same type of criticism at home and from Moscow which had greeted the deal with Darlan during the previous year. Badoglio was an old Fascist and, before falling out with Mussolini in 1940, had led Italian troops in the despicable attack on Ethiopia

---

[13]Churchill, *Closing the Ring*, p. 46.

in 1935; furthermore, he was supporting and supported by an unattractive and antidemocratic monarch, King Victor Emmanuel III. To deal with Badoglio and the king, said outraged liberals, was to give aid and comfort to the very elements for whose destruction the war was supposedly being fought. Military expediency, however, was a stronger argument than doctrinaire idealism; serious armistice negotiations began on the assumption that the Badoglio regime could continue in power.

Badoglio tried to maneuver Britain and the United States into accepting Italy as an ally against Germany rather than as a surrendered enemy. That was too much. Badoglio was required to accept armistice terms giving the Allies an unfettered right to decide Italy's fate. The Allies decided that treatment of Italy would evolve dependent on its behavior and especially on the vigor and sincerity of its resistance to Germany. The surrender was formally proclaimed on September 8, 1943. Italy declared war on Germany and was thereafter treated with increasing leniency. It had surrendered in the expectation of finding surcease from the horror of war, but, ironically, its worst days were yet to come as the Germans fought a grim two-year holding action along the length of the Italian peninsula. Liberation was achieved at frightful cost, and it came only with the defeat of Germany.

The Russians were excluded from all participation in the arrangements for Italian surrender and afterwards from an effective share in the management of Italian affairs. Was this a mistake? Stalin said it was intolerable for Russia to be a mere observer while the United States and Britain made arrangements for Europe. Some American diplomats warned that later Russia could cite the Italian precedent while excluding the United States and Britain from a voice in the affairs of the countries liberated by the Red Army. If Russia had been made a managing partner in Italy, would the Kremlin have abandoned its suspicions and given the West a share in, for example, the political reconstruction of Poland? In retrospect it seems more likely that the Soviets would have exploited their Italian foothold while still excluding the British and Americans from eastern Europe. Thus, the procedure in Italy was probably prudent as a matter of long-term political calculation as well as short-term military expediency. Some postwar observers have gone so far as to condemn the decision to give Russia a seat on the Allied Advisory Council in Italy, even though the council had no power, on the grounds that membership gave respectability to communism and facilitated the return of the Communist party to Italian politics. On the other hand, if the prevention of the division of Europe into spheres of influence was a desirable goal, British and American behavior in Italy was not the way to start.

Because Russia was a powerless observer in Italy, occupation policy was a compromise of British and American views. The British, and Churchill in particular, believed that the Italian monarchy ought to be retained as an element of stability. Churchill also argued that there were few experienced liberal politicians in Italy after twenty-two years of fascism; therefore, it was necessary to work with right-wing figures such as Badoglio. He feared the alternative was communism. The more idealistic Americans urged the establishment of a republic and were unhappy at working with men like Badoglio. Roosevelt and Hopkins believed that Churchill had a dangerous predilection for monarchies and that his motives in trying to protect King Victor Emmanuel were unworthy of a democratic statesman. After months of tedious Anglo-American fencing over Italian politics, Badoglio stepped down and was followed by a succession of unstable governments of generally liberal hue. Finally, in June 1946, general elections and a referendum were held. The Christian Democrats won the largest number of votes and the monarchy was voted down by a 6-to-5 margin in favor of a republic. Thus, American pressure prevailed in the long run.[14]

The contretemps over Italy boded ill for the future. Even more ominous was the hostility between Russia and the Polish government-in-exile in London. In 1919 the proud Poles regained their national independence (lost since the eighteenth century) and proceeded to attack Russia, then weak from the ordeal of revolution and civil war. The resulting Treaty of Riga (1921) pushed Poland's frontier more than 100 miles to the east at Russia's expense. The population of the annexed area was mixed, although more than half were Ukrainians and Russians. The 1921 line lasted until 1939, when Poland was attacked and partitioned by Germany and Russia acting in collusion. The Polish exile government that

---

[14]Norman Kogan, *Italy and the Allies* (Cambridge, Mass.: Harvard University Press, 1956), is a useful survey.

eventually established itself in London looked on Stalin and Hitler as equal enemies. Then came Hitler's invasion of Russia and the formation of the Anglo-American-Soviet coalition against Germany. The London Poles opened diplomatic relations with Moscow, but they could not forget past hatred — nor could Stalin.

The location of the Russian-Polish boundary remained in dispute. The Poles said they could not consent during the war to any retreat from the 1921 line. The Soviets said they insisted upon the western frontier of 1941 as it existed before the German attack. This happened to correspond closely to a boundary suggested at the Paris Peace Conference after the First World War and called the Curzon line, after the British foreign secretary who officially sponsored it. A third of a nation lay between. The Poles, with their country under German occupation, had little material power, and they feared that Roosevelt and Churchill would deal their territory away to Russia. Roosevelt had little sympathy for Poland, but he was careful to avoid an open concession to Russia, largely because he was sensitive to the political power of several million Polish-Americans. His tactic was procrastination and postponement.

Polish Prime Minister Sikorski was tireless in his efforts to change the American position. If Stalin's pretensions were not firmly challenged now, he said in January 1943, Stalin

> will take it for granted that neither the United States nor Great Britain are going to lift a finger to prevent the domination at the close of the war of most of eastern and southern Europe by the Soviet Union, and the imperialistic ambitions of the Soviet Union will be greatly accelerated and enhanced.

Roosevelt told the Polish government "to keep its shirt on."[15] The American argument was that Poland's and the world's security would depend on Russia's willingness to cooperate in the postwar world; therefore, the present time was no time to make trouble.

Meanwhile, the Russians were treating as Soviet citizens all those who had resided in the disputed area before the war. They also had arrested Polish relief agents who were trying to ease the suffering of Polish refugees in Russia. In April 1943 a major crisis erupted when the Germans announced to the world the discovery,

[15] *Foreign Relations, 1943*, vol. 3 (1963), pp. 317, 329.

in the Katyn forest, of mass graves containing the bodies of 8,000 Polish officers allegedly murdered in 1940 by the Russians, who were holding them prisoner. The Germans exploited the propaganda value of this charge to the utmost, and the Poles suspected, correctly, that it was true. Katyn appeared to be the grim answer to the mystery of the whereabouts of thousands of officers who had vanished without trace from Russian prison camps. The London Poles spurned advice to keep silent in the interests of Allied unity and publicly requested an investigation by the International Red Cross. The Soviet government said it was being outrageously slandered, broke diplomatic relations with the Polish government-in-exile, and soon began to organize a largely Communist clique of Poles in Russia to assume the future government of Poland. After the Katyn crisis, the issue of Polish frontiers became less important than the question of who would rule in postwar Poland: a Soviet satellite regime or freely elected successors to the London exile government.[16]

∽

When Stalin refused to meet the president either alone or with Churchill, Roosevelt settled for the Anglo-American conference (Quadrant) in Quebec in August 1943. The coordination of military strategy for western Europe was the principal business of this conference, but Stalin's ominous conduct could not be ignored. Churchill saw "bloody consequences in the future."[17] Roosevelt, however, appeared to retain an undaunted faith in ultimate Soviet good intentions.

As if to prove Roosevelt correct, Stalin began to soften his tone and suggested a meeting in the immediate future of responsible representatives of the three countries pending the time when the Big Three conference could be arranged. A few weeks later, Stalin for the first time said he was ready to meet Roosevelt and Churchill in late November provided that the meeting was held near the Soviet border in Teheran, capital of Iran. Roosevelt and Churchill

---

[16]The episode is placed in its larger context by J. K. Zawodny, *Death in the Forest: The Story of the Katyn Forest Massacre* (Notre Dame, Ind.: University of Notre Dame Press, 1962).

[17]Herbert Feis, *Churchill, Roosevelt, Stalin: The War They Waged and the Peace They Sought* (Princeton, N.J.: Princeton University Press, 1957), p. 172.

agreed on the preliminary meeting on the foreign minister level to be held in Moscow, but the president said the constitutional necessity of keeping in touch with Congress prevented him from going as far as Iran for the larger meeting. Meanwhile, Secretary of State Hull prepared to go to Moscow. Here was his first and only major assignment during the war. The prospect filled him with a sense of exaltation. He believed the Moscow meeting would be a turning point in world history.

The secretary's high expectations grew out of his passionate involvement in preparations for the establishment of a postwar international security organization. Isolated from the president and lacking knowledge of important wartime negotiations, the secretary found solace in the hope that a new league of nations, fulfilling the vision of Woodrow Wilson, would emerge from the war. Hull believed that the tragic rejection of American membership in the League of Nations in 1919–20 resulted partly from Wilson's failure to educate the American people and partly from an evil mixture of partisan politics with foreign policy. He saw it as his mission to prevent the Wilsonian tragedy from happening again. With his eyes more on the past than on the harshness of the present, he organized an extensive planning operation centered in the State Department but reaching out to leaders of both parties in Congress and representatives of many segments of American life. By the autumn of 1943 the result of this work was evident in the overwhelming majorities that passed the Connally resolution in the Senate and the Fulbright resolution in the House, calling on the United States to help establish and maintain an "international authority with power to prevent aggression and to preserve the peace of the world." Hull believed that American isolationism was dead and that, if the Soviet Union would adhere to a declaration on collective security which he would sponsor at the Moscow conference, the millennium might well be at hand.[18]

The three powers approached the Moscow conference in different ways. The Russians proposed that the question of the Anglo-American second front be the only item on the agenda. The British put forward a long list of European political issues for examination. Hull opposed the British approach and argued that

[18] Robert A. Divine, *Second Chance: The Triumph of Internationalism in America during World War II* (New York: Atheneum, 1967).

if the great powers could agree broadly on the idea of collective security, detailed questions could be easily solved later. He concentrated all his efforts on securing passage of a declaration proclaiming that the powers "recognize the necessity of establishing at the earliest practicable date a general international organization, based on the principle of the sovereign equality of all peace-loving states, and open to membership by all such states, large and small, for the maintenance of international peace and security."[19]

The procedure at the conference was a compromise. First, the Russians were satisfied, thanks to skillful statements by the American and British military delegates, that a second front in the spring of 1944 would occur. Then the British brought up a variety of political questions on which Hull avoided expressing an opinion. No specific decisions of importance were reached, but it was agreed to establish a tripartite body, the European Advisory Commission (EAC), to sit in London and consider problems arising out of the liberation of Europe from Nazi domination. The responsibilities and powers of the EAC were left poorly defined. British Foreign Secretary Eden believed the body should be granted broad responsibility, but Hull and Molotov disagreed. The Russians seemed to fear that they might be outvoted, and Hull suspected that the EAC, unless narrowly restricted in its scope, might develop into a regional control body for Europe and thus undermine the general responsibility of the future world organization.

Day after day Hull tried to steer the conference away from details and on to the consideration of the general principles embodied in his declaration on collective security, but he encountered a worrisome obstacle in Russia's unwillingness to accept China as a signatory. The American secretary of state said it was essential to recognize China as one of the four great powers upon which the success of the world organization would depend. "China is too important a factor," Roosevelt and his advisers agreed before Hull's departure for Moscow, "both now and in the future, both because of herself and because of her influence over British India, to be alienated."[20] The Russians, like the British, were dubious concerning China's power and furthermore wished to avoid com-

[19] *Foreign Relations, 1943*, vol. 1 (1963), p. 756.
[20] Ibid., pp. 541–542.

promising their neutrality in the war against Japan by being associated in a political statement with China. Hull told Molotov that there would be no declaration at all if China was not an original signatory. The Russians relented. On October 30 the famed Four Power Declaration was signed, with the Chinese ambassador in Moscow acting on China's behalf.

After the conference adjourned, Hull's jubilation was boundless as he listened to Stalin say privately that Russia would go to war against Japan after Germany was defeated. Unity for global victory and permanent peace seemed complete. Back in Washington in November, the secretary told a joint session of Congress what the Moscow conference signified: "There will no longer be need for spheres of influence, for alliances, for balance of power, or any other of the special arrangements through which, in the unhappy past, the nations strove to safeguard their security or to promote their interests."[21] The applause was deafening. All that remained to bring the optimism of 1943 to a climax was the much-desired but elusive Big Three meeting.

In Moscow Hull had failed to persuade Stalin to make a meeting with Roosevelt possible by traveling farther from Moscow than Teheran. The president then dropped the excuse that he could not maintain adequate communication with Congress in Teheran and gave in to Stalin. On November 11 Roosevelt left Washington and, after stopping at Cairo for a conference with Generalissimo and Madame Chiang Kai-shek, arrived at the American legation in Teheran on November 27. That evening Stalin, warning of security problems, invited the president to stay in the larger and better-protected Russian embassy. Roosevelt accepted and on November 28 established himself in Russian quarters, where he met Stalin for the first time.

In four crowded, disorganized, and exhilarating days the president conferred in formal session and informally at meals with Stalin and Churchill and on several occasions with Stalin alone. Secure in the knowledge that they represented, as Churchill observed, the greatest concentration of power the world had ever seen, the three leaders planned amicably for the final defeat

---

[21] Cordell Hull, *The Memoirs of Cordell Hull*, vol. 2 (New York: Macmillan, 1948), pp. 1314–1315.

of the Axis. Churchill showed his usual interest in a variety of Mediterranean and Balkan operations, but Stalin and Roosevelt chose to permit no dilution of the Overlord plan. The Russians promised to time their great spring offensives so as to give maximum aid to the cross-Channel invasion. Stalin also reaffirmed Russia's intention to enter the war against Japan. Military plans, however, were less important than the political discussions of the conference. Without making a single formal commitment, the three leaders laid down the guidelines that governed the settlement of the war and went far toward meeting Soviet objectives. The Yalta conference of February 1945 is usually considered the great decision-making conclave of the war, but Yalta merely filled in the outline already sketched at Teheran.

Roosevelt's position emerged from days of disconnected conversation in which he cast himself in the role of the genial mediator who could laugh at Churchill's prejudices and win his way to Stalin's heart. When alone with the Soviet leader, however, Roosevelt was less than mediator, for he then laid great emphasis on American disagreement with Britain. For example, he invited Stalin's support in a general liquidation of British and French colonialism. India, they agreed, was an especially difficult problem. The general impression left by Roosevelt in his private talks with Stalin was that the United States was as likely to side with Russia as with Britain in the event of some future disagreement. There is no evidence that Stalin believed this. Some have suggested he suspected a trick.

The attitude Roosevelt displayed toward France at Teheran illustrates his desire to contrast himself with the British. In the year since the North African landings, General de Gaulle had demonstrated his ability to win the support of the French people in North Africa, the overseas colonies, and the underground within France. The British had had their share of problems with de Gaulle, but they acknowledged him as the undisputed French leader. But Roosevelt reacted negatively to the consolidation of de Gaulle's authority and rejected every suggestion that the United States ought to work more closely with the French Committee of National Liberation. On the contrary, the president supported a tentative plan to govern France after liberation by an official responsible directly to the supreme Allied commander, whose job it would be "to hold the scales even between all French political groups sympathetic to the Allied cause."[22] This meant, in effect, treating France more like an occupied than a liberated country. De Gaulle, on the contrary, expected that his committee would be responsible for governing France.

The president seemed bent not only on blocking de Gaulle's drive for authority but also on punishing France as a whole for its failure to resist Germany in 1940. On the way to Teheran he told the Joint Chiefs of Staff that "it was his opinion that France would certainly not become a first class power for at least 25 years."[23] The contrary British expectation, he said, was wrong and merely reflected the British desire to have French military strength at their disposal in the future. Roosevelt expanded on these ideas in conversation with Stalin, commenting that no Frenchman over the age of forty should be allowed to hold office in postwar France, thus disqualifying all those in positions of responsibility at the time of the German victory. He agreed with Stalin that "the French must pay for their criminal collaboration with Germany" and that "the entire French ruling class was rotten to the core."[24] No decisions were made in regard to France at Teheran, but from the drift of Roosevelt's remarks it appeared that he and Stalin were united against Churchill in their determination to treat France almost as an enemy country and to prevent the reestablishment of its military power.

The future of Germany was the most important topic discussed at Teheran. Churchill recommended a moderate reorganization of Germany in order to create political and economic stability. He said Prussia, which he considered the source of German militarism, should be detached and south Germany ought to be associated with the small Danubian states in a confederation. Stalin attacked the idea of a confederation and demanded drastic dismemberment. Roosevelt sided with Stalin and put forward a plan fo the permanent partition of the German state into five weak, self-governing parts and the imposition of an international trusteeship over the heavily industrial Ruhr and Saar regions, the city of Hamburg, and the Kiel Canal. The preservation of this regime

---

[22]Quoted by Julius W. Pratt, *Cordell Hull*, vol. 2 (New York: Cooper Square, 1964), p. 586. This work is one of the series on "The American Secretaries of State and Their Diplomacy," edited by Samuel Flagg Bemis and Robert H. Ferrell.

[23]*Foreign Relations, The Conferences at Cairo and Tehran* (1961), p. 195.

[24]Ibid., pp. 485, 509.

would depend on Russian power, for the president assumed that the American people would demand the withdrawal of American troops shortly after victory. Churchill argued against such schemes, only to be accused by Stalin of harboring a secret affection for Germany.

Roosevelt's habit on these tense occasions was to preserve the generally friendly tone of the discussion by giving good-natured support to Stalin. For example, one night at dinner Stalin said that 50,000 to 100,000 German officers ought to be exterminated (shades of the Katyn massacre). Churchill was appalled and stoutly combated this proposal of "cold blooded execution of soldiers who had fought for their country." Roosevelt, however, tried a macabre joke by saying the figure for execution should be set at 49,000 or more.[25] In the end all agreed that it was too soon to reach final conclusions about Germany and that the European Advisory Commission should be directed to conduct further studies. The rule for Germany, as for every other difficult question at Teheran was: if at first you disagree, postpone.

The three leaders agreed that the future of Poland was a crucial question. Here Churchill took the initiative, saying that Britain had gone to war in 1939 because of Germany's invasion of Poland and was now committed to the reestablishment of a strong, independent country. Stalin, however, blocked any constructive discussion by saying that the Polish government in London was implicated with the Germans and that their agents in Poland were killing partisans. Roosevelt said little on the Polish question in the presence of Churchill, but privately he told Stalin he needed the votes of the 6 or 7 million Americans of Polish extraction in the United States. For this reason, although he could understand Stalin's views on Poland, he could not participate in any decisions until after the elections. Stalin replied that now that the president had explained, he understood.

Many other European issues were discussed in tentative fashion. Roosevelt could truthfully say that he had made no commitments, yet he had made implicit agreements. From them one could project one possible future for Europe. As one American participant at the conference wrote:

> Germany is to be broken up and kept broken up. The states of eastern, southeastern, and central Europe will not be permitted to

[25] Ibid., p. 554.

group themselves into any federations or associations. France . . . will not be permitted to maintain any appreciable military establishment. Poland and Italy will remain approximately their present territorial size, but it is doubtful if either will be permitted to maintain any appreciable armed force. The result would be that the Soviet Union would be the only important military and political force on the continent of Europe.[26]

The president did not permit himself to share these forebodings. He was convinced that a common desire for peace would prompt Stalin to cooperate as one of the "four policemen" of the world as long as the other great powers continued to trust Russia. In that case, no nation need fear Soviet military and political power in Europe.

East Asian questions were not discussed at great length at Teheran. Stalin reaffirmed Russia's intention of entering the war against Japan and indicated that in due time he would expect compensation. Roosevelt agreed that Russia might acquire all of the Kurile Islands and the southern half of Sakhalin from Japan. More important, Dairen in Manchuria could be made a free port in order to give Russia an ice-free outlet, and Russia might also regain some of the special privileges it had enjoyed long ago on the Manchurian railways. Stalin wondered if China would approve of such arrangements. Roosevelt foresaw no difficulties. Churchill was delighted by the discussion and said "that hungry nations and ambitious nations are dangerous, and he would like to see the leading nations of the world in the position of rich, happy men."[27]

Roosevelt left Teheran on December 2 and, after further conferences in Cairo, returned to Washington in triumph. His personal meeting with Stalin had apparently accomplished all and more than he had expected. The year that opened with the proclamation of the doctrine of unconditional surrender was closing with military victory assured, after which the great powers would cooperate in bringing stable peace in Europe. Only in Asia did Roosevelt see major uncertainties. Britain and Russia had recognized China as a great power in principle; could they be persuaded to recognize China in fact? Roosevelt believed that China's attainment of its place as the leader of Asia would mean the end of European colonialism. Would Britain and France withdraw peacefully?

[26] Quoted by Feis, *Churchill, Roosevelt, Stalin*, p. 275.

[27] *Foreign Relations, The Conferences at Cairo and Tehran* (1961), p. 568.

CHAPTER 5

India, China, and Anti-Imperialism

The undeniable importance of wartime disputes between the United States and the Soviet Union for the subsequent development of the Cold War should not blind us to the fact that throughout most of the war President Roosevelt and his advisers were seriously worried about the continued existence of Western, particularly British and French, imperialism. By imperialism they meant rule by Europeans over what later became known as the Third World—economically undeveloped and mostly non-white peoples of Africa and Asia.

The president believed that a refusal by the imperial powers to set colonial peoples on the road to independence was an immediate obstacle to the war effort and in the long run was more likely to produce future wars than anything the Russians might do. Thus, he embarked on a crusade against imperialism in the Allied camp. This crusade enjoyed a high personal priority until the closing months of the war when, with the defeat of the Axis certain, Russian behavior in Europe was perceived by many of the president's advisers as the greater threat to lasting peace. Roosevelt's own commitment to anticolonialism also appears to have waned—perhaps he hoped it would be only temporary—in 1945, when he saw that it was necessary to be concerned, after all, with the reconstruction of France in Europe.

The British at the time and some commentators since have belittled Roosevelt's anti-imperialism as ill-informed, intuitive, and superficial. British Foreign Secretary Anthony Eden, for example, called the president's thinking about India "a terrifying commentary on the likely Roosevelt contribution to the peace, a meandering amateurishness lit by discursive flashes."[1] But each passing decade since Roosevelt's death has confirmed the essential wisdom of his insight if not his profundity.

Anti-imperialism is the oldest ideal of American foreign policy, although the term itself is a product of the late nineteenth century. Since 1776 the United States has deplored the domination of one people by another and has encouraged aspirations for independence everywhere in the world. Although American governments have frequently been untrue to the ideal (for example, in regard to Hawaii, the Philippines, Cuba, Puerto Rico, and Panama), the Roosevelt administration displayed less inconsistency between rhetoric and behavior than most. During the 1930s the United States pledged not to intervene in the internal affairs of Latin America and promised independence to the Philippines. In the Atlantic Charter of 1941 Roosevelt and Churchill proclaimed "the right of all people to choose the form of government under which they will live." Those words became a rallying cry for colonial peoples during and after the war.

In 1942, as the Japanese wave of conquest swept over southeast Asia and threatened India, anti-imperialism became a perceived military necessity as well as an ideal for the United States. "Asia for the Asians," said the Japanese, in an effort to exploit the dependent peoples' hatred for their European masters. At the same time Nazi propaganda was telling Arabs that German victory would bring them independence. In Washington it seemed that the Allies could lose the war if the colonial peoples believed these arguments and cooperated with the Axis. Considering imperialism morally wrong, economically wasteful, and a breeding ground for war, Americans also believed that independence would mean a happy, stable, and prosperous postwar world — prosperous both for former colonies and for the United States, which would develop new markets. American tradition, morality, military necessity, and future economic interest all converged.

The British and French opposed the American crusade to abolish colonial empires. Churchill, for example, announced in Parliament in September 1941 that the Atlantic Charter applied to the enemy, not to India and Burma; in November 1942 he made

[1]Quoted by Christopher Thorne, *Allies of a Kind: The United States, Britain, and the War Against Japan, 1941–1945* (New York: Oxford University Press, 1978), p. 245. This study is rich with material on the colonial question.

the much publicized remark that he had not become the king's first minister "in order to preside over the liquidation of the British Empire."[2] De Gaulle appeared even more intransigent in his determination to preserve French glory and sovereignty over every square mile of France's prewar colonial empire. At the highest level Roosevelt and Churchill never allowed differences over colonialism to jeopardize the Anglo-American relationship in a fundamental way, but their subordinates operating directly in the colonial areas viewed each other with deep and sometimes irrational suspicion. The typical American representative overseas saw the British as arrogant, swaggering snobs determined to maintain their superiority by trampling on the rights of native peoples. The British, in turn, considered the Americans brash, ignorant intruders who preached freedom simply to oust the British and take over the colonial areas for their own selfish purposes.

Americans did not agree on how freedom for colonial peoples should be achieved. Some public figures, like Vice-President Henry A. Wallace and the 1940 Republican presidential candidate Wendell L. Willkie, implied that immediate independence was desirable and practical. President Roosevelt, however, favored a period of transitional trusteeship on the model of American policy toward the Philippines. "Trusteeship is based on the principle of unselfish service," he wrote in September 1941. "For a time at least there are many minor children among the peoples of the world who need trustees . . . just as there are many adult nations or peoples who must be led back into a spirit of good conduct."[3] Sensitive to the need for delicacy in dealing with the British on the colonial question, he moved by indirection and constantly shifted his ground and opinions. His tactics were the despair of more ardent and doctrinaire anti-imperialists.

∽

Asia, where half the world's population lived under some form of imperialism, was the area of greatest American concern.

[2] Quoted by Ruth B. Russell, *A History of the United Nations Charter: The Role of the United States, 1940–45* (Washington, D.C.: Brookings Institution, 1958), p. 79. This volume also contains much on the colonial issue as it was connected with United Nations trusteeship arrangements.

[3] Ibid., p. 43.

Since the nineteenth century, Americans had looked on their country as beloved guide and protector of China against the selfishness of the other great powers. They were less able to recognize the bedrock of self-interest underlying idealistic rhetoric: by opposing colonial control of China, they would be maintaining an open door for American trade and profits. The attitude toward China symbolized by the Open Door notes of 1899–1900 was extended with the coming of the war to include India and the other British, French, and Dutch colonies of Asia. "White nations," said Roosevelt to Soviet Foreign Minister Molotov in 1942, "could not hope to hold these areas as colonies in the long run."[4] The United States also sought to apply its anti-imperial assumptions to the Middle East, but there encountered a cluster of dilemmas (see Chapter 6). Black Africa was too little known, too remote from the fighting, and seemingly too backward to attract attention. A few lower-echelon diplomats were aware of latent turmoil on the African continent, but their pleas for the development of an American policy toward Africa were not heard above the clamor of more urgent problems.

Within Asia the initial object of American concern was India, the world's second most populous country and the core of the British Empire.[5] Americans believed Asia would be permanently secure if, as a result of the war, India gained its freedom and China became firmly established as a great power. But American attitudes toward India were contradictory and uninformed. On the one hand, India was perceived as a land of romance, of tigers, elephants, maharajahs, and virtuous Kiplingesque Englishmen. On the other hand, an even stronger image was evoked by the saintly Mahatma Gandhi, whose only weapons in the fight for freedom were nonviolent resistance and the devotion of his followers. Very little was known in the United States of the bitter feud between the Hindu majority and the large Moslem minority, and less of Britain's complicated efforts since 1917 to prepare India for some form of self-government. Instead of trying to understand the complexity of Indian politics, Americans drew a facile parallel between their own struggle to win independence from

[4] U.S. Department of State, *Foreign Relations of the United States, 1942*, vol. 3 (Washington, D.C.: U.S. Government Printing Office, 1961), p. 581.

[5] A reliable account is Gary R. Hess, *America Encounters India, 1941–1947* (Baltimore, Md.: The Johns Hopkins University Press, 1971).

Britain two centuries before and current Indian aspirations. The parallel had little validity and was bound to mislead.

During the First World War the British government officially declared in favor of the "progressive realisation of responsible government" for India. In the next two decades, however, politicians squabbled endlessly over the meaning of words: what, for example, was "dominion status"? Blood flowed sporadically in the streets. By 1939 the barrier of misunderstanding between the British and Indian leaders was higher than ever. The outbreak of war, staggering British defeats, and the onrushing wave of Japanese conquest brought on a major crisis. Indian leaders, especially in the dominant Congress party, argued that Britain had dragged India into the war without its consent. India was threatened by Japan, they said, only because it was a British base. Why should Indians die to preserve the British Empire? The British reiterated a promise of Indian self-government after the war but said that constitutional issues could not be decided while nations were fighting for their existence. Indians, in turn, distrusted British promises and rightly saw Prime Minister Churchill as an imperialist who would never willingly abandon British sovereignty over India. Churchill's rhetoric was extreme, but his attitudes faithfully reflected the majority of the British government and Parliament.

Even before Pearl Harbor the American government began to interest itself in India on the grounds that the subcontinent's fate was vital to the military security of the United States. Secretary of State Hull discreetly hinted in May 1941 to British Ambassador Halifax (who had served as viceroy of India from 1926 to 1931) that Britain should liberalize its policy toward India, but "nothing came of this approach."[6] In August 1941 John G. Winant, the American ambassador in London, suggested that the United States bring pressure on the British to agree on dominion status for India, but his suggestion was lost in the argument over whether the Atlantic Charter did or did not apply to India. Americans said it applied universally; Churchill said no. His policy was received with dismay in the United States and angry discontent in India. In October 1941 the United States prepared the ground for further intervention by establishing an American dip-

---

[6]Cordell Hull, *The Memoirs of Cordell Hull*, vol. 2 (New York: Macmillan, 1948), p. 1483.

lomatic mission in New Delhi and receiving an Indian agency general in Washington. In the sign language of diplomacy these gestures meant that the United States recognized India's potential for independence.

As the military situation in Asia deteriorated rapidly after Pearl Harbor, both Britain and the United States took further steps. Roosevelt tried to discuss India with Churchill in Washington in December 1941, but he received such a sharp rebuff that thereafter he confined most of his comments to the prime minister on India to writing. Meanwhile, the Japanese were driving the British out of Malaya and Burma. India remained as the only base from which to supply China. Early in 1942 American troops established the necessary airfields on Indian soil. With every Japanese victory, the desire for passive neutrality deepened in India, as did suspicion of British good faith. Churchill rejected the idea of promising India dominion status after the war, with the right of secession from the British Commonwealth. He saw that the Moslem population would consider themselves betrayed by such a development. The Moslem minority feared domination by their Hindu majority enemies in a unified state; by 1942, they were committed to the concept of Pakistan, a separate and independent Moslem realm. The Hindu majority, however, considered the partition of India unacceptable. In the face of these difficulties Churchill withheld a declaration of policy and followed the classic course of deliberate procrastination: he established a special cabinet committee to study the Indian problem. Meanwhile, Roosevelt maintained the pressure on the British to do something and interjected himself more deeply into the situation by appointing Louis Johnson, formerly assistant secretary of war, as his personal representative in India. Johnson, alas, was ill fitted for the mission. Another American called him "coarse, bombastic, and essentially ignorant regarding matters into which he was muscling."[7]

Hoping to break the deadlock and placate the Americans, the British government in March 1942 sent Sir Stafford Cripps, a left-wing member of the Labour party and a man renowned for his advanced views on freedom for India, on a special mission to New Delhi. Louis Johnson, arriving in India at the same time, hovered

[7]John Paton Davies, quoted by Thorne, *Allies of a Kind*, p. 242.

at Cripps's elbow and gave the impression that Roosevelt wished to be the mediator between Britain and India. Cripps carried an offer "for the earliest possible realisation of self-government" after the war, subject to the right of any province to choose separate independence if it desired and to guarantees for the protection of racial and religious minorities. The British insisted on these conditions in order to fulfill their obligations to the numerous semiautonomous princely states and their promise that no settlement would be imposed against the wishes of the Moslems. These arguments were a mixture of sincerity and a deliberate policy of divide and conquer. The Congress party rejected the Cripps proposals. Gandhi is said to have called them "a post-dated cheque on a bank that was obviously crashing."[8] The Congress leaders said they would take nothing less than immediate independence without conditions and charged the British with cynically provoking discord between Hindu and Moslem in order to delay independence indefinitely.

Churchill blamed the Congress party for the failure of the Cripps mission, but Roosevelt — who had been informed by Johnson that agreement had been nearly reached — placed the responsibility on the British. In a strongly worded cable to Churchill, he suggested that the Indians form an interim independent government along the lines of the American Articles of Confederation of the 1780s. After a short period of trial and error, the Indians could then draw up a constitution for a more perfect union. Churchill, however, felt that such a move would mean "ruin and slaughter." Writing after the war, he commented that Roosevelt's "mind was back in the American War of Independence, and he thought of the Indian problem in terms of the thirteen colonies fighting George III at the end of the eighteenth century."[9] Harry Hopkins, in London during this interchange, succeeded in blunting Churchill's annoyance by saying blandly that Roosevelt had no intention of being "drawn into the Indian business except at the personal request of the Prime Minister and then only if he had an assurance both from India and Britain that any plan he worked out would be acceptable."[10]

[8] Reginald Coupland, *The Cripps Mission* (London: Oxford University Press, 1942), p. 52.

[9] Winston S. Churchill, *The Hinge of Fate* (Boston: Houghton Mifflin, 1950), p. 219.

[10] Robert E. Sherwood, *Roosevelt and Hopkins: An Intimate History* (New York: Harper, 1948), p. 524.

By August 1942 the situation, from the American point of view, had reached an intolerable stage. Gandhi and thousands of Congress party leaders had been jailed by the British, and attitudes on both sides were hardening. Worst of all were the reports reaching Washington that many Indians were turning against the United States in the belief that the American troops servicing the airlift to China over "the hump" were in India in order to support British imperialism. Accordingly, a public statement was issued that American forces were in India for the sole purpose of fighting the Axis. Hull then warned Ambassador Halifax that a continued impasse might lead in the United States to "a general movement of agitation against Great Britain and in favor of independence," which would seriously injure Anglo-American relations.[11]

At the end of 1942 Roosevelt decided to send another personal representative to India in order to gather information and indicate American sympathy for Indian aspirations. The man selected was William Phillips, a conservative career diplomat, onetime undersecretary of state, and a close friend of the president. Phillips spent four months in India and returned convinced that the British were acting in a dangerously misguided fashion. He believed that most members of the cabinet in London, except for Churchill, wished independence for India, but he found the Englishmen in India to be a reactionary lot blind to the changes taking place in the world around them and determined to maintain British rule indefinitely. Lord Linlithgow, the viceroy, exemplified this attitude. He wrote that "it is we who have created and developed these great territories, given them peace and good order and held them together, and there are limits to the sacrifices that we can reasonably be expected to make."[12] Phillips wrote to Roosevelt that

> there is one fixed idea in the minds of Indians, that Great Britain has no intention of "quitting India" and that the post-war period will find the country in the same relative position. In the circumstances, they turn to us to give them help because of our historical stand for liberty.[13]

[11] Hull, *Memoirs*, vol. 2, p. 1490.

[12] Thorne, *Allies of a Kind*, p. 356.

[13] William Phillips, *Ventures in Diplomacy* (Portland, Me.: The Author, 1952), p. 362.

Indian leaders suggested that the United States sponsor and preside over an assembly of all Indian groups to discuss the future. Phillips told Roosevelt that the idea of American chairmanship was a necessary guarantee of independence because "British promises in this regard are no longer believed."[14]

Back in Washington, in May 1943, Phillips made an impassioned plea to the president for a forceful American policy.

> If we do nothing and merely accept the British point of view that conditions in India are none of our business, then we must be prepared for serious consequences in the internal situation in India which may develop as a result of despair and misery and anti-white sentiments of hundreds of millions of subject people.[15]

Roosevelt was impressed by what Phillips said but did not want to risk another Churchillian outburst by mentioning India again directly to the prime minister, who was also in Washington at that moment. Accordingly, the president sent Phillips to see Churchill at the British embassy and urge that the time was ripe to bring the Hindus and Moslems of India together. Churchill paced the room in anger and prophesied a bloodbath in India if Britain made the type of concessions which the United States was urging. Phillips decided it was hopeless to argue. Roosevelt agreed. At that moment he had no desire to place obstacles in the way of Anglo-American agreement on the cross-Channel invasion.

Phillips sought in a variety of ways during the remainder of 1943 to prod the American government into bringing effective pressure on the British. He wrote repeatedly to Roosevelt and gave impressive testimony before the Senate Foreign Relations Committee to the effect (according to Senator Vandenberg) "that F.D.R. should tell Churchill that he either yields to a reasonable settlement of the Indian independence questions . . . or that American troops will be withdrawn from that sector."[16] The president, however, had ceased to appeal directly to the British on India and was about to turn momentarily to Russia for support in his anti-imperial crusade.

---

[14]Ibid., p. 377.

[15]Ibid., p. 388.

[16]Arthur H. Vandenberg, Jr., ed., *The Private Papers of Senator Vandenberg* (Boston: Houghton Mifflin, 1952), p. 53.

At Teheran, in November 1943, Roosevelt made colonialism the chief topic of conversation in his first meeting alone with Stalin. The heart of the discussion, as recorded in the minutes, went as follows:

> THE PRESIDENT . . . felt it would be better not to discuss the question of India with Mr. Churchill, since the latter had no solution of that question, and merely proposed to defer the entire question to the end of the war.
>
> MARSHAL STALIN agreed that this was a sore spot with the British.
>
> THE PRESIDENT said at some future date, he would like to talk with Marshal Stalin on the question of India; that he felt that the best solution would be reform from the bottom, somewhat on the Soviet line.
>
> MARSHAL STALIN replied that the India question was a complicated one, with different levels of culture. . . . He added that reform from the bottom would mean revolution.[17]

The president never found another opportunity to discuss India with Stalin. When they met again at Yalta in 1945, too many other topics competed for attention. Meanwhile, the president sought to connect the question of India and all colonialism in Asia with his campaign to make China a great power.

❧

President Roosevelt found an ally in anticolonialism in Chiang Kai-shek. The generalissimo was a bitter critic of the British and felt, as did Roosevelt, that the existence of colonialism in Asia played directly into the hands of the Japanese. Chiang also had vague ideas, which Roosevelt encouraged, of playing a role in the departure of the British from India. In February 1942 Generalissimo and Madame Chiang visited Gandhi in India. Churchill appealed directly to Chiang not to intervene publicly, and Chiang kept official silence. However, he did write sympathetically to Roosevelt of Gandhi's indictment of the British; later, when Gandhi was imprisoned, he raised a storm of protest, which Churchill deeply resented.

Thus, Roosevelt and Chiang were lined up against Churchill. As a result, it was impossible for Churchill to distinguish Roose-

---

[17] *Foreign Relations, The Conferences at Cairo and Tehran, 1943* (Washington, D.C.: U.S. Government Printing Office, 1961), p. 486.

velt's campaign to establish China as a great power from the Sino-American diplomatic attack on the Asian possessions of the British Empire. The president's repeated suggestions that the British ought to turn over the colony of Hong Kong to China strengthened Churchill's defensive and resentful attitude. (Some British officials asked sarcastically what American territory Roosevelt proposed to hand over to the Chinese.) In resisting the idea of China as one of the four great powers, Churchill commented in October 1942 that such spurious status for China would simply mean "a faggot vote on the side of the United States in any attempt to liquidate the British overseas Empire."[18] Americans, in turn, suspected that the British wanted a weak China in order to protect their imperial position and perhaps even return to the days of European spheres of influence in Asia.

By trying to get China to be an instrument for the abolition of colonialism, Roosevelt was seeking to inspire Chiang Kai-shek with a sense of his importance in the world and thereby compensate for the inability of the United States to provide heavy military support for the China theater. There was also a growing feeling among Americans that direct involvement in colonial areas, with inevitable association with the imperial powers, would tarnish the American image. "By concentrating our Asiatic effort on operations in and from China we keep to the minimum our involvement in colonial imperialism," wrote one of the president's advisers. "We engage in a cause which is popular with Asiatics and the American public. We avoid the mutual mistrust and recrimination over the colonial question, potentially so inimical to harmonious Anglo-American relations."[19]

In line with this advice, Roosevelt wrote to Chiang Kai-shek about his general idea of trusteeship after the war for colonial peoples — a system under which a designated great power would be responsible for ruling and educating a former colony, as a parent governs a child, until it was ready for independence. His favorite specific example was French Indochina (by which was meant primarily those provinces comprising what is now Vietnam), then completely under Japanese occupation. Roosevelt

---

[18]Churchill, *The Hinge of Fate*, pp. 507–508.

[19]Memorandum by John Paton Davies, *Foreign Relations, The Conferences at Cairo and Tehran*, p. 372.

believed that France was a disgracefully decadent nation that had opened the door to Hitler in Europe and Japan in southeast Asia. Under no circumstances, he said again and again in 1942 and 1943, should France be allowed to return to Indochina; instead, the area should be placed under joint Chinese and American trusteeship in preparation for independence. "France has had the country — thirty million inhabitants — for nearly one hundred years," he noted, "and the people are worse off than they were in the beginning."[20] British objections should be disregarded, Roosevelt said, because they were afraid of the impact of the trusteeship concept on their own colonies.

Roosevelt's convictions about Indochina were reinforced by a belief in the economic and strategic importance of southeast Asia and by his antipathy to Charles de Gaulle, whose leadership of postwar France the president wished to prevent. Until 1944, when the defeat of the Axis was finally in sight, the future of Indochina remained theoretical. But in that year Roosevelt, confronted with the need to make practical decisions and with growing opposition to his ideas within his own government, began to weaken. At the same time he lost his faith, as we shall see, in China's ability in the foreseeable future to act as a responsible great power. Thus, he acquiesced in growing British involvement in military planning for Indochina and allowed them to train French forces for eventual return. By the eve of his death in April 1945, he had shifted to the position of saying that the French could return provided they would promise eventual independence for Indochina, but his policies were not clear either to the public or within the American government.[21]

The confusion of American policy at the time of Roosevelt's death is well illustrated by the small Office of Strategic Services (OSS) mission which operated in Indochina in the closing months of the war. The OSS was the forerunner of the CIA. In the summer of 1945, in preparation for the Japanese surrender, several OSS officers led by Colonel Archimedes Patti parachuted into Indochina. Patti was an anticolonial liberal who believed that Roosevelt's earlier policy of preventing the restoration of French

---

[20]Ibid., p. 872.

[21]An excellent article is Walter LaFeber, "Roosevelt, Churchill and Indochina: 1942–45," *American Historical Review*, 80 (December 1975): 1277–1295.

rule was still in effect. No one told him otherwise. As the Japanese surrendered, Patti made contact at Hanoi with the Vietnamese Communist leader Ho Chi Minh. Patti advised Ho on a declaration of independence from France (with the words taken from the American Declaration of July 4, 1776), and sent Ho's appeals on to Washington for support. But Patti, heir to Roosevelt's anticolonialism, could not prevail over a new pro-French attitude that was gaining ascendancy in the Truman administration or against the belief that Ho, as a Communist, was not an authentic spokesman of the people.[22] Thus, to summarize a complicated series of events, the French returned without a word of complaint from the United States. None of Ho's messages were acknowledged. Patti's mission ended in confusion and among accusations from the French that he was some sort of Communist. And by the end of 1946 the French and the Vietnamese, led by Ho, were at war, a war that would eventually be inherited by the United States.

President Roosevelt did not criticize the Dutch, who in the Netherlands East Indies (now Indonesia) had a larger southeast Asian empire than the French. This was because of his admiration for Dutch resistance to Germany and Japan and because the Dutch government-in-exile had promised to convene a constitutional convention after the war to arrange the details of self-government for their colonies. The president also seemed to feel a special kinship with the country of his ancestors, in contrast to his visceral aversion to the French.

The climax of Roosevelt's anti-imperialism and of his efforts to flatter Chiang Kai-shek came in November 1943 at Cairo, where the two met for the only time during the war. The situation in China was normal — that is, bad and getting worse. Militarily, China was still last on the list of American priorities; the volume of supplies carried by the airlift from India was still a pitiful trickle, and no firm plans had been made to clear the Japanese out of Burma and thus open a truck route into the besieged country. American Chief of Staff General George C. Marshall supported a major Burma operation vigorously, but the drain on resources for Mediterranean operations repeatedly led to the cancellation or postponement of plans.

[22] Archimedes L. A. Patti, *Why Viet Nam?: Prelude to America's Albatross* (Berkeley, Calif.: University of California Press, 1980).

American inability to supply China with military equipment on a scale comparable to that provided Britain and Russia was the greatest external obstacle to China's effectiveness in the war. The greatest internal obstacle was the mutual hostility between the Nationalist government of Chiang and the Chinese Communists in the north. Chiang's Kuomintang party and the Communists had cooperated in the 1920s, but then they had fallen upon each other in grim, sporadic civil war. In the mid-1930s the Communists, led by Mao Tse-tung and Chou En-lai, had saved themselves from annihilation by the heroic "long march" from the coastal south to the remote north. The all-out Japanese attack of 1937 produced very little cooperation between the two Chinese groups, for Chiang Kai-shek seemed at all times more committed to the elimination of his rivals than to fighting the Japanese. Only with difficulty had Americans persuaded Chiang not to take direct military action against the Communists. The problem from the American point of view was complex: how do you support a regime and forge an effective fighting force against the Japanese when the material resources are lacking and when the regime will not make peace within its own country?

American military authorities could not agree on the best way to avert disaster. General Claire Chennault, head of American air forces in China and a favorite of Chiang, urged concentration on bombing operations against the Japanese. This idea appealed to Chiang because it would mean he could conserve his ground troops to use against the Communists. General Stilwell, the senior American officer in China and Chiang's bluntly antagonistic chief of staff, argued that air power could do little if the Chinese could not control the ground. If bombing began to annoy the Japanese, they would simply capture the airfields from which the planes took off. Stilwell urged the United States to demand that Chiang reform his corrupt and inefficient military machine. Chiang hated him for this. Corruption was the basis of his rule, the currency with which he paid for support.

Roosevelt hoped that these dismal facts could be more than counterbalanced by talking face to face with the generalissimo. At Cairo he made a valiant effort and there, in the shadow of the pyramids, unfolded the vision of a glorious future for China. Japan was to be driven to unconditional surrender, Korea made independent after a period of trusteeship, and, according to the public declaration of Cairo issued after the meeting, "the territory that Japan has so treacherously stolen from the Chinese, such as Manchuria and Formosa, will of course be returned to the Republic of China. All of the conquered territory taken by violence and greed by the Japanese will be freed from their clutches."[23] In other words, Japan was to be reduced to the dimensions it had at the time of Commodore Perry's arrival in 1853. Roosevelt also affirmed his determination that China should take its place "on an equal footing in the machinery of the Big Four Group and in all its decisions."[24]

The generalissimo and the president returned to their respective countries in a heady mood. Chiang soon reported jubilantly to Roosevelt on the effect of the Cairo Declaration in China: "The whole nation is articulate to a degree that has never been known before in unanimously hailing the Cairo Declaration as a sure sign-post leading the Far East toward post-war peace. . . ." The president carried the same optimism to the American people in an address on Christmas Eve, 1943: "I met in the Generalissimo a man of great vision, great courage, and a remarkably keen understanding of the problems of today and tomorrow. . . . Today we and the Republic of China are closer together than ever before in deep friendship and unity of purpose."[25] But rhetoric cannot long withstand reality. After 1943 even Roosevelt's cheerful faith in China began to waver. As his faith declined, so did the vigor of his crusade against imperialism.

Military developments partly explain the waning of American anti-imperial diplomacy. Idealistic sympathy for the freedom of all peoples remained after 1943, but when colonial areas ceased to be threatened directly by the Axis, the attention of American leaders turned elsewhere. India, for example, was out of danger in 1944; thus, there was no military reason to antagonize the British by criticizing their inability to reach agreement with Indian leaders. A few idealistic opponents of colonialism continued to write memoranda within the State Department, but as the end of the war approached, they encountered opposition from the United

[23] *Foreign Relations, The Conferences at Cairo and Tehran*, p. 403.
[24] Ibid., p. 323.
[25] Herbert Feis, *The China Tangle* (Princeton, N.J.: Princeton University Press, 1953), pp. 109–110.

States Navy and Army, which wanted to take over strategically important islands in the Pacific without any limitations on American control.

China's military plight remained desperate until 1945, but its strategic importance in the war as a whole declined rapidly during 1944. Originally, American planners believed that air bases in northeast China would have to be established in order to defeat Japan, but in 1944 it became apparent that an advance from island to island across the Pacific provided a quicker and easier route to the Japanese homeland, a route fully under American military control unencumbered by the necessity of dealing with allies. With this shift in strategic expectations, all possibility of raising the military priority of the China theater was lost.

The frustrations of trying to persuade the Chinese to help themselves, however, did more to change the American outlook than military considerations. Throughout 1943 American observers in China grew more bitterly critical of the Chiang Kai-shek regime. They reported venality and corruption everywhere; stubborn resistance to political, social, and economic reform; low morale; a general unwillingness to fight; and a readiness to sit back and let the United States defeat Japan. In many places the Chinese had relaxed into an undeclared armistice with the Japanese and were trading across enemy lines. At the same time the Chinese Communists in the north were gaining strength. Their land-reform measures were apparently winning the enthusiastic support of the population in the constantly expanding area that the Communists controlled. The morale and fighting ability of the Communist divisions, compared with the sloth and apathy of Chiang's badly led armies, seemed refreshing to American observers. The Communists said they wanted to cooperate with the Nationalist government to expel the Japanese, but month by month Chiang was allocating more of his forces as a barrier against the Communists. Full-scale civil war was becoming an ominous possibility. This would add to the difficulty of defeating Japan and, in the long run, would shatter the hope of a stable postwar Asia under the leadership of China as one of the "four policemen."

By 1944 Roosevelt and his advisers recognized that pledges of support for China's future as a great power and intimate exchanges about the folly of British imperialism provided no remedy for China's ills. Huge dollar loans and gestures such as the relinquishment of extraterritorial rights were also futile, for they did not contribute to the political unity of the country. Thus, the United States adopted as a prime political objective the unification by peaceful means of the Nationalist and Communist forces, and for this purpose it sent high-ranking envoys to persuade, cajole, and mediate. Vice-President Henry A. Wallace, who arrived in Chungking in June 1944, was the first.

Wallace, like most Americans who became entangled with China during the war, underestimated the difficulty of bringing the Nationalist and Communist factions together. Assuming that all Chinese should share a basic identity of interests, Wallace told Chiang that "nothing should be final among friends."[26] Chiang said he was willing to grant political amnesty to the Communists if they gave up their separate territory and placed their troops under his command — if, in short, they put themselves completely in his power. The Communists, seeing clearly what Chiang was proposing, said they believed in the unity of China but insisted on keeping control of their territory and eighteen divisions. Wallace left China in a pessimistic mood. "Chiang, at best, is a short-term investment," he reported to the president. "It is not believed that he has the intelligence or political strength to run post-war China. The leaders of post-war China will be brought forward by evolution or revolution, and it now seems more like the latter."[27]

The next special envoy to try his hand bringing the irreconcilable factions together was General Patrick J. Hurley, one of the president's favorite troubleshooters. But Hurley, in contrast to Wallace, was an unshakeable supporter of Chiang. He believed in unity, but only on Chiang's terms. If anyone disagreed, Hurley marked that person as an enemy and sought his removal. Thus, in October 1944 Roosevelt, on Hurley's recommendation, recalled General Stilwell and replaced him with General Albert C. Wedemeyer, an ideological anti-Communist satisfactory to Chiang.[28]

[26] Ibid., p. 147.

[27] Quoted by Michael Schaller, *The U.S. Crusade in China, 1938–1945* (New York: Columbia University Press, 1979), p. 163.

[28] Hurley's extraordinary and often bizarre career is described by Russell D. Buhite, *Patrick J. Hurley and American Foreign Policy* (Ithaca, N.Y.: Cornell University Press, 1973). On Stilwell, Barbara W. Tuchman, *Stilwell and the American Experience in China, 1911–1945* (New York: Macmillan, 1970), is immensely readable.

Hurley's most vitriolic attacks were reserved for a small group of Foreign Service officers — most notably John Paton Davies and John S. Service — who reported what they honestly believed to be true: that Chiang would lose and the Communists would win. It was therefore in the interest of the United States to reach an understanding with the Communists in order to prevent them from falling under Russian control. Hurley considered these thoughts close to treasonous. His denunciations of Davies, Service, and others ultimately led to a purge of the most knowledgeable "China hands" from the Foreign Service.

If China was to become an effective fighting ally, extensive changes would have to be made in the character and behavior of the Nationalist government. But what could the United States do if its friendly advice was ignored? Since the war was being fought to prevent nations from intervening in each other's affairs, coercion of China would be improper. On the other hand, it would be equally improper and distasteful to allow Chiang Kai-shek to use American aid to impose what many called a Fascist regime on an unwilling people.

The existence of the Chinese Communists sharpened the horns of the dilemma over how, if at all, to intervene. Knowing little of Communist ideology or recent Chinese history, some Americans assumed that the Nationalists and Communists could be brought happily together. To please the United States, Chiang gave lip service to the idea of cooperation, but inwardly he believed it was essential for him to destroy the Communists before they destroyed him. These facts were not understood in Washington at the time, and the American government continued to hope that the goals of victory over Japan, nonintervention, democracy, and Chinese unity could somehow all be achieved together.

CHAPTER 6

The Middle East

Opposition to British and French imperialism was a central theme of American diplomacy throughout most of the war in the Middle East as well as in Asia. If the Middle East fell, the way would be open for the dreaded juncture of German and Japanese forces along the southern rim of Asia, the Axis would gain control of limitless petroleum resources, and the supply route through the Persian Gulf to Russia would be blocked. Americans believed that British imperialism in the region played into the hands of the enemy. The petroleum was also perceived as of crucial importance for the long-range security and prosperity of the United States. Someday oil reserves in the United States and the Western Hemisphere would be depleted. Oil experts disagreed as to when that day would come, but all agreed that it was essential for Middle Eastern supplies to be brought under American control.

Americans believed that the United States possessed unique moral prestige among the peoples of the Middle East and that the British, in contrast, suffered ill repute because of their high-handed imperial methods. "Goodwill toward the United States," observed Secretary of State Hull in 1942, "has become . . . a deep-seated conviction on the part of the peoples in this area, due mainly to a century of American missionary, educational and philanthropic efforts that have never been tarnished by any material motives or interests."[1] The United States, therefore, sought to expand American influence while urging the end of imperial controls and the completion of independence for all Middle Eastern countries. It was assumed that leaders and peoples of the region,

[1] U.S. Department of State, *Foreign Relations of the United States, 1942*, vol. 4 (Washington, D.C.: U.S. Government Printing Office, 1963), p. 27.

inspired by the ideals of the Atlantic Charter and looking to the United States for guidance, would present a united front against the Axis. And after the war Americans would be able to reap the award of expanded and secure access to oil.

The United States was the last of the great powers to intervene in the political convulsions that, in this century, have transformed the predominantly Moslem lands stretching from North Africa to Afghanistan. The American government was relatively uninterested when the First World War spawned or accelerated the developments that have given the Middle East its explosive instability: the final disintegration of the Ottoman Empire, the rise of Arab nationalism, the blossoming of the Zionist dream of a Jewish homeland in Palestine, and the changing nature of modern warfare and economic security that made oil the single most essential ingredient of modern power.

Between 1919 and 1939 American economic interests (most notably a concession to oil companies in Saudi Arabia) grew, but politically the United States remained only slightly involved— protesting, for the record, several British moves that we perceived as blocking potential American oil interests but otherwise being passive. Meanwhile, the Arab countries, recent appendages of the Ottoman Empire, acquired varying degrees of nominal independence while chafing under British or French (in Syria and Lebanon) control. The Arabs had little sense of common purpose beyond their hatred of the embryonic Jewish homeland in Palestine, administered under British mandate. The Palestine question slumbered in the 1920s but erupted in the 1930s because Nazi persecutions of Jews gave new vitality to Zionism. During the war, the United States for the first time confronted the insoluble problem of how to respond to Jewish aspirations and simultaneously retain Arab friendship, which was deemed necessary for both strategic and economic reasons.

After 1939 the United States began for the first time to take a sustained political interest in the Middle East, but at the time of Pearl Harbor American involvement was still minute compared to the pervasive British influence. Military planners of the two countries agreed early in 1942 that the region was a British sphere of responsibility. But no sooner had the agreement been made than the Americans began to suggest that the British alter their political behavior to conform more closely to the spirit of the Atlantic Charter. As the American military and economic contribution to the defense of the area mounted, suggestions became hard-edged and insistent. The United States is paying the bill, said many American diplomats active in the region, and therefore should call the tune—especially when the British are making enemies with their domineering and insensitive ways.

By 1943 the sphere-of-influence agreement had been replaced by an American perception that the United States should assert predominant influence whenever it so decided. The British, unhappy and resentful, believed the United States was aiming as much at postwar economic advantage, at British expense, as at the defeat of Hitler. The British were not entirely wrong. The decline of their power, to be dramatically revealed by the Suez crisis of 1956, was already far advanced. In a showdown, the British could not prevail against American opposition. As Americans gained responsibility and power, however, they acquired something of the British point of view and discovered that simple reliance on the precepts of the Atlantic Charter could not, for example, make Russia cooperate in Iran, safeguard strategic oil reserves, or solve the deadly conflict between Arab and Jew.[2]

Egypt provides an example of the process. No country had a higher strategic importance for Great Britain. Egypt meant the Suez Canal, the foothold in North Africa, control of the Middle East as a whole, and the route to India. The country, under de facto British military occupation since 1882, was nominally independent; but in Cairo, headquarters for all British operations in the Middle East, the British ambassador dictated to the Egyptian government literally at gunpoint. Egyptians were understandably resentful. A few politicians close to King Farouk hoped for Axis victory.

A major crisis came in February 1942, when King Farouk threatened to install an anti-British prime minister. The British ambassador summoned troops to surround the palace and forced the king to accept a British candidate, Nahas Pasha, as prime

---

[2] A succinct survey is Barry Rubin, *The Great Powers in the Middle East, 1941–1947* (London: Cass, 1980).

minister. The British were trampling on Egypt's right to conduct its own internal affairs, yet King Farouk was a dissolute and reactionary monarch surrounded by a clique of politicians who came close to sympathizing with Nazi Germany. Americans disagreed on what, if anything, the United States should do. Wallace Murray, longtime head of the Near Eastern division in the State Department and an impassioned critic of British imperialism, believed the United States should take Farouk's side and complain formally. He argued that Farouk was likely to emerge as "a martyr in the eyes of his people and a rallying point for disaffection, sabotage and attacks directed at the British." Undersecretary of State Sumner Welles disagreed. How would we feel, he asked, if the British intervened in our relations with a Latin American country? Murray challenged the validity of the analogy, but Welles prevailed: the United States did nothing.[3] The immediate crisis passed. Prime Minister Nahas cooperated with the British and remained in power until October 1944, by which time the Axis threat had receded.

こ∿ゆ

The British considered Egypt vital because it controlled strategic lines of communication. They considered Iran vital for its oil. Iran (known as Persia until the 1930s) at the time had the world's third largest proven reserves of oil—after the United States and the Soviet Union. The oil was almost entirely in the hands of the Anglo-Iranian Oil Company, in which the British government itself owned a majority interest.

For more than a century Iran had sought to gain political bargaining power by playing the major powers off against each other. Britain and Russia were the main players in this game, but with the outbreak of World War II the Shah of Iran showed an alarming interest in cultivating the Germans. In August 1941 the British and Russians decided the situation was too serious for them to be squeamish about respecting Iranian sovereignty. The Russians in the north and Britain in the south jointly occupied Iran in order to prevent the country from falling under German

[3]See *Foreign Relations, 1942*, vol. 4 (1963), pp. 68–71, for the argument between Murray and Welles.

control. The British also threw out the reigning Shah and replaced him with his son (the same who ultimately was driven from the country in 1979 by Ayatollah Khomeini's revolution). The United States accepted the military necessity of this infringement on Iranian sovereignty but pressured Russia and Britain into signing a treaty with Iran by which they pledged to respect Iranian independence and to withdraw their troops no later than six months after the end of the war. The Iranian government, however, distrusted both Britain and Russia and asked the United States for support. The American minister in Teheran, Louis Dreyfus, and State Department officials in Washington listened with sympathetic and anti-British ears. The British, Dreyfus reported, were seeking a stranglehold on the Iranian economy out of selfish commercial and political motives. In Washington Wallace Murray read these reports and predicted that "sooner or later the United States would have to assume a dominant role in Iran."[4] The Americans bombarded London with unwelcome advice and filled Iran with a host of special advisers and administrators in order to encourage the Iranians and keep an eye on the British. The most persuasive American adviser was Arthur Millspaugh, a consultant who played a major role in directing the Iranian economy and in offering advice on how to limit British influence. The United States also extended lend-lease aid directly to Iran, thereby reducing the country's economic dependence on Britain, and improved and managed the railroad from the Persian Gulf over which supplies flowed to Russia. This "Persian corridor" was an indispensable alternative to the U-boat-infested Arctic route.

That the Soviet Union also posed a threat to Iranian independence was a fact that complicated the simple American anti-British outlook. Notwithstanding their pledges to respect Iran's sovereignty, the Russians busily encouraged separatist movements in the region under their occupation, obstructed the carrying out of American technical aid in their zone, refused to allow Iranian troops to enter their area to deal with tribal disturbances, and intensified famine conditions by diverting Iranian wheat production. In March 1942 the Iranian government asked the United States for a specific declaration of support against Soviet designs. Here was a dilemma. How could Russia be deterred or even warned

[4]Ibid., p. 190.

without adding to Stalin's already ominous distrust of the West? The United States had to remain silent. As Welles explained to the Iranian minister, "It would not only be inappropriate, but positively prejudicial, for this Government — out of a clear sky insofar as it was concerned — to make any public declarations concerning the independence and integrity of Iran."[5]

In the face of disquieting Russian behavior, the United States became less critical of the British in Iran and the British more responsive to American opinion. But given the president's overriding policy of avoiding irritating confrontations with Russia, little could be done to make the Soviets act in a more cooperative and considerate manner. In Moscow in October 1943, Secretary of State Hull and Foreign Secretary Eden failed to win Soviet acceptance of a tripartite declaration on Iran; but a few weeks later, at the first Big Three summit conference in Teheran, Stalin acquiesced. Roosevelt, Churchill, and Stalin thereupon issued a public declaration of support for Iranian independence and promised some postwar economic aid as compensation for the country's wartime suffering. The Russians' deeds, however, continued to contradict their words. In 1944 they bullied the Iranian government with tough talk and ostentatious military maneuvers in an effort to secure exclusive oil concessions in the north. Britain, it should be remembered, already controlled Iran's southern oil fields. Iran was able to withstand Soviet pressure for the moment. As the war neared its end and tension between Russia and the West increased in many areas, American convictions about Iran's importance were stronger than ever; but now they saw the Soviet Union, not Britain, as the principal threat.

The American approach toward Iran during the war was a blend of humanitarian sentiment and self-interested calculation. President Roosevelt and some of his advisers saw Iran, much as many Americans had seen and still saw China, as a friendly, backward land eager to accept American tutelage in everything from agricultural reform to finance, education, and police organization. Roosevelt said he was "thrilled by the idea of using Iran as an example of what we could do by an unselfish American policy. We could not take on a more difficult nation than Iran. I should like, however, to have a try at it." For the State Department

---

[5] *Ibid.*, p. 275.

this meant social as well as economic reform. As one commentary noted in 1944: "One of the main tasks . . . is to break this stranglehold of the entrenched classes and to insure for the mass of the Iranians a fairer share in the proceeds of their labor." No one asked at the time whether the United States could achieve such an objective. American self-interest focused — to quote another State Department policy paper in 1944 — on "the possibility of sharing more fully in Iran's commerce and in the development of its resources; the strategic location of Iran for civil air bases; and the growing importance of Iranian and Arabian oil fields."[6]

Across the Persian Gulf from Iran lies Saudi Arabia, an isolated desert land whose vast petroleum resources were yet to be fully measured but would eventually be known to exceed those of all other countries in the Middle East. Saudi Arabia was the creation of King Ibn Saud, a tribal chieftain who since 1914 had defeated all rivals and extended his authority over the sparse and scattered population of a country three times larger than Texas. Ibn Saud's rise had been encouraged by the British, from whom he received political support and a small financial subsidy. In 1933 no oil had yet been discovered in Saudi Arabia, but in that year King Ibn Saud granted a vast concession in the eastern part of the country to the Standard Oil Company of California, which soon merged its Arabian interests with the Texas Company in a firm eventually named the Arabian American Oil Company (Aramco). In 1938 the Americans struck oil.

With the outbreak of war in 1939 the British, anxious to preserve the confidence of all Arab peoples, stepped up their political activities in Saudi Arabia and increased their payments to Ibn Saud to compensate for revenues lost by the wartime suspension of the pilgrim traffic to Mecca, Islam's most holy shrine. The United States, in turn, established diplomatic representation in the country for the first time by opening a legation at Jidda in April 1942 and provided the country with a technical mission to advise on irrigation. Mutual Anglo-American suspicion began to mount. Representatives of American oil interests charged that British activity was designed to oust them from the concession. They argued that, since the British were dependent on lend-lease

[6]Rubin, *The Great Powers in the Middle East*, pp. 90–96.

aid, the subsidy to Ibn Saud was, in effect, an application of American money against American interests. This argument was heeded in Washington, and in February 1943 Saudi Arabia was declared eligible for direct lend-lease aid. Anglo-American rivalry accelerated throughout 1943. Ibn Saud sent two of his sons on an official visit to Washington. The United States, urged on by the oil companies, granted a large loan and, late in the year, dispatched a military advisory mission, an action resented by the British, who had not been consulted. Meanwhile, in Jidda, the American minister said that his British colleague was trying to turn Ibn Saud against the United States. The Foreign Office in London denied this charge but did reassign its representative at the request of the State Department.

The situation in Saudi Arabia coincided with a near panic in the United States over the long-term adequacy of domestic American and Western Hemisphere oil reserves. Oil experts in 1943 reported that for the first time in history consumption was exceeding the rate of new discoveries in the United States. Although the amount of oil remaining in the United States ultimately turned out to be greater than the wartime estimates, the sudden sense of strategic vulnerability permeating the American government was comparable to that felt in the 1970s.

The prime mover of oil policy in the American government was Secretary of the Interior Harold L. Ickes. He told President Roosevelt that by 1944 the United States would not be able to produce enough oil to meet both military and civilian requirements. It was essential, he said, to acquire a "sovereign" control over Saudi Arabian oil reserves. Ickes and others explored a variety of means to this end. The United States government might buy out the private American companies in Arabia — an idea that was politically explosive because it ran against the grain of American free enterprise ideology; it might negotiate with the companies for an option on a stated amount of production; or it might build a pipeline from the Persian Gulf to the Mediterranean in order to be independent of British facilities. Ickes did succeed in establishing the government-owned Petroleum Reserves Corporation to carry out whatever program was decided upon. The corporation made grandiose plans that seemed to challenge simultaneously the principle of private ownership, State Department responsibility for foreign policy, and the British.

Lord Beaverbrook, Ickes's counterpart in the British cabinet, was on guard. "Oil," he said, "is the greatest single post-war asset remaining to us . . . we should refuse to divide our last resource with the Americans."[7] But eventually the two governments, noting Soviet ambitions in the Middle East and realizing that the region contained enough oil for both, discovered the advantages of cooperation over a rivalry which, if unchecked, threatened to excite public opinion in both countries and damage Anglo-American relations. Accordingly, an agreement was signed on August 8, 1944, whereby the United States and Great Britain pledged themselves to respect each other's concessions and to pursue broad policies of nondiscrimination aimed at the orderly development of petroleum resources. Although the agreement paid lip service to the ideals of the Atlantic Charter, it is noteworthy that the oil-producing countries of the Middle East were not consulted in its drafting. In that respect it was a relic of old-style imperialism rather than an indication of how the future would be shaped. The agreement lessened wartime Anglo-American antagonism, although it was never formally ratified because of opposition in the United States Senate.

The smaller countries of the Middle East also called forth American diplomatic attention. Afghanistan, wedged between Russia and British India and fearing both, looked with sympathy on Germany, from which the country had received extensive technical aid. Here was a potential trouble spot on the path of a possible German invasion (should the Soviet Union fall) of India and, in any event, a source of unrest spreading across the border and tying down troops needed elsewhere. Conscious that the British were disliked by the Afghans, the United States moved after Pearl Harbor to develop closer relations with the country. A legation was opened in Kabul in 1942 (Afghanistan, in turn, opened a legation in Washington in 1943), special arrangements were made to facilitate trade between the two countries, and a group of American teachers and irrigation experts were sent to Afghanistan. The United States saw itself as a big brother protecting

[7]Quoted by Irvine H. Anderson, *Aramco, the United States, and Saudi Arabia* (Princeton, N.J.: Princeton University Press, 1981), p. 85. See also Michael B. Stoff, *Oil, War, and American Security* (New Haven, Conn.: Yale University Press, 1980). Anderson and Stoff together provide superb coverage of wartime oil policy in the Middle East.

Afghanistan from alleged Russian and British diplomatic bullying. Noting that Afghanistan remained tranquil throughout the war, Secretary of State Hull later concluded that the United States had won a friend.

Iraq, lying between Iran and Syria, was close to the scene of combat and, like Egypt, a British sphere. Great Britain controlled Iraq, once called Mesopotamia, as a League of Nations mandate until 1932 and afterward under special treaty arrangements. Iraqi politicians were intensely nationalistic, generally anti-British, and receptive to German propaganda. In the spring of 1941 a pro-German politician, Rashid Ali, staged a military coup. The legitimate regent (for King Feisal, then still a child) was forced to flee for his life disguised as a woman and riding out of Baghdad under a rug in the back seat of the American minister's car. The Iraqi army then surrounded the tiny British garrison at the Habbaniya air base while the Germans prepared to send planes from Vichy-controlled Syria and Lebanon. The United States agreed that the British were justified in using all the force at their disposal. Rashid Ali was proclaiming his devotion to Iraqi independence, but his actions were serving the interests of Germany. Heavy fighting broke out on May 1, 1941. Fortunately, the Germans — who were preparing for the coming invasion of Russia — sent insufficient aid. The outnumbered British forces triumphed. Rashid Ali escaped to Turkey and the regent came back to Baghdad. In 1942 the United States made Iraq eligible for lend-lease aid, and the next year the country declared war on the Axis.

Syria and Lebanon, lying between Iraq and the Mediterranean and comprising the region known as the Levant, presented another kind of problem. These two small countries had been detached from the old Ottoman Empire after the First World War and placed under French administration as League of Nations mandates destined for eventual independence. After the fall of France in 1940, they continued for a short time under Vichy control until, after heavy fighting in June and July of 1941, they were occupied by a joint British and Free French force. Like the Iranian occupation and the Iraqi intervention, this action was taken to prevent the countries from falling under German control. General de Gaulle promised independence to Syria and Lebanon, but he held the countries under repressive political control while the British remained responsible for military defense. This dual arrangement led to a sharp Anglo-French altercation. The British accused the French of intending to withhold independence indefinitely and demanded that the Syrians and Lebanese be allowed to hold elections. De Gaulle, in turn, denounced the British for encroaching on his authority and said that he intended to uphold the honor of France in the Levant.

In September the American representative in Beirut reported that Anglo-French relations were at the breaking point and that de Gaulle would use force if necessary. Throughout the crisis some American diplomats said that the United States should support the British, but others said that the British were championing independence as a cynical ruse designed to oust the French and obtain exclusive control for themselves. The American position was further complicated, until the North African invasion of November 1942, by the desire to maintain relations with the Vichy government, which still claimed legal rights in Syria and Lebanon. Thus, American recognition of the independence of the countries would antagonize both Vichy and de Gaulle and might aid an allegedly nefarious British scheme. On the other hand, a refusal to sympathize with the ideal of independence would be inconsistent with the Atlantic Charter and might tarnish the image of the United States in the eyes of the Syrian and Lebanese people. The only practical course was a pose of impartiality.

In October 1942 the British and French reached a temporary accord. For several months relative calm prevailed. In the summer of 1943 the long-postponed elections were held, and in both Syria and Lebanon strongly nationalist, anti-French cabinets were formed. When the Lebanese government in November attempted to curtail French power, de Gaulle caused the imprisonment of the Lebanese president and those members of the cabinet who could be found. Churchill denounced these "lamentable outrages" and won American support against de Gaulle. "What kind of France is this," he asked in a telegram to Roosevelt, "which, while itself subjugated by the enemy, seeks to subjugate others?"[8] The French, faced with the possibility of losing Anglo-American military aid, freed the Lebanese politicians. Roosevelt and his advisers were now convinced that French imperialism in the Levant

[8] *Foreign Relations, The Conferences at Cairo and Tehran, 1943* (Washington, D.C.: U.S. Government Printing Office, 1961), p. 189.

was a greater threat than British schemes. Accordingly, in 1944 the United States extended formal diplomatic recognition to Syria and Lebanon while significantly withholding an acknowledgment of France's special position. De Gaulle's heavy-handed methods had converted the United States from an impartial mediator into an unequivocal opponent of France's continued presence in the Levant. Ironically, the British were less critical of French policy in 1944 because of a desire to see France restored as a major factor in the balance of power.

The last wartime crisis in Syria and Lebanon took place in the spring of 1945. The French wanted treaties with the two countries recognizing France's sphere of influence. The Syrian and Lebanese governments refused to negotiate. De Gaulle thereupon sent troop reinforcements to Syria and presented his terms for a treaty as an implied ultimatum. The Syrians would not buckle under and heavy fighting broke out between French and Syrian troops in Damascus at the end of May. The British intervened with a military force vastly superior to that of the French, ordered a cease-fire, and compelled the French troops to withdraw from the city. President Truman supported the British. Thus, as the war ended, the French imperial position in Syria and Lebanon had been irrevocably impaired.

By 1945 the initial anti-British bias of American policy had been softened everywhere in the Middle East. But one agonizing problem remained unresolved: the future of Jewish settlement in Palestine. Nothing in wartime diplomacy so burdened British and American leaders with a sense of inescapable tragedy, for the issue of a Jewish homeland was inextricably linked to the Holocaust — Hitler's extermination of millions of European Jews — and to the question of whether more could have been done to save those who were sent to the gas chambers. The fundamental American and British response was to say that the best way to save the Jews was to defeat Hitler. But was this an excuse behind which leaders refused to face the full enormity of the extermination policy and take specific measures to deal with it — such as bombing the rail lines used by Hitler to transport the victims, publicizing the atrocities, retaliating explicitly for what was happening, and providing plans for the displaced to settle? Were these failures partially the result of a lack of sympathy, amounting to anti-Semitism, among some American officials in the State Department? As long as the Holocaust is remembered, these questions will haunt the Anglo-American conscience.

The issue was complicated by commitments to the Arabs that the British felt they could not honorably break and which they considered essential as a means of keeping Arabs out of the German camp. It was further complicated by the counterpressure of American public opinion, which sympathized overwhelmingly with the aspirations of Jews for large-scale immigration into Palestine in spite of British commitments to the Arabs. But neither the administration nor the Congress felt enough domestic pressure to open the United States to large-scale immigration.[9]

Modern Zionism, the movement to establish a Jewish state in Palestine, was born in the nineteenth century and became a factor in world politics during the First World War. The British government, having encouraged Arab nationalism as a weapon against Turkey (Germany's ally), felt the need to satisfy Jews throughout the world, including those in the United States, by supporting the idea of a permanent Jewish homeland. The result was the famed Balfour Declaration, issued by British Foreign Secretary Arthur Balfour on November 2, 1917:

> His Majesty's Government view with favour the establishment in Palestine of a National Home for the Jewish people, and will use their best endeavours to facilitate the achievement of this object, it being clearly understood that nothing shall be done which may prejudice the civil and religious rights of non-Jewish communities in Palestine, or the rights and political status enjoyed by Jews in any other country.

Few documents have created as much acrimony. Zionists and Arabs, ignoring the carefully qualified wording, saw the declaration as an unequivocal promise or a base betrayal. The United States, in the person of President Woodrow Wilson, gave vague approval to the declaration but refused to assume any responsibility for its implementation.[10]

In the 1920s the British acquired a League of Nations mandate for Palestine and tried to govern in a manner that would gloss over the contradictory wartime gestures to Arab and Jew. At

---

[9]Henry L. Feingold, *The Politics of Rescue: The Roosevelt Administration and the Holocaust, 1938–1945* (New Brunswick, N.J.: Rutgers University Press, 1970).

[10]The best account is Leonard Stein, *The Balfour Declaration* (New York: Simon & Schuster, 1961).

first few Jews migrated to Palestine and the issue of Zionism faded. Then came Hitler's persecutions of German Jewry and the recrudescence of anti-Semitism elsewhere in the world. Zionism and the flow of immigrants revived. Palestinian Arabs resisted by force and, during the late 1930s, the British had to put down a bloody rebellion. In 1939, with war imminent, the British government decided that the goodwill of the Arabs and the security of the Middle East would have to take priority over the plight of Jews. In the White Paper of May 1939 the British repudiated the Zionist part of the Balfour Declaration and promised the Arabs that Jewish immigration to Palestine would not exceed 75,000 in the period to March 31, 1944, after which immigration would be under Arab control. In other words, Jews would then be excluded. The White Paper also restricted the right of Jews to buy land in Palestine and promised eventual independence for Palestine under the Arab majority. If the policy of the White Paper prevailed, the Zionist dream would be dead.

The White Paper was so obviously an act of desperation that the Arab peoples doubted British sincerity and continued to be receptive to Nazi propaganda. Jews were sickened. It seemed that the British government had sacrificed them because it knew that under no circumstances would they give aid to Hitler. The only course for the Jewish community in Palestine was, in the words of David Ben Gurion, to "fight the war as if there were no White Paper, and the White Paper as if there were no war."[11] This meant offering Jewish units for combat under British command. It also meant the encouragement of illegal immigration, the stockpiling of arms for use within the country, and constant, articulate propaganda against the British policy.

The American government found it impossible to adopt a consistent policy on Palestine. Public and congressional sympathy for Jewish immigration into Palestine and the establishment of a Jewish homeland was clear, organized, powerfully expressed— and unimpressed by arguments over the military expediency of currying favor with the Arabs when the very existence of European Jewry was at stake. In the words of a statement signed by 63 senators and 182 congressmen, all of whom belonged to the American Palestine Committee:

[11] Quoted by George Kirk, *The Middle East in the War* (London: Oxford University Press, 1952), p. 13.

It shall be the common purpose of civilized mankind to right this cruel wrong insofar as may lie in our power, and, above all, to enable large numbers of the survivors to reconstruct their lives in Palestine where the Jewish people may once more assume a position of dignity and equality among the peoples of the earth.[12]

On the other hand, as the British were quick to point out, every expression of sympathy for the goal of a Jewish Palestine was resented by the Arabs who claimed, with some reason, that the creation of a Jewish state in their territory against their will would be a violation of the Atlantic Charter. The Arabs, however, were unable to influence American public and congressional opinion.

Officially, the American government took refuge in platitudes about trust, cooperation, and peaceful settlement of all disputes — while affirming that full responsibility for all decisions involving Palestine lay with the British government. Secretary of State Hull tried to please both sides by declaring: "The Jews have long sought a refuge. I believe that we must have an even wider objective; we must have a world in which Jews, like every other race, are free to abide in peace and honor."[13] Privately there was a tendency in Washington to put the primary blame for the Palestine dilemma, as for other Middle Eastern problems, on the British. Wallace Murray in the State Department condemned the British "for having permitted, and even encouraged, the Arabs to establish a vested right in that burning question." He implied that the British were deliberately creating discord in order to maintain their imperial position in the Middle East. He believed that the United States had the moral authority to work out a settlement between Arab and Jew. "Our reputation in the Arab World is solidly established on confidence and good faith in our motives. This is an asset no longer possessed by the British and one which they should therefore be glad to exploit jointly with us."[14]

President Roosevelt, sensitive to the political power of 5 million Jewish Americans, maintained an active interest in Palestine. He had no precise ideas on how a settlement could be reached but characteristically made many suggestions. In 1942 he was attracted to the idea of winning King Ibn Saud's support for a Jewish home-

---

[12]*Foreign Relations, 1942*, vol. 4 (1961), p. 550.

[13]Ibid., p. 548.

[14]Ibid., pp. 555–556.

land by offering him generous economic aid and the possibility of becoming "boss of bosses" for the Arab world. American Middle Eastern specialists thought this an absurd idea. In 1943 the president turned to one of his favorite panaceas, trusteeship, and suggested that Palestine should be administered jointly by a Jew, a Christian, and a Moslem — thereby recognizing its status as a Holy Land for three religions. He also toyed with the idea of a federal union between Palestine and the neighboring Arab states. He optimistically believed that the Arabs would get over their prejudices and ultimately welcome Jewish leadership and technology in developing the economy of the Middle East for the benefit of all.

As the presidential election of 1944 approached, Roosevelt and Hull came under increasing pressure to define the government's position and to compel the British to modify their policy for the benefit of the Zionists. The British did make a small concession by stating that limited Jewish immigration could continue after the deadline of March 31, 1944, set by the White Paper of 1939. This did not satisfy American opinion, and early in 1944 resolutions were introduced in the House and Senate calling on the U.S. government to secure free entry of Jews into Palestine with "full opportunity for colonization so that the Jewish people may ultimately reconstitute Palestine as a free and democratic Jewish commonwealth." The State and War Departments succeeded in having these resolutions quashed in committee on the argument that their passage would endanger the lives of American servicemen in the Middle East. But at the same time the president assured Jewish leaders that he disapproved of the British White Paper and would see that "when future decisions are reached full justice will be done to those who seek a Jewish National Home." Also, both major parties inserted pro-Zionist planks in their 1944 platforms, and Roosevelt in October gave a promise that, if reelected, he would find the means of establishing a Jewish commonwealth in Palestine. The State Department did its best to explain away these political pledges issued for home consumption by assuring Middle Eastern rulers that no decision on Palestine should be reached without "full consultation with both Arabs and Jews." But the president, as Secretary of State Hull observed, "talked both ways to Zionists and Arabs, besieged as he was by each camp."[15]

[15] Cordell Hull, *The Memoirs of Cordell Hull*, vol. 2 (New York: Macmillan, 1948), p. 1525.

At the Yalta conference, in February 1945, the Palestine question was not raised, much to the disappointment of Zionist leaders who were hoping for a Big Three declaration in support of their goal. Then, on his return from Yalta, Roosevelt held a series of surprise meetings on board the cruiser *Quincy* with King Farouk of Egypt, Emperor Haile Selassie of Ethiopia, and King Ibn Saud of Saudi Arabia. Churchill, as Harry Hopkins commented, was disturbed by the president's action "because he thought we had some deep laid plot to undermine the British Empire in these areas." Although there was some underlying justification for Churchill's uneasiness, he need not have worried on this occasion. The meetings with Farouk and Haile Selassie were largely ceremonial and the talk with Ibn Saud dealt exclusively with Arab opposition to Zionism. Roosevelt listened with apparent fascination as the colorful chieftain told of his determination to end Jewish immigration. "I gained the impression," wrote Hopkins, "that the President was overly impressed by what Ibn Saud said."[16] This seems to have been the case, for back in the United States Roosevelt remarked to Congress on March 1 that "I learned more about the problem, the Moslem problem, the Jewish problem, by talking with Ibn Saud for five minutes than I could have learned in exchange of two or three dozen letters."[17] The remark was typical Roosevelt flippancy, but it sounded ominous to Zionist ears.

One month later Roosevelt was dead. Meanwhile, as the Allies occupied defeated Germany, the full story of the gas chambers, crematoria, and extermination camps was revealed to the world. The knowledge had been available before 1945, but American leaders and the American people had refused really to believe something so horrible. President Harry S. Truman reacted in a compassionate way. The surviving remnant should be immediately admitted to Palestine, he said. In Palestine the British confronted a wave of terrorism by Zionist militants (one of whose young leaders was Menachem Begin). In August 1945, Prime Minister Clement Attlee (who had succeeded Churchill after the Labour party's victory in the July 1945 elections) suggested to Truman

[16] Robert E. Sherwood, *Roosevelt and Hopkins: An Intimate History* (New York: Harper, 1948), pp. 871–872.

[17] Quoted by Kirk, *The Middle East in the War*, p. 327.

that an Anglo-American committee of inquiry be sent to Palestine. The president agreed but did not waver from his pro-Zionist convictions. When the state of Israel, after three more years of bloodshed and turmoil, declared its independence in 1948, the United States was the first country to extend diplomatic recognition. The Zionist dream was fulfilled, thanks in considerable measure to American support. But conflict between Jew and Arab remained a primary cause of instability in the Middle East.

Turkey was the only Middle Eastern country fortunate and skillful enough to maintain more than nominal independence during the war; it was also the only country of the region in which the United States and Great Britain did not suspect each other's motives. There was some friendly Anglo-American rivalry for diplomatic prestige and occasional disagreement over methods, but since neither country could impose its will on Turkey, they cooperated quite well through four years of delicate and highly involved diplomacy.

The old Ottoman Empire, defeated and discredited during the First World War, disappeared in 1918. Kemal Ataturk, a brilliant political tactician, then led the country through a social, economic, and political revolution. By the time of his death in 1938, he had created in Turkey the rudiments of a stable and promising state. Ataturk's lieutenants, who governed during the war, sought to protect that achievement and to maintain Turkey's independence regardless of which side won the great struggle raging around its borders. The Turks pursued this goal by exploiting the bargaining power of the country's strategic location as the bridge between Europe and the Middle East, its control of the Dardanelles waterway between the Mediterranean and the Black Sea, its economic resources, and its rugged (although poorly equipped) army. Masters of calculated vacillation, the Turks teetered between Axis and Allies and won favors from both before finally declaring war against Germany in February 1945, just in time to receive an invitation to the United Nations conference in San Francisco. These tactics infuriated British and American diplomats but compelled a grudging admiration.

In the first years of the war, Turkey balanced a nonaggression treaty with the Soviet Union (1925) and a defensive alliance with Britain (1939) against a nonaggression pact with Germany (1941) and received lend-lease aid from the United States. Neither side could afford to provide the massive amounts of weapons Turkey would demand for entering the war and neither could afford the damage it could inflict as an enemy. Thus, through 1942, both sides paid for its neutrality by supplying some arms, economic aid, and high prices for Turkish products. Early in 1943 Churchill, enraptured by his perennial vision of a great campaign in the eastern Mediterranean and the Balkans, decided the time had come to bring Turkey into the war. Roosevelt at Casablanca told the prime minister to "play the hand" and see what he could do.[18] Churchill went to see President Ismet Inonu in Turkey in January 1943 and was momentarily beguiled into thinking he had succeeded in his mission—although Inonu seems to have used the Churchill talks as a lever to get better treatment from Germany.

British, American, and Russian leaders agreed at the end of 1943 to ask Turkey again to enter the war. The request, culminating in a Roosevelt-Churchill-Inonu meeting in Cairo in December, failed because the Turks were able to exploit small differences in attitude between the United States and Great Britain. Roosevelt, shifting from the position he had taken at Casablanca, now wanted to assert his primacy in diplomacy with Turkey. His instinctive method was to hint that the United States was more sensitive than Britain to Turkey's needs. Turkey's position was that it was eager to go to war provided the Allies could protect it from German attack. It then made exorbitant demands for equipment and air cover. American military planners, dubious of Turkey's usefulness as a belligerent and dogmatically opposed to Churchill's eastern strategy, were unwilling to divert resources from the buildup for the cross-Channel invasion. Meanwhile, Germany, informed of every Allied move by a spy in the British embassy in Ankara, applied successful counterpressure.

As the date for the invasion of France approached, Turkey was still neutral. It was also still receiving aid from both sides and was supplying Germany with chrome, a material vital for the

[18]Winston S. Churchill, *The Hinge of Fate* (Boston: Houghton Mifflin, 1950), p. 699.

production of armament steel. At last Britain and the United States decided they could afford to get tough. Military aid was curtailed and Turkey was threatened with a blockade if it refused to end the chrome shipments to Germany. Turkey complied. The success of the cross-Channel invasion then removed all doubt as to which side would win. In August 1944 Turkey broke diplomatic relations with the Axis and in February 1945 declared war on Germany.

But in March 1945 the Soviet Union denounced the 1925 non-aggression treaty and gave every indication that it now regarded Turkey, in the words of the American ambassador in Ankara, "in much the same light as it does Poland, Rumania, and Bulgaria."[19] In June Moscow presented terms for a new treaty that, if accepted, would indeed turn Turkey into a Soviet dependency. The stage was thus set for one of the early crises of the Cold War. Turkey was a bridge in more ways than one.[20]

ᏻᎧᏻ

The United States began its wartime diplomacy in the Middle East with the simple theory that opposition to imperialism would help defeat the Axis, enlarge American access to oil, and ensure lasting peace. By 1945 the Axis threat was gone and British and French imperial power had been radically reduced, but the region was as explosively insecure as it had been on the day of Pearl Harbor. By 1945 it was clear to most American leaders, if not quite yet to the public, that the Middle East — like the world as a whole — was too full of contradictions and uncertainty for diplomacy by slogan. It was also clear that the war could not have been won without an abundant supply of oil. Those whose job it was to think about American security and the growth of the American economy knew that the Middle East was one region from which the United States would not readily retreat.

---

[19]Quoted by Rubin, *The Great Powers in the Middle East*, (1980), p. 193.

[20]For more detail, see Edward Weisband, *Turkish Foreign Policy: Small State Diplomacy and Great Power Politics* (Princeton, N.J.: Princeton University Press, 1973).

CHAPTER 7

The Future of Germany

Until 1944 military necessity gave orders to diplomacy. American leaders concentrated on those things which they believed would hasten victory; they had relatively little time to think deeply about the shape of the postwar world. They used the leverage of lend-lease aid to the British to win a grudging commitment to a postwar world with low tariff barriers, and they espoused a generalized devotion to a world security organization to take the place of the League of Nations. But as long as Nazi Germany held the continent of Europe from the Russian plain to the English Channel, President Roosevelt considered it premature to make detailed plans. He rested optimistically with untested assumptions about the peace that would emerge after Hitler's ruthless day was done. The peaceable cooperation of the "four policemen" would suppress war. The world would become increasingly democratic and all nations would cooperate politically and economically.

The climax of this optimism came, it will be recalled, late in 1943 when Roosevelt, Churchill, and Stalin met for the first time at Teheran. In the glow of military success, the Big Three put aside their earlier squabbles over strategy and amiably looked ahead. Prime Minister Churchill felt some uneasiness over how the Soviet Union would behave once the Red Army rolled into central Europe, but the president appeared to have few qualms. The tide of victory had not yet surged far enough to put his happy assumptions about Soviet-Western cooperation to the test. But with the successful cross-Channel landing in France in June 1944 and the simultaneous Russian advance through Poland, diplomacy entered a new phase. Soon the Allies would be on German soil.

116

GERMANY IN DEFEAT

Victory was almost at hand. The time had come to give specific substance to vague hopes. What should be done with the vanquished enemy and with the surrounding belt of liberated states?

Americans agreed that all traces of the Nazi regime must be eliminated from the country and that Germany must be deprived of the power to wage aggressive war. They could not agree, however, on the means to these ends or on the relationship that ought to exist between Germany and the rest of Europe. Nor could they agree on the role the United States or the Soviet Union would play in maintaining the peace. So profound was the disagreement within the American government that the United States as late as the Yalta conference of February 1945 was still without a consistent, thoroughly reasoned program for Germany. Thus, it became necessary in the hectic, final days of the war to accept a cluster of improvised arrangements — which were the source of discord for decades to come.

How one approached the treatment of Germany was related to fundamental, often unconscious, assumptions about the causes of the Second World War in particular and all war in general, and thus of assumptions concerning how war in the future could be prevented. President Roosevelt's assumptions were clear and simplistic: Germans by their national character were warlike. Germany caused the war. If Germans were punished and the country was permanently weakened through dismemberment, disarmament, and economic controls, then there would be peace. Roosevelt yielded to no one in his readiness to punish Nazi leaders, but he believed all Germans shared responsibility for the regime.

Although no American leaders would exonerate Germany of guilt, few were as simplistic as the president. Secretary of State Hull, for example, believed that the primary causes of war were economic: restrictive trade policies that choked trade, caused unemployment, made people vulnerable to the appeal of totalitarian leaders, and aggravated international tension into armed conflict. Peace, therefore, depended not so much on what happened to Germany in isolation but on the creation of a liberal international economy into which Germany would be integrated.

A third view, embryonic in the United States until after the war, attributed war to a collapse of the balance of power. During the war this view was more British, and specifically Churchillian, than American. It held that Germany's population, resources, and geographic position were essential elements in the postwar world. If they were not organized under Western auspices, they would be organized by the Soviet Union — with disastrous results. In time the second and third attitudes became reinforcing as the Soviet Union came to be perceived as the obstacle to a liberal economic system and thus as a potential cause of war. Most American leaders during the war showed a mixture of attitudes, shifting according to time and circumstances from an emphasis on revenge to a call for reconstruction. Most, with the exception of Roosevelt, believed that the future of Germany was inseparable from all other aspects of the peace including, above all, the nature of relations with the Soviet Union.

Although Americans differed profoundly in their visions of Germany's future, the United States government was absolutely steadfast on one crucial point: a refusal to deal with anti-Hitler Germans who hoped to overthrow the führer and negotiate a peace with the West as a means of saving Germany from Communist influence. Stalin's suspicions in this regard were unfounded. At no time did the United States contemplate a separate peace. The German officers who in desperation attempted to assassinate Hitler on July 20, 1944, hoped they could save Germany in this manner. Hitler survived and put the plotters to death. Even had they killed Hitler, they would have been unsuccessful. The Russians condemned them as reactionaries who were striving to salvage German capitalism and militarism,[1] and it seems unlikely that Roosevelt would have jeopardized his hopes for amicable relations with the Soviet Union by dealing with them. His and Churchill's insistence on "unconditional surrender" was sincere, not a cover for betrayal.

At Teheran in November 1943, President Roosevelt had casually outlined his personal scheme for drastic dismemberment of Germany and had supported Stalin's opposition to Churchill's moderation. Nothing was decided at Teheran, although the newly created European Advisory Commission (EAC) was assigned the task of working out details for the forthcoming tripartite occupation of Germany. Within a year the EAC had drafted an instrument of surrender, marked out zones of occupation for the three powers, and recommended the establishment of an Allied Control Council to exercise overall supervision while national commanders retained supreme authority in the separate zones. Other matters, including the crucial issue of dismemberment, remained undecided. Meanwhile in Washington, three departments — State, War, and Treasury — were competing for the decisive voice in the formulation of American policy toward Germany. Roosevelt remained aloof from the internal debate while passionately held differences produced intense conflict among his advisers.

Officers of the State Department believed that the primary responsibility for advising the president on German policy was theirs. By late 1943 the department had reached the moderate conclusions that it maintained throughout the war. An important memorandum of September 23, 1943, for example, argued that

---

[1] Vojtech Mastny, *Russia's Road to the Cold War* (New York: Columbia University Press, 1979), p. 165.

Germany should be granted a tolerable standard of living and an opportunity for economic recovery. Forced partition was folly, for it would create a lasting grievance and thus might lead to new threats of war. The nation should remain unified but under a decentralized federal government. A healing peace would leave a minimum of bitterness and would contribute to the reconstruction of Europe as a whole. The army, preparing for occupation duty, reached similar moderate conclusions. The spirit of the army's draft "Handbook for Military Government in Germany," completed in the spring of 1944, was sympathetic to reform rather than vengeful punishment. Germany was to retain its centralized administration and much of its industry, which was essential to the well-being of the European and indirectly to the American economy. After a short period of occupation, American troops would withdraw and Germany, denazified and demilitarized, could govern itself. This early planning was calm, humane, and constructive—assuming that an economically revived and unified Germany would not again threaten European security. It was designed to create stable conditions and minimize the burden of occupation duty for the American army. German civilian officials, except for a few of high rank who were indelibly tainted with nazism, were to remain on their jobs. But the army handbook suffered from two fatal flaws: it was out of tune with public opinion inflamed by reports of Nazi atrocities and it did not enjoy the support of the president.

The man who compelled the president to turn his attention to German policy was Secretary of the Treasury Henry Morgenthau, Jr. Conscious that finance was the fuel of wartime foreign policy, Morgenthau and a corps of energetic assistants had steadily expanded the Treasury's role in foreign affairs at the expense of the State Department, a fact keenly resented by Secretary of State Cordell Hull. Morgenthau, friend and neighbor to Roosevelt at Hyde Park, also enjoyed more personal influence with the president than any other member of the cabinet. Thus, when he decided to intervene on the German question, the secretary of the treasury's impact was startling and immediate.[2]

---

[2]For the secretary of the treasury's wide-ranging foreign policy interests, see John M. Blum, *From the Morgenthau Diaries*, vol. 3: *Years of War, 1941–1945* (Boston: Houghton Mifflin, 1967).

During the summer of 1944, while the president postponed consideration of German policy, Morgenthau and his assistants took critical note of the trend of thinking in the State and War Departments. They were particularly appalled by the army's draft handbook. On a flying trip to Europe in August, Morgenthau conferred with General Eisenhower and Ambassador John G. Winant, the American representative on the EAC, and then returned to Washington determined to force a showdown. He showed the offending handbook to Roosevelt and argued that unless the direction of American planning was radically changed, Germany would emerge from the war with its power to commit aggression intact. The president agreed. "It is of the utmost importance that every person in Germany should realize that this time Germany is a defeated nation," Roosevelt said in a scolding memorandum for Secretary of War Henry L. Stimson. And to Morgenthau he remarked: "We have got to be tough with Germany and I mean the German people, not just the Nazis. You either have to castrate the German people or you have got to treat them in such a manner so that they just can't go on reproducing people who want to continue the way they have in the past."[3] These comments reflected the widely held belief that one cause of the Second World War was the German sense that they had been betrayed, not beaten, into an unfair peace in 1918–19, and a second belief, more popular in the day of Theodore than Franklin Roosevelt, that nations behave according to innate national character. Wolves eat meat; Germans make war. Roosevelt added that he did not want the German people to starve, "but . . . if they need food to keep body and soul together beyond what they have, they should be fed three times a day with soup from Army soup kitchens . . . they will remember that experience all their lives."[4]

Morgenthau, heartened by the president's support, carried on his fight in a special cabinet committee on Germany consisting of himself, Hull, and Stimson. The detailed Treasury plans, as they unfolded in September, ran parallel to the extreme suggestions put forward by Roosevelt and Stalin at Teheran. Germany should be required to pay heavy reparations in kind and through forced

[3]Quoted by Warren F. Kimball, *Swords or Ploughshares? The Morgenthau Plan for Defeated Nazi Germany* (New York: Lippincott, 1976), p. 96.

[4]Cordell Hull, *The Memoirs of Cordell Hull*, vol. 2 (New York: Macmillan, 1948), p. 1603.

labor but not through long-term production (which would be possible only if German industry were rebuilt). Large slices of territory should be distributed among Germany's neighbors: the area north of the Kiel Canal to Denmark; the Saar and much of the Rhineland to France; East Prussia and southern Silesia to Russia and Poland. The remaining core should be partitioned into two weak, rural states and an industrial sector under international control which

> should not only be stripped of all presently existing industries but so weakened and controlled that it cannot in the foreseeable future become an industrial area — all industrial plants and equipment not destroyed by military action shall either be completely dismantled or removed from the area or completely destroyed, all equipment should be removed from the mines and the mines shall be thoroughly wrecked.[5]

Stimson, Hull, and their assistants considered that the Treasury's ideas were dangerous folly. Such treatment, they argued, would require permanent military occupation of Germany in order to hold down a sullen and hate-filled populace. More important, it would do enormous damage to the economy of Europe as a whole, which could not function without German industry. As Stimson observed:

> This war more than any previous war has caused gigantic destruction. The need for the recuperative benefits of productivity is more evident now than ever before throughout the world. Not to speak of Germany at all or even of her satellites, our allies in Europe will feel the need of the benefit of such productivity if it should be destroyed.

Recovery must come quickly, he added, "to avoid dangerous convulsions in Europe."[6] The secretary of war was here touching a theme that would, after 1945, become a fundamental tenet of American European policy — that economic suffering was a breeding ground for totalitarianism; therefore, if a stable and prosperous European economy, with Germany at its core, were not reestablished, Soviet communism was likely to spread. His

---

[5] Ibid., p. 1605. After his resignation from the cabinet in 1945, Morgenthau published a description of his "plan" in *Germany Is Our Problem* (New York: Harper, 1945).

[6] Henry L. Stimson and McGeorge Bundy, *On Active Service in Peace and War* (New York: Harper, 1948), p. 572.

implicit assumption was that wars are caused not by particular warlike nations but by social instability and totalitarianism.

Stimson, deeply disturbed by the ascendancy of the Morgenthau program, went to Roosevelt to plead for moderation. The interview, on the eve of the president's departure for the second Quebec conference with Churchill, filled the secretary with despair. His diary tells the story:

> I have been much troubled by the President's physical condition. He was distinctly not himself Saturday. He had a cold and seemed tired out. I rather fear for the effects of this hard conference upon him. I am particularly troubled . . . that he is going up there without any real preparation for the solution of the underlying and fundamental problem of how to treat Germany. . . . I hope the British have brought better trained men with them than we are likely to have to meet them.[7]

Roosevelt took no one to Quebec specifically to advise on German policy. Stimson remained in Washington. So did Secretary of State Hull, whose nonparticipation was rationalized by the fact of poor health. Suddenly, as the conference opened, Roosevelt sent for Morgenthau.

The secretary of the treasury flew to Quebec and plunged immediately into separate but tacitly connected discussions with Churchill on the treatment of Germany and postwar American aid to Britain. At first the prime minister resisted Morgenthau's drastic proposals for Germany. He said he had no intention of seeing Britain chained to a dead body. Morgenthau, however, tried to tempt the prime minister with the vision of British export trade booming thanks to the elimination of German competition. Whether or not Morgenthau influenced Churchill with this neomercantilism, the prime minister was gratified by the accord signed on September 15, 1944, by which the United States tentatively agreed to supply Britain with $6.5 billion in postwar aid. On the same day Churchill dictated a short memorandum incorporating and even strengthening the essence of what soon became known as the Morgenthau plan. "This programme for eliminating the war-making industries in the Ruhr and in the Saar," concluded the memorandum, "is looking forward to converting Germany into a country primarily agricultural and pastoral in character."

[7] Ibid., p. 575.

Churchill and Roosevelt then initialed their agreement: "O.K. F.D.R. W.S.C. 15/9."[8] Morgenthau later denied that he and Churchill had bargained American aid to Britain for British support for his drastic plan. Technically, there was no bargain, and yet it is hard to conceive of one agreement having been reached without the other.

Morgenthau's triumph at Quebec marked only the first round in the battle over German policy. Back in Washington, Hull and Stimson prepared the counterattack. At the same time the Morgenthau plan, whose substance had been leaked to the press, was receiving far more public criticism than approval. In Germany the Nazi propaganda machine found itself with a highly exploitable issue. The German people were told that the Morgenthau plan was a "satanic plan of annihilation" inspired by Jews; it revealed the meaning of "unconditional surrender"; Germany had no alternative but to fight to the death.[9] Roosevelt, sensitive to the need to avoid controversy on the eve of the presidential election, began to waver. He wrote to Hull on September 29 that "no one wants to make Germany a wholly agricultural nation again, and yet somebody down the line has handed this out to the press. I wish we could catch and chastise him."[10] To Stimson the president admitted that he had signed the Quebec memorandum without much thought and that he now believed that "Henry Morgenthau pulled a boner."[11] Characteristically, the president decided that the best way out of an embarrassing situation was postponement. "I dislike making detailed plans for a country which we do not yet occupy," he wrote to Hull on October 20.[12]

Thus, as the second Big Three meeting, arranged for Yalta in the Crimea, grew near, American policy was still in flux. Preliminary agreement, however, had been reached on the zones of Ger-

[8]Ibid., p. 577. See U.S. Department of State, *Foreign Relations of the United States, The Conference at Quebec, 1944* (Washington, D.C.: U.S. Government Printing Office, 1972), pp. 323–361, for extensive documentation.

[9]Forrest C. Pogue, *The Supreme Command* (Washington, D.C.: U.S. Government Printing Office, 1954), p. 342.

[10]*Foreign Relations, The Conferences at Malta and Yalta, 1945* (Washington, D.C.: U.S. Government Printing Office, 1955), p. 155. Hereafter *Foreign Relations, Yalta.*

[11]Stimson and Bundy, *On Active Service*, p. 581.

[12]*Foreign Relations, Yalta*, p. 158.

many that the three powers would occupy. Initially, the British proposed that Russia occupy eastern Germany, Britain the northwest, and the United States the southwest. All agreed on the Russian zone, but Roosevelt refused to have American troops in the southwest, a region dependent on lines of communication through France. The president was obsessed with the idea that France after the war would be convulsed by revolution, and he feared that American troops in southwest Germany might be trapped. He wanted the American zone in the northwest, with direct lines of communication and escape through North Sea ports. He assumed, and said repeatedly, that the American people would not tolerate the presence of American troops in Europe for more than two years after Germany's surrender. He wanted withdrawal of those troops to be as easy as possible, unencumbered by European political turmoil. Postwar France was Britain's problem, he said, and the United States was determined to keep hands off. Roosevelt's vague apprehensions were well expressed in a bantering telegram he sent to Churchill on February 29, 1944:

> "Do please don't" ask me to keep any American forces in France. I just cannot do it! I would have to bring them all back home. As I suggested before, I denounce and protest the paternity of Belgium, France, and Italy. You really ought to bring up and discipline your own children. In view of the fact that they may be your bulwark in future days, you should at least pay for the schooling now![13]

The British pointed out that American armies were advancing toward Germany on the southern flank with the British on the north. Chaos would result from any attempt to switch places for the occupation. They also argued that France after the war would be a strong and stable partner, not a victim of revolution. A compromise was worked out. The United States took the southwestern zone plus an enclave enclosing the ports of Bremen and Bremerhaven in the northwest and a written guarantee of transit rights across the British zone.

In 1943 Roosevelt told the Joint Chiefs of Staff that "the United States should have Berlin," and the War Department had dutifully sketched out a huge American zone stretching to and including the German capital. But such a pretension could not be

---

[13] Quoted by William M. Franklin, "Zonal Boundaries and Access to Berlin," *World Politics*, 16 (October 1963): 1–31, at p. 19.

maintained, and during 1944 the three powers agreed that Berlin, 110 miles within the Russian zone, would be divided into sectors of occupation as a microcosm of Germany as a whole. The question of a Russian guarantee of access rights from the west into Berlin was deferred on the theory that arrangements could be made more easily when Germany was actually in Allied hands. After Germany's surrender, such an agreement was worked out easily enough with Marshal Georgi Zhukov, the commander of Soviet forces in Germany.

By the end of 1944, an increasing number of American officials were beginning to argue that the United States was too trusting of the Russians, too wedded to optimistic assumptions about postwar cooperation. They were moved to these conclusions primarily by the harsh and even brutal way the Soviets were imposing their will and political system on Poland (see Chapter 8). The time has come, said these dissenters, to face the fact that the Russians intend to take whatever they can get and regard American acquiescence as weakness. While giving lip service to such ideals as democracy and self-determination, the Soviet government would use every means at its disposal to dominate as much of Europe as possible. One of the most articulate spokesmen for this position was Averell Harriman—whom, ironically, Roosevelt had sent as ambassador to Moscow in late 1943 as someone sympathetic to the Soviet Union in place of the too critical Admiral Standley. Soviet behavior had changed Harriman's mind. "It is particularly noteworthy," he wrote, "that no practical distinction seems to be made [by Russia] . . . between members of the United Nations whose territory is liberated by Soviet troops and ex-enemy countries which have been occupied."[14] Harriman was thinking especially of Poland.

Harriman and others argued that it was imperative for the United States to have a realistic understanding of Soviet intentions and to bargain accordingly. It was foolish to give and give and never ask. "In all cases where our assistance does not contribute to the winning of the war," suggested the head of the American military mission in Moscow, "we should insist on a quid pro quo. . . . When our proposals for collaboration are unanswered after a reasonable time, we should act as we think best and inform

[14] *Foreign Relations, Yalta*, p. 450.

them of our action."[15] President Roosevelt, however, showed little outward sign of heeding such advice, and as a result filled some Americans with a sense of angry desperation. For example, Secretary of the Navy James Forrestal, perhaps the most extreme ideological anticommunist in the cabinet, wrote in September 1944 to a friend that

> whenever any American suggests that we act in accordance with the needs of our own security he is apt to be called a god-damned fascist or imperialist, while if Uncle Joe suggests that he needs the Baltic Provinces, half of Poland, all of Bessarabia and access to the Mediterranean, all hands agree that he is a fine, frank, candid and generally delightful fellow who is very easy to deal with because he is so explicit in what he wants.[16]

This unresolved difference of opinion in regard to Russia had a direct bearing on American policy toward Germany. One attitude suggested that Roosevelt at Yalta should go down the line in supporting Stalin's views on Germany and thereby ensure Soviet trust and cooperation. The other attitude suggested that Roosevelt should move warily, listen carefully to what Churchill had to say, and use American economic power as an inducement to make the Soviets behave in a reasonable fashion. Those who took the first attitude stressed the importance of the permanent destruction of Germany as a factor in European politics. They were not worried over the prospect of Russian military power in Europe because they believed it was possible to influence the Russians to work cooperatively for a lasting peace. Those who held to the second attitude argued for preservation of German economic strength as the nucleus of a reconstructed Europe strong enough to resist Soviet expansion. The president, as he prepared to leave for Yalta after his inauguration to a fourth term, had retreated from the extreme position of the Morgenthau plan but was far from ready to shape policy toward Germany in terms of opposition to Russia.

Prime Minister Churchill was deep in gloom on the eve of Yalta. "This may well be a fateful conference," he wrote to Roosevelt in January 1945, "coming at a moment when the great allies are so divided and the shadow of the war lengthens out before us.

[15] Ibid., p. 449.

[16] Walter Millis, ed., *The Forrestal Diaries* (New York: Viking, 1951), p. 14.

At the present time I think the end of this war may well prove to be more disappointing than the last."[17] British military planners advocated a strategic spear thrust by fast compact units across northern Germany to Berlin. This idea, with its strong political implications in relation to Russia, was rejected in favor of General Eisenhower's preference for a measured advance on a broad front — a strategy that risked no unnecessary lives (the ferocious German counterattack at the Battle of the Bulge in December had made Eisenhower wary). Eisenhower would have changed his strategy if Roosevelt had told him that it was politically important to get to Berlin before the Russians, but this the president was unwilling to do. Why, indeed, should there be a race to Berlin, since the occupation zones had been drawn and agreed?

Roosevelt and Churchill were letting history determine their opinions while simultaneously urging one another to lead his country in an escape from the past. Roosevelt, fearing a repetition of 1919–20, when President Wilson had been repudiated by a nation retreating into political isolation, was sure that public opinion would prevent him from committing American troops to postwar duty in Europe. He did not deny that American withdrawal would leave Russia dominant on the Continent, especially if Germany were reduced to permanent impotence, but he hoped that Russian cooperation would make Soviet power an asset rather than a threat to American security and world peace. He was not certain that these pleasant things would happen, but he saw no practical alternative to proceeding in ways most likely to bring them about. Churchill, wedded to the British tradition of opposing the domination of Europe by any single power, thought that Roosevelt's readiness to trust Russia was unrealistic. If Western values were to survive, the prime minister maintained, the United States would have to abandon its historical isolation and take on permanent responsibility for the balance of power in Europe in partnership with Great Britain. Roosevelt avoided direct argument with Churchill on this issue, but his most trusted advisers developed the American rebuttal that British reliance on the balance of power would lead to more war. They believed Britain must abandon its historical tradition and put its trust in a world security organization based on full cooperation among the four

[17] *Foreign Relations, Yalta*, p. 31.

great powers. As the president and the prime minister flew in their separate planes over the Black Sea to Yalta on February 3, 1945, neither was ready to accept the other's point of view; each was preparing to argue for that program for postwar Germany which best suited his concept of what the future held in store, particularly the future of Soviet-Western relations.

President Roosevelt was a dying man at Yalta. Photographs and the testimony of those who were there bear witness to his haggard, shrunken appearance. His once strong face was flabby and dark with fatigue. His broad shoulders drooped beneath the folds of his cape. Historians and medical authorities disagree over whether the power of the president's mind had also declined in the months since Teheran. But Roosevelt had never delighted in arduous intellectual combat or prolonged attention to detail, and he now seemed more reluctant than ever to engage in argument. Impatient and weary, he seemed eager to patch together quick agreements and hasten the conference to its end. What impact, if any, the president's health had on the results of the conference is a controversial question. Some of his defenders deny that his mind had lost its edge. The president knew exactly what he was doing, they say, and served the interests of his country well by negotiating the best agreements that could be obtained under the circumstances; where satisfactory agreements could not be obtained, he astutely arranged for decisions to be postponed. Some critics, on the other hand, charge that Stalin scored a great diplomatic victory over the noncommunist world because Roosevelt was too ill and too naive to resist. Such accusations are hard to sustain, because on a variety of issues the president's lack of physical and mental energy led him to accept Churchill's position rather than Stalin's.[18]

As an introduction to the discussion of the German question, Roosevelt said he hoped Stalin would repeat the toast offered at Teheran to the execution of 50,000 officers of the German Army. "I am more bloodthirsty in regard to Germans than I was a year ago," the president said. "Everyone is more bloodthirsty now," Stalin replied, "for the Germans are savages who seem to hate the

---

[18]Diane Shaver Clemens, *Yalta* (New York: Oxford University Press, 1970), analyzes the conference negotiations in terms of traditional bargaining and compromise in which neither side won or lost.

creative work of human beings with a sadistic hatred."[19] The president agreed. The next day in plenary session Stalin, doubtless believing that he enjoyed the president's support, pressed for an immediate decision in favor of the dismemberment of Germany. Churchill, who had always looked on dismemberment with misgiving, played for time. Before a decision is made, said Churchill, there must be "elaborate searchings by experienced statesmen on the historical, political, economic and sociological aspects of the problem and prolonged study by a subcommittee." We need not go into details now, answered Stalin, but we can reach a decision. No, said Churchill, there must be further study.

Roosevelt showed signs of impatience at the lengthy remarks of Churchill and Stalin. "I still think the division of Germany into five states or seven states is a good idea," the president said. "Or less," interjected Churchill, before launching into what appeared to be another long speech. At this point Secretary of State Edward R. Stettinius, Jr., who had replaced Hull after the 1944 elections, passed a note to the president. "We can readily agree to referring this [to] the 1st meeting of Foreign Ministers," it said. The president was grateful for the suggestion. Let us ask the foreign ministers to report on "the best method for the study of plans to dismember Germany," he said.[20] This was done.

Stettinius showed a greater readiness to support the British position in the meetings of foreign ministers than did Roosevelt in the plenary sessions. The result was a compromise formula by which the three Allies agreed to take such steps "including the complete dismemberment of Germany as *they deem requisite for future peace and security.*"[21] The word "dismemberment" was included to meet the Russian demand and Roosevelt's own strong personal preference, but the qualifying phrase, here given in italics, meant that no one was committed to anything. A committee was established in London to study procedure. Thus, British wishes were met. President Roosevelt seemed to favor a decision on dismemberment, but the stubborn resistance of the British stood in the way. A weary president took the road marked "post-

---

[19] *Foreign Relations, Yalta*, p. 571. I have altered the indirect form of the minutes to first-person discourse.

[20] Ibid., p. 614.

[21] Ibid., p. 978; italics added.

ponement," thus avoiding open disagreement. Possibly if his health and energy had allowed, he would have made a greater effort to fight through to a decision — with results that would have been even less satisfactory to the West.

The president's weariness may also have been a significant factor in his acquiescence in the French demand for a zone of occupation in Germany. At Teheran, it will be recalled, Roosevelt had spoken of France with unmitigated contempt. France, he believed at that time, had forfeited the right to a position of postwar power, should be deprived of its colonies, and should be prevented from rearming for the foreseeable future. But since Teheran, France had been liberated and General de Gaulle had confounded Roosevelt's expectations by winning the support of an overwhelming majority of the French people. During most of 1944 Roosevelt, unreasonably influenced by his personal antipathy to de Gaulle, had refused to extend formal recognition to the general as head of the provisional government of France. The president persisted in his belief that recognition of de Gaulle by the United States would abet a plot to fasten a dictatorship on the French people and would thereby hasten the revolution which was to engulf the country after the war. At the same time the president suspected that Churchill's interest in seeing France restored as a military power was part of the prime minister's misguided infatuation with the discredited principle of the European balance of power. Events finally forced the president's hand. General Eisenhower, as supreme Allied commander, had to deal with someone in the civil administration of liberated France. De Gaulle had the authority and the organization; there was no one else with whom Eisenhower could work. Belatedly, in October 1944, the United States recognized what it could no longer deny: de Gaulle, for the time being at least, was the government of France.

De Gaulle, indignant that recognition had come so late, pressed on with that unrelenting devotion to the single ideal of the glory of France which became so familiar in later decades. He demanded and gained membership for France in the European Advisory Commission (EAC), insisted on being invited to the next Big Three conference (but was not), and declared that France must have its zone of occupation in Germany. In December 1944 he made an independent approach to Stalin — much to British and American consternation. The result was a Soviet-French treaty of mutual assistance. De Gaulle gained the prestige he desired and successfully refused the price asked by Stalin: recognition by France of the Lublin government in Poland, a Soviet puppet. Churchill, meanwhile, was encouraging de Gaulle's aspirations — not because he found the general a comfortable ally (indeed, Churchill once quipped that of all the crosses he had to bear, the most burdensome was the cross of Lorraine) but because the impending departure of American power from Europe made the reconstruction of France a necessity.

Roosevelt was not happy with de Gaulle's success, but by the autumn of 1944 there was little he could do to stem it. After Hull's departure from the cabinet, he had no adviser who shared his deep anti-French prejudices. On the contrary, a State Department "briefing book" memorandum prepared for his guidance at Yalta declared that the United States ought to help France regain its strength and influence in the interests of winning the war and preserving the peace. "It is likewise in the interest of this Government to treat France in all respects on the basis of her potential power and influence rather than on the basis of her present strength."[22] Worn down by the weight of advice at home and constant pleading from Churchill, Roosevelt, in January 1945, decided to support the French bid for a zone of occupation in Germany. At Yalta, Stalin resisted the idea of a French zone and French membership on the Control Council for Germany, but he finally agreed after having won concessions in other areas. The French zone, shaped like an hourglass in the valley of the Rhine, was carved from the original American and to a lesser extent the British zones. France also gained a sector in Berlin.

Reparations took up much time at Yalta and touched the heart of the different ideas held by the three powers concerning Germany's future. Here the Russians seized the initiative by demanding that Germany be stripped of $20 billion worth of reparations, with half going to the Soviet Union. Reparations would take the form of heavy industrial equipment (the Russians suggested that 80 percent of Germany's machinery ought to be removed), commodities, and forced labor — payments in kind rather than in currency. Removal of capital goods would take place during the first two years; payments from production would last for ten years.

²²Ibid., p. 300.

Here was a Morgenthau plan with a vengeance, justified on the grounds of the terrible damage inflicted by Germany on the Soviet Union. Roosevelt was sympathetic to the Russian position. The British would have none of it. They recalled the poisonous impact of the reparations tangle after the First World War. No single issue had been so bungled or had contributed so much to the economic and political chaos leading to renewed war. The British would have preferred no reparations at all, but now they said it was impossible to fix a dollar amount and that $20 billion was outrageously high, far beyond Germany's capacity to pay and keep its population alive at the same time. The Russians disagreed.[23]

Roosevelt and his advisers had great difficulty in devising American policy. They too remembered the fiasco of reparations and war debts following the First World War, and they were determined to avoid a situation in which the United States ended up paying any part of the bill. (In the interwar period, American banks had made large loans to Germany while Germany made some reparations payments, and the Allies had made small repayments on war loans from the United States. The Germans defaulted on the loans, making the United States, in a phrase of the time, into "Uncle Sucker.") Thus, Americans wanted any assessment to be within Germany's ability to pay. But Roosevelt wanted to avoid giving the impression that the United States was ganging up with Great Britain in a callous effort to prevent the Soviet Union from gaining compensation for its grievous suffering. Again, postponement for further study was the better part of wisdom. An arrangement was made for a three-power reparations commission to sit in Moscow and take $20 billion (half for Russia) "as a basis for discussion." The British refused to be associated with any stated sum but were outvoted.

Roosevelt saw reparations from Germany as something the Soviet Union deserved. After his death, American policy shifted to a view of reparations as one of several bargaining tools — along with continued lend-lease aid and a possible reconstruction loan — by which the United States might secure Soviet cooperation on a whole range of issues. President Truman and those who advised him on reparations were tough bargainers and far less sympathetic

---

[23]See Bruce Kuklick, *American Policy and the Division of Germany: The Clash with Russia over Reparations* (Ithaca, N.Y.: Cornell University Press, 1972).

to Russia's condition than Roosevelt had been. They procrastinated deliberately on a Russian request for a reconstruction loan (never granted), manipulated lend-lease in a manner perceived as hostile by Russia, and ultimately blocked a reparations agreement for Germany as a whole in favor of allowing each occupying power to do what it wished in its own zone. This outcome shut Russia off, as intended, from access to the bulk of Germany's industrial resources, which were located in the western zones. It also contributed significantly to the economic and political division of Germany, which was to be a major cause and result of the Cold War.

The Big Three did agree "that the question of the major war criminals should be the subject of enquiry by the three Foreign Secretaries for report in due course." This led to the convening of the tribunal at Nuremberg late in 1945, at which surviving Nazi leaders (Hitler, among others, escaped trial by committing suicide) were tried, convicted, and sentenced to death or imprisonment. The Nuremberg trials and parallel trials of Japanese leaders in Tokyo have been both praised and condemned. On the one hand, they were a potentially constructive contribution to international law and the maintenance of peace by establishing the existence of punishable "crimes against humanity," by convicting leaders of conspiracy to wage aggressive war in violation of treaties, and by affirming that obedience to orders is no defense for the commission of illegal acts. On the other hand, they were an example of "victors' justice." The Russians, for example, sat in judgment but were not themselves subject to scrutiny for any crimes committed under Stalin's orders.

One of the lesser agreements signed by military authorities at Yalta seemed routine at the time, but within months it would lead to tragedy. It declared that the Russians and the Western Allies would automatically return each other's nationals liberated from German prisoner of war camps. The primary Western motivation behind the agreement was to secure the prompt and efficient return of American and British prisoners. But when Germany surrendered and the exchanges began, it turned out that the Russians regarded all of their nationals in German hands as real or potential traitors. Many were executed—even in sight of the American or British liaison officers involved in the exchanges. Others were sent to Siberia. Some Russians had joined the German units fighting against the Soviet Union, but most were honest prisoners of war. This brutal and indiscriminate treatment, demonstrating such utter disdain for individual justice, was a shocking accompaniment to the celebration of victory.[24]

As Roosevelt returned from Yalta to Washington, the potential shape of postwar Europe bore slight resemblance to what he had envisioned in 1943 and 1944. The decision to refer the issue of dismemberment to the foreign ministers was, as it turned out, the end of the question. Nothing more was done. The Morgenthau plan had been tacitly renounced by Britain and the United States, although some of its flavor still lingered in the directive known as JCS (for Joint Chiefs of Staff) 1067, which was soon to be issued as a guide for American occupation policy. Dismemberment became an eventual and unintended reality of the Cold War. Assistant Secretary of War John J. McCloy, a leading architect of a moderate and constructive policy toward Germany, described JCS 1067 as "harsh enough to win Russian support and yet moderate enough to prevent total chaos."[25] More important, the directive was considered temporary. Policy could and did shift to meet changing circumstances, and throughout the spring and summer of 1945 McCloy, Stimson, and others labored to see that it shifted in the direction of moderation. Morgenthau continued to fight a rearguard action in behalf of his ideas, but without success. In July 1945, when President Truman refused to take him to the Potsdam conference, he resigned — part of the exodus of former Roosevelt advisers who retained an optimistic outlook on the possibilities of collaboration with the Soviet Union.

But even Roosevelt in his final days began to realize that policy toward Germany might have to take account of Soviet hostility. He rejected to the end the call from Churchill that a showdown with Russia be faced while the West still had the military power to reinforce its diplomatic opinions, but his confidence was shaken by the ruthless character of Russian behavior throughout eastern and central Europe. His confidence in Stalin had reached a peak at Teheran and then continued on a slightly descending plateau until Yalta, when it momentarily climbed again. In April, the month he died, he was not yet disillusioned, but neither was he as ebulliently confident as before. No one can say what course he would have followed had he lived.

---

[24]See Mark R. Elliott, *Pawns of Yalta: Soviet Refugees and the American Role in Their Repatriation* (Urbana, Ill.: University of Illinois Press, 1982).

[25]John L. Snell, *Wartime Origins of the East-West Dilemma over Germany* (New Orleans, La.: Hauser, 1959), p. 180.

CHAPTER 8

The Fate of Poland and the Collapse of the Alliance

President Roosevelt's assumptions about the possibilities of happy cooperation with Russia in the establishment of a peaceful democratic world were subjected to greater strain by Soviet behavior toward Poland than by any other issue. Poland was the first victim of Hitler's war and the immediate cause of Britain's entry into the war — but Poland was also the victim of Soviet expansion in the period (1939–41) of collusion between Hitler and Stalin. For the British and Americans, therefore, a free postwar Poland was a goal with a powerful emotional appeal.

But from the Soviet point of view, Poland was the historic avenue of invasion from the west. Thus, a "friendly" Poland was an essential requirement of Soviet national security. Furthermore, as the Soviets saw it, the territory acquired in 1939 simply returned to Russia what Poland had taken by force at the end of World War I.

Roosevelt hoped that Western and Soviet goals for Poland could be simultaneously achieved, and he made every possible concession to Soviet views. Part of the difficulty was the impossibility of reconciling staunch American opposition to a division of postwar Europe into spheres of influence — one for the West and one for the Soviet Union — and at the same time being sensitive to the Soviet Union's fears about its security. For Stalin, a Soviet sphere of influence in eastern Europe was as essential for security as a sphere of influence under the Monroe Doctrine in the Western Hemisphere was to Americans. Roosevelt failed, and so did

President Harry S. Truman in that brief interval before he decided, in anger, that Russia could no longer be trusted to honor the principles of the Atlantic Charter. The Soviets imposed a totalitarian Communist system on Poland. The fate of Poland symbolized the collapse of the dream of Allied unity and the beginning of decades of open and ominous conflict.

Until the closing months of the war, the American government wished to avoid entanglement in the bitter quarrel between Moscow and the Polish government-in-exile in London. It was folly to jeopardize victory over Germany, the chance of Russian entry into the war against Japan, and the dream of postwar unity by raising an issue that was sure to anger the Russians. Furthermore, before 1945 it was far from clear in Washington whether Russia or Poland had the stronger case. Was the Soviet demand for the Curzon boundary line, set at the Paris Peace Conference in 1919 but overthrown by the Poles, so unreasonable? And was it not fair for Moscow to insist on a "friendly" Polish government? Roosevelt was also worried that millions of Polish-Americans might vote against him in the 1944 election if a controversy over Poland erupted, and he was forced to support the Russian position in public. Finally, there was the tradition of American noninvolvement in purely European political questions. Roosevelt, underestimating the readiness of the American people to assume permanent postwar responsibility, believed it was unwise to take a position that Congress and the American people would not allow him to back up with anything stronger than words.

At Teheran at the end of 1943, Roosevelt had conveyed the impression to Stalin that he accepted Russian ideas on Poland but could not openly endorse them for domestic political reasons. Increasing evidence that Soviet intentions in Poland were a travesty of Western concepts of political freedom and self-determination did not shake the president from this stance. Polish Prime Minister Stanislaw Mikolajczyk — replacing Wladyslaw Sikorski, who had been killed in an airplane accident in July 1943 — was tireless in his efforts to win British and American support against Russia. It was a frustrating task. Churchill tried to convince Mikolajczyk that Poland should accept the Curzon line and agree to remove some of the more extreme anti-Soviet members from the London government-in-exile. The Polish leader replied that he was willing to discuss boundaries but could make no final decisions before the war was over, and he refused to allow the Soviets to dictate the membership of his cabinet. Mikolajczyk's freedom of action was, in fact, very limited by the dependence of the London government-in-exile on the underground resistance movement in Poland. Without the underground's support, the exiled politicians could not hope to return to power in Poland at war's end.

In June 1944 Mikolajczyk, after being put off several times, received an invitation to visit Roosevelt in Washington. The president was his usual affable self and characteristically implied that the United States was a more reliable friend to Poland than was Britain. Mikolajczyk left Washington in improved spirits but without a shred of substantive support. He did not really expect the United States to back Poland in a showdown with the Soviet Union, but he had no other place to turn for help.

Meanwhile, the Red Army had advanced beyond the Curzon line and was nearing the outskirts of Warsaw. The Soviet government, having broken diplomatic relations with the Polish government in London in the spring of 1943 because of the controversy over the Katyn forest massacre, announced that the civil administration of liberated Poland was in the hands of the Committee of National Liberation in Lublin. The committee was composed of puppets of Moscow.

Thus, in midsummer 1944, it appeared that Moscow was bent on ignoring the London Poles altogether. Mikolajczyk — in desperation and in response to pressure from Churchill and Roosevelt — went to Moscow at the end of July in a futile effort to make peace with Stalin. At that moment the Warsaw uprising, the most heart-rending single episode of Polish-Soviet relations, began. The Polish underground inside Warsaw gave its allegiance to the government-in-exile in London but nevertheless was jubilant at the approach of the Red Army which, by July 31, was within 12 miles of the city. The underground — determined to liberate the city themselves rather than wait for the Russians and perhaps encouraged by radio broadcasts from Moscow — on that day attacked the German troops in the city. They faced German tanks, machine guns, and planes with almost no arms of their own. The Russian advance stopped while for two months the Germans annihilated the underground fighters, who happened to be potential rivals to the Lublin committee waiting safely behind Soviet lines. The Russians claimed that their long pause was justified on tactical

POLAND AFTER YALTA

grounds. That may have been true, but the delay also served to shape the political future of Poland in Russia's favor. The underground took a great risk in order to liberate the city. The Russians had the power to ensure the underground's failure, and they used it.

The leaders of the uprising sent poignant pleas for help. Stalin refused to act. The uprising, he said, is the work of criminals and irresponsible agitators. Churchill, however, persuaded a reluctant Roosevelt to join him in asking Stalin for permission to land British and American planes behind Soviet lines after dropping supplies to the freedom fighters in Warsaw. Stalin replied with a brutal refusal. "I do not see what further steps we can take at the present time," said Roosevelt to Churchill. The prime minister proposed telling Stalin the planes would come with or without permission. The president rejected this idea and invoked the need to have Soviet support against Japan. Churchill could not act without American agreement, but afterwards he wrote that he would have liked to have told Stalin, "We are sending our aeroplanes to land in your territory after delivering supplies to Warsaw. If you do not treat them properly all convoys will be stopped from this moment by us." By now time was running out in Warsaw. Frantically, Churchill continued to seek Roosevelt's support, sending three long telegrams on September 4 alone. The president, however, had been informed that the uprising was over (actually resistance continued until October 2). "There now appears to be nothing we can do," he told Churchill.[1]

∽

Some American officials were reluctant to irritate the Soviet Union over Poland because of their intense desire for Russian cooperation in laying the foundations of a postwar world security organization — the second coming of the Wilsonian vision of a league of nations. President Roosevelt himself was far from being a dedicated Wilsonian. He preferred great-power control (the "four policemen") to a new league but permitted true believers like Secretary of State Hull to orchestrate a remarkable upwelling of public and congressional support. For millions of Americans, lasting peace depended on the formation of a new, effective world organization. In September 1943 the House of Representatives passed the Fulbright resolution in favor of such an organization by 360 to 29; a similar resolution passed the Senate in November by an 85-to-5 vote. On the international level, Secretary of State Hull at Moscow in October 1943 engineered a declaration in favor of a world organization signed by the United States, the Soviet Union, Great Britain, and China. It was the greatest moment of Hull's life; the glorious and once repudiated vision of his hero, Woodrow Wilson, appeared to have been redeemed. Hull wrote:

> I was truly thrilled as I saw the signatures affixed. Now there was no longer any doubt that an international organization to keep the

---

[1] Winston S. Churchill, *Triumph and Tragedy* (Boston: Houghton Mifflin, 1953), pp. 139–144.

peace, by force if necessary, would be set up after the war. As I signed, I could not but recall my long personal battles on behalf of the old League of Nations. Now it was probable that the United States would be a member of the new security organization.[2]

The next step was a conference of the four signatories of the Moscow Declaration, to be held in the late summer of 1944 at Dumbarton Oaks, a lavish estate on the outskirts of Washington. There the general structure of the world organization — a Security Council with permanent (great-power) and rotating members and a General Assembly for all — was sketched out. All agreed that there should be a great-power veto in the Security Council, but there was an impasse over what exactly could be vetoed: decisions only or everything. Could a great power prevent a grievance against it by a smaller power — Poland against Russia or Mexico against the United States, for example — from even being discussed? That idea was repugnant to American liberal opinion. The answer, and the next step in the formation of the organization in which such hope was being invested, would await the meeting of Roosevelt, Churchill, and Stalin at Yalta. During the Cold War, Soviet use of the veto was frequently condemned by Americans, but it should be pointed out that it was Roosevelt, even more than Stalin, who insisted on this protection for the great powers and on the limitation of decisions by a majority in the world organization.

Many British diplomats and some Americans believed that enthusiasm in Washington for the potential of a world organization was excessive and was diverting attention from more pressing practical problems. George F. Kennan, then counselor of the American embassy in Moscow and later a leading historian and commentator on Soviet-American relations, warned:

> An international organization for the preservation of peace and security cannot take the place of a well-conceived and realistic foreign policy . . . and we are being . . . negligent of the interests of our people if we allow plans for an international organization to be an excuse for failing to occupy ourselves seriously and minutely with the sheer power relationships of the European peoples.[3]

---

[2] Cordell Hull, *The Memoirs of Cordell Hull*, vol. 2 (New York: Macmillan, 1948), pp. 1314–1315.

[3] Quoted by Herbert Feis, *Churchill, Roosevelt, Stalin: The War They Waged and the Peace They Sought* (Princeton, N.J.: Princeton University Press, 1957), p. 436.

Roosevelt, however, was determined to occupy himself as little as possible with those power relationships until after the election. Not so Prime Minister Churchill. Seeing that all of Poland would soon be in Soviet hands, he flew to Moscow in October 1944 in a further attempt to bring about an accommodation between Poles and Russians. Ambassador Averell Harriman stood by as an observer, not a participant, and thereby symbolized Roosevelt's detachment. Representatives of the puppet Lublin regime and Prime Minister Mikolajczyk joined in these Moscow conversations, but no progress was made. In November, Mikolajczyk, despondent over the feebleness of British and American support and under criticism from right-wing associates for having gone to Moscow, resigned. The reorganized Polish cabinet was more rigidly anti-Soviet than the old. At the beginning of 1945 the deadlock over Poland seemed more hopeless than ever. The Polish government in London refused to accept the Curzon line as a boundary and the Soviets just as adamantly refused to consider any other. On that issue the London Poles could not win, for both Churchill (publicly) and Roosevelt (privately) were supporting the Curzon line or something close to it as a fair boundary. The one chance for an independent Poland appeared to be the formation of a representative government combining members of the London group, the Lublin committee, and other leaders from inside Poland. But neither the Poles in London nor the Soviets, speaking through the Lublin committee, were willing to give a share of real power to the other side. Few Americans appreciated how slight were the chances of a satisfactory settlement.

Although Poland was the primary purpose of Churchill's trip to Moscow, he was also anxious to reach an accord with Stalin on a division of responsibility in southeastern Europe—a region where President Roosevelt had disclaimed a desire for American political involvement. Before looking at Churchill's famous "percentages" deal with Stalin, it is necessary to describe briefly the situation in each of the five countries involved.[4]

Rumania, having fought on the German side, surrendered to the Allies in September 1944. This meant surrendering to the Russians, for there were no British or American troops in Rumania—

---

[4]Geir Lundestad, *The American Non-Policy Towards Eastern Europe, 1943–1947* (New York: Humanities Press, 1975), is a useful country-by-country survey.

or in Bulgaria or Hungary. The American Joint Chiefs of Staff noted that "from the military point of view, the present Rumanian situation is analogous to the Italian situation. . . ." In political terms this meant that the United States and Great Britain had the same influence in Rumania as the Russians in Italy — that is, almost none. Some officials in the State Department lamented this fact but could do nothing about it.

Bulgaria's situation was only slightly different. During most of the war Bulgaria was at war with Great Britain and the United States but not with the Soviet Union. During 1944 the British and Americans conducted talks with Bulgarian representatives in Cairo, looking toward an armistice that would detach the country from Germany on terms more lenient than unconditional surrender. The Soviet Union seemed willing to let the Western powers take the lead in Bulgarian matters. But suddenly, in September 1944, Russia declared war on Bulgaria and sent an army across the border. In Bulgaria, a right-wing government was overthrown and replaced by a coalition in which Communists were prominent. Soon Bulgaria surrendered. The armistice negotiations took place in Moscow. Now the Russian position was as predominant as in Rumania. The United States and Great Britain accepted an accomplished fact and — in the words of an American diplomatic observer — "gave the Russians considerable reason to believe that Rumania and Bulgaria were being abandoned to their exclusive domination."[5]

Hungary was also a satellite of Germany and a particularly obnoxious one, whose government was almost as brutal in its persecution of Jews as the Nazis. Hungary was within the Soviet sphere of military operations. Although the United States took a somewhat deeper interest in the desirability of a democratic postwar government for Hungary than it did in the cases of Rumania and Bulgaria, the outcome was essentially the same. Some right-wing Hungarians approached the United States in hopes of securing American support in opposing the Soviet Union after the war. They were rebuffed. Hungary surrendered in January 1945 and the Soviet Union proceeded to dictate the nature of the country's political regime.

[5] Ibid., p. 260. See also Michael M. Boll, "U.S. Plans for a Postwar Pro-Western Bulgaria: A Little-Known Wartime Initiative in Eastern Europe," *Diplomatic History*, 7 (Spring 1983), 117–138.

Yugoslavia was a different story. The country had been attacked by the Germans in 1941 and occupied since, with a Yugoslav government-in-exile established in London under King Peter. Within Yugoslavia, two groups of partisans operated in the mountains, fighting the Germans and each other. The group led by the fiercely independent Communist Josip Broz Tito was the more powerful. The rightist group under Draga Mihailovic was supported by the government-in-exile but bore the taint of collaborating with the enemy. In 1944 the British were trying to end the Yugoslavian civil war and to persuade Tito to accept the government-in-exile. The United States agreed with this objective.[6]

Greece was also wracked by civil war. After beating off an Italian invasion in 1940, Greece was invaded and occupied by Germany while the government of King George II went into exile in Egypt. Many Greeks hoped the king would never return. He was an extreme conservative of German origin who had shown considerable sympathy for Hitler before the war. Two guerrilla forces maintained the fight against the Germans and a bloody civil war against each other. As in Yugoslavia, the left-wing group, the EAM–ELAS, had more popular support and was more powerful than its rightist foe, the EDES. When the Germans withdrew in October 1944, the British sent troops to Greece and, in bloody fighting, suppressed—for the moment—the EAM–ELAS. Communists were prominent in the leadership of the EAM–ELAS, but it would be a mistake to describe the situation in Greece as simply Communists vs. the right. It was, in fact, a complex civil war among Greeks over the kind of country they would have. The British were motivated by Greece's strategic importance in the eastern Mediterranean astride the communications lines to the Middle East. They backed the side that, regardless of its popularity among Greeks, would provide the best protection for Britain's strategic interests.[7]

Now let us return to Churchill and Stalin in Moscow. Churchill's first objective was to have a free hand in Greece. His second objective was to retain some power and influence in Yugoslavia, neighbor to both Greece and Italy. His larger plan was to divide

[6] For more details see Walter R. Robertson, *Tito, Mihailovic and the Allies, 1941–45* (New Brunswick, N.J.: Rutgers University Press, 1973).

[7] Lawrence S. Wittner, *American Intervention in Greece, 1943–1949* (New York: Columbia University Press, 1982), is a well-documented account.

Europe into spheres of influence that would enable each of the two sides—the Soviets and the British—to suppress civil war without fearing intervention by the other. This objective had to be pursued with deliberate deception, for it ran directly counter to the American insistence that spheres of influence were unacceptable, an immoral relic from an earlier and more dismal age. That Churchill was exploring this course as late as October 1944 demonstrates that his confrontational stance vs. the Soviet Union, which became so evident in the spring of 1945, was not of long standing. In the fall of 1944, Churchill was more bent on appeasing the Soviet Union than was Roosevelt.

Churchill decided that a direct appeal to Stalin for a spheres-of-influence agreement was necessary. During the previous summer he had received a disapproving response to this idea from Secretary of State Hull; but now, in Moscow, he obtained Roosevelt's vague approval—at least for a temporary agreement to cover arrangements while eastern Europe was still a theater of military operations. Accordingly, in a scene that his own memoirs have made famous, the prime minister jotted down a proposed country-by-country division of "predominance": Rumania—90 percent for Russia and 10 percent for the others; Greece—90 percent for Great Britain "(in accord with U.S.A.)" and 10 percent for Russia; Yugoslavia and Hungary—50:50 percent; Bulgaria—75 percent for Russia and 25 percent for the others. Stalin examined the paper and penciled a tic mark of approval. In Churchill's words:

> After this there was a long silence. The pencilled paper lay in the centre of the table. At length I said, "Might it not be thought rather cynical if it seemed we had disposed of these issues, so fateful to millions of people, in such an offhand manner? Let us burn the paper." "No, you keep it," said Stalin.[8]

It is a mistake to put too much importance on the precise figures in this agreement but also important not to underrate the significance of Churchill's initiative. His subsequent explanations that the arrangements were proposed as no more than temporary expedients are not convincing. The next day Soviet Foreign Min-

---

[8] Churchill, *Triumph and Tragedy*, pp. 227–229. Albert Resis, "The Churchill-Stalin Secret Percentages Agreement on the Balkans, Moscow, October, 1944," *American Historical Review*, 83 (1978): 368–387, demonstrates that Churchill was being less than candid in maintaining that he intended only a temporary arrangement.

ister V. M. Molotov tried to revise them in Russia's favor. It made no difference. The Soviet Union assumed 100 percent control wherever its troops were on the scene—Rumania, Bulgaria, and Hungary. Tito in Yugoslavia gained control of the country through his own efforts and, by 1948, while remaining Communist, had gained his independence from the Soviet Union.

Great Britain had its way in Greece and proceeded with the suppression of left-wing forces in a manner that to many Americans, conservatives and liberals alike, seemed no different than Soviet behavior in its sphere. Many suspected Churchill of intending to impose the unpopular monarchy on the Greek people against their will. President Roosevelt was privately indignant. His son Elliott recalled him saying:

> How the British can dare such a thing! The lengths to which they will go to hang on to the past! I wouldn't be surprised if Winston had simply made it clear he was backing the Greek Royalists! That would be only in character. But killing Greek guerrillas! Using British soldiers for such a job![9]

Officially the United States avoided direct criticism of the British, while letting them know the angry state of much American public opinion. The Greek government, with British support, won that round of the civil war. An armistice was signed in February 1945. But this civil war would resume in 1946, and in 1947 the United States assumed the British role of supporting a right-wing government against an insurgency. That, of course, was the occasion of the proclamation of the Truman Doctrine, a landmark in the Cold War.

Poland was not included in the Churchill-Stalin deal, although in conversation the two leaders expressed mutual dislike for the Polish exile government. Furthermore, the virtual free hand that Churchill secured to manipulate the Greek government and suppress Communists there made it difficult for him to protest against Russian intervention in Polish internal affairs. Churchill seems to have discarded his recent indignation over Soviet behavior during the Warsaw uprising.

---

[9] Quoted by John O. Iatrides, *Revolt in Athens: The Greek Communist "Second Round," 1944–1946* (Princeton, N.J.: Princeton University Press, 1972), pp. 213–214.

But Roosevelt, after his election victory. began to give more attention to Polish affairs. In November 1944 he urged Stalin to allow Poland to keep the important city of Lvov and the surrounding oil fields, although they were located on the Soviet side of the Curzon line. Stalin was unreceptive. More important than frontiers, however, was the question of how the postwar government would be formed. By free elections with a genuine choice of candidates and without intimidation of voters? Or by Soviet-style elections with a single slate of candidates and the use of terror as an ingredient in the political process? The reports that Ambassador Harriman was sending from Moscow at the end of the year were not optimistic. The Soviets, he said, appear bent on the domination of internal Polish affairs. Any Pole who would not accept Soviet policies would be conveniently branded a Fascist. In short, the Soviet concept of the terms "friendly" and "independent" as applied to Poland and other neighboring states, warned Harriman, appeared "to mean something quite different from our interpretation."[10]

At the same time it appeared that Moscow was on the verge of recognizing the Lublin committee as the government of Poland, thus further closing the door on the London government-in-exile — which was still recognized, although without enthusiasm, by the United States and Britain. Roosevelt appealed to Stalin not to recognize the Lublin committee before they had a chance to talk face to face, "which I hope will be immediately after my inauguration on January 20."[11] Stalin replied with a denunciation of alleged criminal terrorist activity by agents of the Polish government-in-exile operating in Poland. He said he had no reason to delay recognition of the Lublin committee. Roosevelt answered, in a telegram prepared for his signature by the Department of State, that he was "disturbed and deeply disappointed" by Stalin's statement but still hoped Russia would postpone recognition of a group that obviously did not represent the people of Poland.

---

[10]Telegram of December 28, 1944, U.S. Department of State, *Foreign Relations, The Conferences of Malta and Yalta, 1945* (Washington, D.C.: U.S. Government Printing Office, 1955), p. 65. Harriman's richly documented account of his wartime experience is W. Averell Harriman and Elie Abel, *Special Envoy to Churchill and Stalin, 1941–1946* (New York: Random House, 1975).

[11]*Foreign Relations, Yalta,* p. 218.

I cannot ignore the fact that up to the present only a small fraction of Poland proper west of the Curzon Line has been liberated from German tyranny, and it is therefore an unquestioned truth that the people of Poland have had no opportunity to express themselves in regard to the Lublin Committee.[12]

The president had never spoken so bluntly, but Stalin was unmoved. The Soviets recognized the Lublin committee on December 31 as the provisional government of Poland. Meanwhile, according to a report from Harriman, which was brought specially to the president's attention on January 12, 1945, the Soviets in Poland and throughout eastern Europe were

employing the wide variety of means at their disposal — occupation troops, secret police, local communist parties, labor unions, sympathetic leftist organizations, sponsored cultural societies, and economic pressure — to assure the establishment of regimes which . . . depend for their existence on groups responsive to all suggestions emanating from the Kremlin.[13]

The State Department, whose role in policy was expanding, prepared a detailed analysis of desirable objectives in Poland for the use of the American delegation at Yalta. In seeking a truly democratic and independent Poland, the department said, "We should endeavor to prevent any interim regime from being established which would exclude any major element of the population and threaten to crystallize into a permanent government before the will of the population could become manifest." Specifically, the United States should resist the growth of power by "the so-called provisional government at Lublin," which seemed to owe its existence largely to the Red Army and the NKVD (the Soviet secret police). The United States should insist on free elections under effective supervision. In regard to boundaries, the department suggested the Curzon line plus Lvov and the oil fields on the east, but it warned against the plan, proposed by Churchill and agreed upon at Teheran, to place Poland's other boundary far to the west at Germany's expense.

[12]Sent December 30, 1944; ibid., p. 224.
[13]Ibid., p. 450.

By including a large section of German territory in Poland and the probable transfer of some eight to ten million Germans, the future Polish state would in all probability be forced to depend completely on Moscow for protection against German Irredentists' demands and in fact might become a full-fledged Soviet satellite.[14]

It was one thing to describe American aims; another thing to achieve them. These State Department advisers argued that the Soviet's position could be modified only by hard bargaining, a readiness to apply pressure by withholding favors, and a willingness to do without Soviet assistance in some other areas. President Roosevelt was prepared to do none of these things. In the short term, he did not want to annoy the Soviets over an issue like Poland when his military advisers said that Russia's participation in the war against Japan was necessary to save untold thousands of American lives. Over the long term, the president believed Soviet cooperation in the postwar world to be far more important than Poland's boundaries or Stalin's actions in an area so much and so inevitably under Soviet supervision. His fear of arousing Soviet suspicions prevented him from considering sanctions in the form of a reduction or suspension of American aid. On the contrary, Secretary of the Treasury Morgenthau was urging in January 1945 that the United States offer Russia a $10 billion low-interest loan (as compared with $6 billion for which the Soviet government had asked and $6.5 billion tentatively promised to Great Britain). Rejecting the recommendation of State Department officials that economic aid to Russia should be used as a bargaining tool, Morgenthau argued that a generous "gesture on our part would reassure the Soviet Government of our determination to cooperate with them and break down any suspicions the Soviet authorities might have in regard to our future action." He also suggested to Roosevelt that the "credit to Russia would be a major step in your program to provide 60 million jobs in the post-war period."[15] Although negotiations for a loan ultimately collapsed, the secretary of the Treasury's proposal is important as an indication of the currents of thought then swirling around the president.

A strong American stand on Poland was also inhibited by the desire to commit Russia unequivocally to the world security organ-

14 Ibid., pp. 230–232.
15 Ibid., pp. 315, 321.

ization. Although the Dumbarton Oaks conference had been hailed as a success, the crucial issue of the veto and several other problems had yet to be decided. If these issues could not be solved at Yalta, there might not be a world security organization. The implicit connection between the American dream of a world organization and the problem of Soviet behavior in Poland illustrates two conflicting concepts of national security. The Russians appeared to seek security through domination of neighboring nations. Alternatively, the world organization, envisioned by American idealists, would enable all nations large and small to live without fear of attack. There would be no need for any nation to impose its will on weaker neighbors in order to build walls against potential enemies, as Russia seemed to be doing in Poland. The only way to persuade Russia to abandon its old-fashioned concepts, Americans argued, was to demonstrate that the new system could become a reality. On the other hand, direct criticism and opposition to Russian plans in Poland would confirm the Soviets in their suspicions and thus defeat the basic American purpose. This circle of precarious "ifs" was completed by Secretary of State Stettinius's fear that the American people would reject membership in the world organization, as they had done in 1919, if Russia refused to permit genuine independence for Poland.

On the question of the extent of the veto in the Security Council of the new organization, the Russians retreated from their Dumbarton Oaks position that the great powers should be able to veto everything—including discussion. They agreed somewhat ambiguously that the veto would not block simple discussion, only Council votes for action. Furthermore, no power would veto a recommendation for the peaceful settlement of a dispute to which it was a party, although it could block anything stronger than a pious call for peaceful settlement. This compromise was quite satisfactory to President Roosevelt. No more than Stalin did he want the United States to be subject to coercion arising out of a complaint of some small power. They agreed that the United Nations could work only if the great powers were unanimous.

Russia won on another, less important United Nations issue. It was granted three votes in the General Assembly (after having asked at Dumbarton Oaks for sixteen). Roosevelt considerd this unimportant, for he never intended the General Assembly to be anything more than a debating society. But, in order to protect himself against possible public outrage concerning these three votes, the president secured British and Russian agreement to support an American bid for three votes should it prove necessary. It never did. The Big Three also agreed that San Francisco would be the location for the meeting to draft the charter of the organization, that the meeting would begin on April 25, 1945, and that only those states which had declared war on Germany would be invited. Churchill's fears that the world organization would meddle with British colonialism were allayed by an agreement that trusteeship status would apply only for former League of Nations mandates, territory detached from the enemy, and areas placed voluntarily under trusteeship by the governing power. These agreements were received by the American delegation with rejoicing. Their faith in the potential of the new organization made it easier to accept compromise agreements on issues such as Poland.

The Yalta agreement on Poland was a tissue of words over a chasm of still unresolved differences. The only point firmly nailed down was the Polish-Soviet border. The boundary was drawn along the Curzon line with very slight deviations in Poland's favor. Lvov and the oil fields became Russian. The Russians pressed for a Polish-German boundary along the Oder and western Neisse rivers. Roosevelt and Churchill agreed that Poland should receive some compensation at Germany's expense, but the Oder-Neisse line was excessive. "It would be a pity," said Churchill, "to stuff the Polish goose so full of German food that it dies of indigestion."[16] It was decided to postpone decision, but the Russians went ahead anyway, deporting Germans from the disputed area and turning the territory over to Poland.

The most important and controversial aspect of the agreement on Poland dealt with the character of the new Polish government. The Russians proposed that the provisional government recognized by them (i.e., the Lublin committee) be enlarged by the addition of "some democratic leaders from Polish émigré circles" and then recognized by Britain and the United States.[17] The British and Americans objected to the word "émigré" to describe the London Poles and to the dominant position of the Lublin committee. Their preference was for a completely reorganized government

[16]Ibid., pp. 717, 725.
[17]Ibid., p. 716.

that would be truly diverse, not monolithically subservient to the Soviet Union. The Russians argued back that the government they recognized was fully representative and was already functioning; furthermore, supervised elections were an insult to Polish independence. The British and Americans, anxious for agreement, gave in. Churchill felt he could not protest too strongly, since Stalin was supporting Britain's scarcely democratic attempts to create a government in Greece suitable for British interests. The Russians won their objective: the new government was to be formed by reorganization of "the Provisional Government which is now functioning in Poland." The British and American ambassadors in Moscow were to consult with Molotov and various Poles for this purpose. The reorganized government was to be recognized by all three major powers. There would be unsupervised elections in which all "democratic and anti-Nazi parties" could participate.[18] The words were idealistic but the meaning ominous, given Stalin's opinion that most of the Poles associated with the London government-in-exile were akin to Nazis.

Roosevelt had no inclination to probe deeply into developments elsewhere in eastern Europe, although some Americans argued that the United States should be concerned about any and all violations of the principles of the Atlantic Charter. The United States at Yalta did propose that the three powers proclaim their good intentions in the form of a "Declaration on Liberated Europe." The Soviet Union and Britain agreed. By this document the three governments agreed to cooperate in helping the peoples of liberated Europe and the former Nazi satellites "to form interim governmental authorities broadly representative of all democratic elements in the population and pledged to the earliest possible establishment through free elections of governments responsive to the will of the people." The Big Three further agreed to consult each other and concluded with a rhapsodic invocation of the "principles of the Atlantic Charter."[19]

The Americans at Yalta had no desire to poke too hard at these tender words. "We really believed in our hearts that this was the dawn of a new day," said Harry Hopkins, who was at Yalta but too ill to sit at the conference table. "We were absolutely certain

[18] Ibid., p. 980.
[19] Ibid., pp. 977–978.

that we had won the first great victory of the peace—and, by 'we,' I mean all of us, the whole civilized human race."[20]

This optimism quickly began to crumble. Early in March Harriman, in Moscow, reported that the Soviets were placing obstructions in the way of calling representative Poles together to form a new government. No Westerner could tell what was happening inside Poland because Russia would not allow observers into the country. Tales of intimidation and mass political arrests, however, were plentiful. On March 13 Churchill cabled Roosevelt: "Poland has lost her frontier. Is she now to lose her freedom? . . . [W]e are in presence of a great failure and an utter breakdown of what was settled at Yalta." British strength, he said, was insufficient to move the Soviets; "combined dogged pressure" was necessary.[21] The president reacted negatively and denied that a breakdown of the Yalta agreement had occurred. Significantly, he emphasized in a cabinet meeting three days later that he was having difficulty with the British, not the Russians. "In a semi-jocular manner of speaking, he stated that the British were perfectly willing for the United States to have a war with Russia at any time and that, in his opinion, to follow the British program would be to proceed toward that end."[22]

President Roosevelt may have been preparing to alter his attitude toward Russia during the final weeks of his life, but the evidence is too fragmentary to support a firm conclusion. The president was disturbed by Stalin's unwillingness to send Foreign Minister Molotov to the approaching San Francisco conference for the founding of the world security organization. He was deeply pained by Soviet accusations of Anglo-American perfidy in the abortive negotiations for the surrender of German armies in Italy. He also admonished Stalin over Poland and admitted to Churchill on April 11 that we "shall have to consider most carefully the implications of Stalin's attitude and what is to be our next step." And yet on the day he died (April 12), the President sent Stalin a friendly message and cabled to Churchill, "I would minimise the Soviet problem as much as possible, because these problems, in one form or another,

[20] Robert E. Sherwood, *Roosevelt and Hopkins: An Intimate History* (New York: Harper, 1948), p. 870.

[21] Churchill, *Triumph and Tragedy*, p. 426.

[22] Memorandum by the assistant secretary of the navy, who attended the meeting; Walter Millis, ed., *The Forrestal Diaries* (New York: Viking, 1951), pp. 36–37

seem to arise every day, and most of them straighten out. . . ."[23]
If a new and harder attitude toward Russia was grappling with the
old assumptions within the president's mind on that soft spring
day, the old assumptions were still on top.

∾

In relation to the tasks confronting him, no man was ever less
prepared to assume the presidency than Harry S. Truman. After
an ordinary career in domestic politics and without the opportunity to be briefed by Roosevelt (who was out of the country for
much of the time between inauguration day and his death), Truman knew little more about problems of foreign policy than any
intelligent reader of the newspapers. But he was a man of blunt
courage and common sense, and he was ready to seek advice and
to make decisions. Sometimes he could be quick to the point of
rashness, but to those in the American government who had privately deplored Roosevelt's calculated ambiguity and talent for
procrastination, Truman was a refreshing contrast.[24]

During his first weeks in office, President Truman attempted
to follow the broad lines of Roosevelt's policies. He lacked both
the desire and the information to strike out in new directions. He
was encouraged by Stalin's announcement that, in tribute to
Roosevelt's memory, Molotov would attend the San Francisco
conference after all. This gesture seemed to indicate that the
Soviets truly intended to support a world organization. At the
same time, Truman and his advisers resisted, just as Roosevelt had
resisted, Churchill's pleas that Anglo-American troop dispositions
be used as levers against Russia. The chance to capture Berlin
before the Russians did was passed by. Also, American troops
waited for several days near Prague, capital of Czechoslovakia, so
that Soviet troops might occupy the city. And then, after the German surrender, troops under Eisenhower's command were quickly
withdrawn westward to the original lines of zonal demarcation.

By relinquishing a belt of German territory up to 100 miles in
depth, the United States was meeting its obligations with scru-

---

[23] Churchill, *Triumph and Tragedy*, pp. 439, 454.

[24] An excellent introduction is Robert J. Donovan, *Conflict and Crisis: The Presidency of Harry S. Truman, 1945–1948* (New York: Norton, 1977).

pulous care. Churchill, however, was downcast. He argued that
the West should hold every possible acre on the grounds that the
Soviets had already violated their obligations in Poland as well as
in every other eastern European country under their control. The
Russians were drawing "an iron curtain" across the continent,
Churchill warned on May 12, and it was imperative to save as
much of Europe as possible before American armies were withdrawn.[25] In the eyes of most of Truman's advisers, Churchill's recommendation was wrongheaded and dangerous. If followed it
would destroy all hopes for cooperation with Russia, hopes now
associated with the cherished memory of President Roosevelt.

Meanwhile, President Truman accumulated information and
began to form his own conclusions. The Polish question above all
else caused him to doubt the possibility of easy cooperation with
Russia. He was not ready to force a showdown, for his military
advisers said Russia's entry into the war against Japan was still a
necessity; but when Molotov passed through Washington on his
way to San Francisco, the president gave the Soviet foreign minister a stern lecture on Russian misbehavior in Poland. "I have
never been talked to like that in my life," said Molotov, according
to Truman's account. "Carry out your agreements and you won't
get talked to like that," Truman replied.[26] The president's natural
inclination was to be as tough with the Soviets as they were with
him. Where Roosevelt had muffled disagreement, Truman bel-
ligerently welcomed confrontation. In this he was supported by
Churchill and at home by Secretary of the Navy Forrestal. But he
decided to suspend judgment until he had a chance to meet
Churchill and Stalin.

Events immediately preceding the last wartime Big Three
conference, held in the Berlin suburb of Potsdam in July 1945,
seemed for the moment to support the validity of the old Rooseveltian assumptions and to discredit the Churchillian alternative.
In preparation for this meeting, Truman sent two special emis-
saries to confer with Churchill and Stalin respectively during the
final week of May. Joseph E. Davies, famed for his uncritical enthusiasm for the Soviet Union, went to London; and Harry Hopkins,

[25] Churchill, *Triumph and Tragedy*, pp. 572–574.
[26] Harry S. Truman, *Memoirs*, vol. 1: *Year of Decisions* (Garden City, N.Y.:
Doubleday, 1955), p. 82.

near death and performing his last overseas mission, went to Moscow. Davies berated Churchill for harboring unwarranted suspicions of Russia. "Are you willing to declare," Davies asked, "that you and Britain were wrong in not supporting Hitler who expressed a similar determination to oppose Russia?" Churchill showed admirable self-control while listening to this tirade, but Davies told Truman that the prime minister "was basically more concerned over preserving England's position in Europe than in preserving Peace." This attitude, said Davies, "could and does undoubtedly account for much of the aggressiveness and so-called unilateral action on the part of the Soviets since Yalta."[27]

At that moment Hopkins, who was in general agreement with Davies's analysis and whose illness since the Teheran conference had insulated him from the full impact of Soviet hostility, was in Moscow conducting amiable conversations with Stalin. His purpose was to convince the Soviet leader that the United States was opposed to Churchill's anti-Russian policies but at the same time was disturbed by the increasing difficulty of reaching agreement with the Soviets on a variety of issues. Specifically, Hopkins succeeded in ending yet another impasse which had developed at the San Francisco conference over the precise nature of the veto in the Security Council of the new world organization. This made it possible for the Charter of the United Nations to be signed on June 25, 1945. The charter, said Truman to the delegates in San Francisco, "is a solid structure upon which we can build a better world. . . . Between the victory in Europe and the final victory in Japan, in this most destructive of all wars, you have won a victory against war itself."[28]

Hopkins also reached agreement with Stalin on which Poles, in addition to the Lublin group, would be invited to Moscow to create the reorganized government envisioned at Yalta. This agreement led to the establishment of the Provisional Polish Government of National Unity on June 28. Two-thirds of this government consisted of Lublin Poles, but Mikolajczyk was second deputy prime minister. Within a week the London government-in-exile was disbanded and diplomatic recognition was extended to the new government by the United States and Britain.

[27] U.S. Department of State, *Foreign Relations, Conference of Berlin (Potsdam),* vol. 2 (Washington, D.C.: U.S. Government Printing Office, 1960), pp. 73, 77.

[28] Truman, *Memoirs,* vol. 1, p. 289.

Thus matters stood on July 7 when President Truman boarded a cruiser for his trip to Europe and the Potsdam conference. Now that Germany was defeated, the United Nations established, and the Polish question quiet for the moment, his thoughts were dominated by two questions concerning Asia. First, how soon and by what methods would Japan be defeated? Second, would Russia cooperate in the establishment of a unified China under the leadership of Chiang Kai-shek?

CHAPTER 9

The Atomic Bomb, Japan, and Russia

On August 6, 1945, Hiroshima was annihilated by an atomic bomb dropped from an American B-29. The Soviet Union declared war on Japan August 8. A second bomb destroyed Nagasaki August 9. The next day the Japanese government offered to surrender and on August 14 accepted American terms.

Even as they rejoiced that the war was over, all thoughtful people trembled in the presence of victory's awful companion: the knowledge that the United States had perfected and demonstrated humanity's capacity to destroy the world. In after years the American conscience has been plagued by this cataclysmic deed. Was it necessary? Did responsible leaders consider the consequences of the act and give adequate thought to withholding the bomb or demonstrating its power to Japan before it was used against human populations? And were the Japanese merely the helpless victims — while the real target, in terms of an intimidating message to be conveyed, was the Soviet Union? The answers to these questions depend on one's opinion of the ability of leaders, in times of stress, to transcend old ways of thinking, incomplete information, overloaded administrative machinery, and the momentum of a program rushing toward climax. They also depend on one's conclusions concerning the nature of the general conflict and specifically the nuclear arms race between the United States and the Soviet Union — a subject beyond the scope of this book.

What can be said with assurance is that the men who decided to drop the bombs acted conscientiously and with a sense of responsibility according to their own standards. The decision was tragic, but there seemed no other reasonable choice at the time.

The first circumstance was that the secrecy, uncertainty, timing, and revolutionary character of the atomic project prevented the American government from thinking in a sustained way about the bomb's potential as a factor in diplomatic and military calculations until the last three months of the war, and even then the calculations were sporadic and poorly coordinated. Knowledge of the bomb, notwithstanding the enormous size and number of installations required for its development, was restricted to a handful of scientists and a very small number of military and political leaders. For example, Admiral William D. Leahy, the president's personal chief of staff, did not learn of the bomb until September 1944. Commenting then as an expert on explosives, he said he doubted the thing would work. The secretary of state was not told the secret until January 1945, and until the day of Hiroshima so few people were aware of the bomb that it was impossible to use the knowledge of the new weapon at the lower and intermediate levels, where detailed military and political plans are made. Furthermore, even those scientists who were confident of the theoretical soundness of the bomb were not sure the device would explode under combat conditions. It seemed wise to make calculations as if no bomb existed. If it worked, so much the better.

Timing also inhibited thorough high-level consideration of the bomb's implications. The first firm forecasts that an operational bomb would be ready in August 1945 were not made by the scientists until December 1944. From December until his death in April 1945, President Roosevelt was too occupied with the closing stages of the war in Europe and the myriad political problems with Russia to give more than occasional thought to the meaning of the bomb. Harry Truman knew nothing of the bomb before he became president, and the problems competing for his attention were, if anything, more numerous and complex than those that Roosevelt had faced. Both presidents understood on the verbal level that an explosive a thousand times more destructive than anything in existence was being prepared. But in a war where thousand-bomber raids had already turned cities to infernos and where tens of millions had died, the political imagination could not comprehend the problem humanity was about to confront. For example, the British bombing of Dresden, Germany, in July 1943 started firestorms that consumed 300,000 buildings and killed over 100,000 people. The American "conventional" incendiary

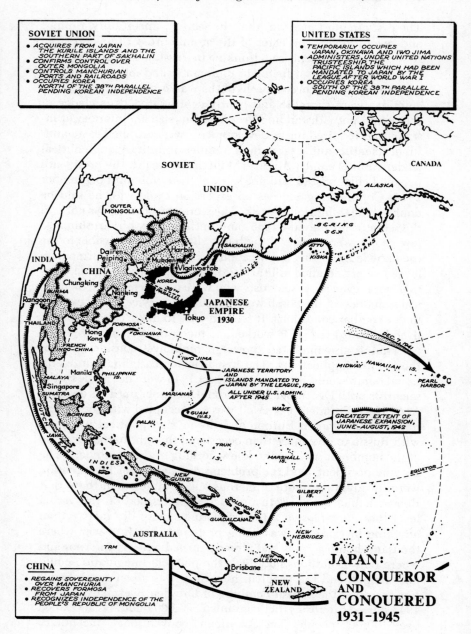

SOVIET UNION
- ACQUIRES FROM JAPAN THE KURILE ISLANDS AND THE SOUTHERN PART OF SAKHALIN
- CONFIRMS CONTROL OVER OUTER MONGOLIA
- CONTROLS MANCHURIAN PORTS AND RAILROADS
- OCCUPIES KOREA NORTH OF THE 38TH PARALLEL PENDING KOREAN INDEPENDENCE

UNITED STATES
- TEMPORARILY OCCUPIES JAPAN, OKINAWA AND IWO JIMA
- ADMINISTERS, UNDER UNITED NATIONS TRUSTEESHIP, THE PACIFIC ISLANDS WHICH HAD BEEN MANDATED TO JAPAN BY THE LEAGUE AFTER WORLD WAR I
- OCCUPIES KOREA SOUTH OF THE 38TH PARALLEL PENDING KOREAN INDEPENDENCE

CHINA
- REGAINS SOVEREIGNTY OVER MANCHURIA
- RECOVERS FORMOSA FROM JAPAN
- RECOGNIZES INDEPENDENCE OF THE PEOPLE'S REPUBLIC OF MONGOLIA

JAPAN:
CONQUEROR
AND
CONQUERED
1931–1945

bombs dropped on Tokyo in March 1945 burned over 17 square miles and killed 84,000.

Scientists who did comprehend could communicate words but not true understanding to their military and political superiors. It should be added that even the scientists persistently underestimated the bomb's explosive power although not its potential for future development. The December 1944 estimates envisioned a device equal to 500 tons of TNT (equal to only twenty-five of the very biggest conventional bombs used during the war). The bolder guessers increased this to 5,000 tons on the eve of the first test at Alamogordo, but this estimate was vastly exceeded in actuality. The Hiroshima bomb was equal to 20,000 tons of TNT. More important, the scientists vastly underrated the dangers of radioactivity. One estimate on the eve of Hiroshima was that the radioactive danger zone would extend less than a mile from the point of explosion.

Also, one must not underrate the influence of sheer momentum. Tens of thousands of people and $2 billion had been devoted to the largest scientific project in the world's history, undertaken to win a war. Germany, the rival in the first atomic arms race, had surrendered before the bombs were ready, but Japan was still fighting and taking American lives. American leaders could not easily contemplate refraining from using a weapon developed at such cost and capable, as they correctly believed, of shortening the war.

German physicists in the 1930s published papers pointing to the theoretical probability of atomic explosives. Albert Einstein, living as a refugee in the United States, warned President Roosevelt in late 1939 and advocated an American research program. Roosevelt listened. A secret research and development program began almost immediately on a small scale and in 1942 grew rapidly into the code-named Manhattan project — with the British as junior partners and the Soviet Union deliberately excluded from participation or knowledge (although the Soviets were informed by spies of what was taking place). If some of Roosevelt's advisers had prevailed, the British also would have been excluded, lest they reap an unearned postwar advantage in the commercial uses of atomic energy from research carried out 90 percent by the United States. The urgency behind the project flowed from fear that German scientists might get there first. Fortunately for the Allies, Hitler did not give his atomic scientists adequate support, the scientists followed some false leads, and in the event did not come close to attaining a bomb. But the war with Japan was still on. Thus, the international history of the bomb has two overlapping contexts: the war in Asia and the relationship of Russia with the West.[1]

⌯

American military and political planning for the defeat of Japan initially hinged on China. But by 1944, as we have seen, early hopes that China would soon have the stability and unity necessary to perform the role of policeman for Asia were shattered. China was a military liability, not a firm base for an invasion of Japan. By 1944 also, the United States Navy had acquired a large margin of supremacy over the Japanese Navy. American amphibious forces were taking island after island in the Pacific, pushing the Japanese steadily back and closing in on the home islands, which were now coming under heavy bomber attacks from Pacific bases. In October 1944 forces led by General Douglas MacArthur retook the Philippines. The next month a new-generation heavy bomber, the B-29, began to bomb Japan from bases on the island of Saipan. China was no longer needed militarily.

Nevertheless, American military planners anticipated horrendous casualties before Japan was finally defeated. Japanese troops on outlying islands fought with suicidal ferocity and in 1945 began using the grimly effective kamikazes, planes loaded with explosives and flown in deliberate suicide collisions against American ships. Americans feared that the Japanese in the homeland might fight to the last grandmother, conceivably killing or wounding as many as a million American troops. These fears made American leaders desperately eager for a promise from Moscow that the Soviet Union would enter the war against Japan.

Stalin said Russia would declare war at a suitable time and for a price. At Yalta, in February 1945, the precise deal was struck. The Soviet Union promised to enter the war against Japan "in two or three months after Germany has surrendered," and by separate

---

[1] The scientific and administrative history of the bomb is traced in enormous detail by Richard G. Hewlett and Oscar E. Anderson in the first volume of the official history of the Atomic Energy Commission, *The New World, 1939–1946* (University Park, Pa.: Pennsylvania State University Press, 1962).

agreement the United States confirmed its promise to supply huge quantities of military equipment for Russian forces in the Far East. Stalin also expressed his "readiness to conclude with the National Government of China a pact of friendship and alliance between the U.S.S.R. and China in order to render assistance to China for the purpose of liberating China from the Japanese yoke." In the optimistic atmosphere of Yalta, where the United States took much on faith, Americans interpreted this to mean that Russia would support the Nationalists as the postwar government of China and would not back the Chinese Communists. This was good news, which seemed to increase the possibility of bringing Nationalists and Communists amicably together and thus averting civil war in China.

In return Russia was granted the objectives that Stalin had outlined at different times during the previous two years. Russia would get the Kurile Islands and then regain the southern part of Sakhalin (lost after the Russo-Japanese War of 1904–05) directly from Japan. Outer Mongolia, claimed by China as part of its territory, would remain under Russian control in the form of the nominally independent Mongolian People's Republic. Russia's "pre-eminent interests" in the principal ports and railroads of Manchuria were to be recognized and safeguarded through vaguely defined arrangements reminiscent of old-style sphere-of-influence imperialism. This impression was not weakened by the agreement's glib assurance "that China shall retain full sovereignty in Manchuria."[2]

Chiang Kai-shek was not informed of the extensive concessions that Roosevelt made to Russia at China's expense, a fact which was an egregious violation of the spirit of the Atlantic Charter and a measure of Roosevelt's loss of faith in China as a responsible great power. This "sellout" of China, when it became known, was a major indictment advanced by critics of Roosevelt's diplomacy. It cannot be defended in terms of ideals, but at the time secrecy seemed justified by the need to prevent Japan from learning of Russia's intentions of entering the war in Asia and by the conviction that no secrets were safe in Chinese hands. President Roosevelt was committed, however, to obtaining Chiang

---

[2]U.S. Department of State, *Foreign Relations, The Conferences at Malta and Yalta, 1945* (Washington, D.C.: U.S. Government Printing Office, 1955), p. 984.

Kai-shek's approval of the Russian claims, made without his knowledge, at a time designated by Stalin. This implied that the United States would support Russia in the event of Chinese unwillingness to give in. Each of the Big Three signed the accord, although Churchill did so against the advice of Foreign Secretary Eden. The prime minister later excused himself by saying that he had not participated in drawing up the agreement and that he had no wish to interfere in an area that was the primary responsibility of the United States.

No significant changes occurred in the Asian outlook in the two-month interval between the Yalta conference and President Roosevelt's death on April 12. The American military continued to say that Russian participation in the war against Japan was essential. The reports that President Truman received about Asia during his first weeks in office were conflicting but predominantly optimistic in regard to Russian intentions. Most advisers believed that the Yalta accord remained a satisfactory basis for Asian diplomacy. For example, Patrick Hurley, the American ambassador to China, visited Churchill in London and Stalin in Moscow during the week of Roosevelt's death and reported that Stalin was in agreement with the American policy of seeking the peaceful unification of the feuding Chinese factions under the leadership of Chiang Kai-shek. Hurley, however, suspected that the British hoped for a weak and disunited China in order to preserve their hold on Hong Kong and their general imperial position in Asia.

Hurley's report was confirmed six weeks later by Harry Hopkins who, it will be recalled, was sent by Truman to see Stalin in preparation for the approaching Big Three meeting. Stalin reaffirmed for Hopkins his devotion to the goal of a unified China under Chiang Kai-shek and said that he would welcome a visit from Chinese Foreign Minister T. V. Soong in order to draw up a Sino-Soviet treaty. Furthermore, he would allow representatives of the Nationalist government to enter Manchuria with the Red Army. Stalin added that "the United States must play the largest part in helping China to get on their feet; the Soviet Union would be occupied with its own internal reconstruction and Great Britain would be occupied elsewhere." He also said that the Soviet Union supported the American idea of the Open Door policy —

that is, a policy of commercial nondiscrimination of all nations in China. Hopkins was delighted.[3]

If Hurley and Hopkins were right, there was no Far Eastern problem. Russia would attack Japan in August, after amicably negotiating a treaty with the Chinese Nationalist government based on the Yalta accord. As the Japanese were rapidly expelled, representatives of the Nationalist government would assume the civil administration of China. The Communists, belittled by Stalin and lacking Soviet support, would have no choice but to accept Chiang Kai-shek's leadership. China, under American tutelage and open to American trade, would at last begin the climb toward unity, democracy, and prosperity. But this latest version of the century-old China dream was sharply challenged by some officials in Washington, most notably by Joseph C. Grew, acting secretary of state while Stettinius headed the American delegation at the San Francisco conference. Taking note of the pattern of Soviet behavior in Europe, Grew, in May 1945, predicted ominously that "the Far East will in due course be brought into the same pattern. Once Russia is in the war against Japan, then Mongolia, Manchuria, and Korea will gradually slip into Russia's orbit. . . . As soon as the San Francisco Conference is over," he urged, "our policy toward Soviet Russia should immediately stiffen, all along the line."[4]

Which brings us to the atomic bomb as an element in relations between Russia and the West. At the beginning of the vast project to develop a bomb, all concerned took it for granted that the weapon would be used if it would shorten the war and save lives. Roosevelt and Churchill promised, on August 19, 1943, at the first Quebec conference, that neither the United States nor Great Britain would use the weapon against each other, or against the enemy without the other's consent, or would give atomic information without the other's consent to any third power. From 1942 onward, however, many of the scientists on the project became

[3]U.S. Department of State, *Foreign Relations, Conference of Berlin (Potsdam)*, vol. 1 (Washington, D.C.: U.S. Government Printing Office, 1960), p. 45.

[4]Joseph C. Grew, *Turbulent Era: A Diplomatic Record of Forty Years, 1904–1945*, vol. 2 (Boston: Houghton Mifflin, 1952), p. 1446.

increasingly apprehensive over the postwar role of the new weapon. Gradually they became convinced of three axioms about atomic weapons. The first axiom was that there were no secrets; the basic scientific principles were known; no modern nation could be prevented for long from acquiring its own bomb. The second axiom was that there was no defense; atomic weapons would decisively overturn the old balance between offensive and defensive weapons in favor of the offense. The third axiom was that atomic weapons could not be controlled by the old system of balance of power and competitive international rivalry.

Certain that Russia had the scientific capability to develop the bomb within a very short time (four years after the United States was a common estimate), they foresaw a potentially catastrophic arms race unless atomic energy was placed under effective international control. The fact that Russian intelligence had gained information about the bomb, as Roosevelt knew, added credence to such predictions. The most prominent scientist to articulate this view was Niels Bohr, émigré Nobel laureate from Denmark. In 1944 Bohr approached both Churchill and Roosevelt with the urgent plea that the Soviet Union be informed of the atomic project and invited immediately to join in the creation of a system of international control. Roosevelt, as was his wont, gave Bohr the impression that he agreed. But Churchill was openly hostile, for he saw an Anglo-American monopoly as a means of containing the Soviet Union and assuring British postwar power. Churchill persuaded Roosevelt, and at Hyde Park, on September 18, 1944, they initialed one of the most important documents of the war and of the atomic age. It deserves to be quoted in full:

1. The suggestion that the world should be informed regarding Tube Alloys [code name for the project], with a view to an international agreement regarding its control and use, is not accepted. The matter should continue to be regarded as of the utmost secrecy; but when a "bomb" is finally available, it might perhaps, after mature consideration, be used against the Japanese, who should be warned that this bombardment will be repeated until they surrender.
2. Full collaboration between the United States and the British Governments in developing Tube Alloys for military and commercial purposes should continue after the defeat of Japan unless and until terminated by joint agreement.

3. Enquiries should be made regarding the activities of Professor Bohr and steps taken to ensure that he is responsible for no leaking of information, particularly to the Russians.[5]

The Hyde Park memorandum defined Roosevelt's position until his death and inhibited the pursuit of any alternative. It demonstrates that while Roosevelt hoped for postwar collaboration with the Soviet Union and was willing to make concessions to Russian interests in eastern Europe and northeast Asia, he was unwilling to go so far as to share what he realized was a weapon of revolutionary potential. Even had he been so inclined, he would have had to overcome not only Churchill's resistance but also the suspicious anti-Soviet attitude of General Leslie Groves, head of the Manhattan project.

The person whose responsibility it was to advise the president on atomic matters was Secretary of War Henry L. Stimson. Despite his age (seventy-eight in 1945) and the burden of his many duties, Stimson thought more deeply on the subject than anyone else in a position of high responsibility. Stimson was attracted by the arguments for international control but bothered by the problem of whether the Russians could be trusted as long as they remained a closed, totalitarian society. Perhaps, he mused, the offer of participation in atomic development through international control could persuade the Russians to liberalize their own society. In May 1945 Stimson convened a broad interdepartmental policy group, known as the Interim Committee, to deal with fundamental atomic issues and prepare advice for Harry Truman, the new president.

Within three months the bomb would be ready for use against Japan. At the same time, Russia, if true to the Yalta timetable, would enter the Asian war. Truman would soon meet with Stalin. A cluster of momentous, interconnected decisions could no longer be postponed. Stimson thought constantly of the problem of postwar control, but he, the president, and their closest advisers believed that the first necessity was to end the war as quickly as possible with the least loss of American life. The bomb, despite its awful implications for the future of humanity, had to be considered first as a means toward that immediate end.

[5]Quoted by Martin J. Sherwin, *A World Destroyed: The Atomic Bomb and the Grand Alliance* (New York: Knopf, 1975). This is an indispensable study.

Several times it was suggested — most articulately by a group of scientists associated with the atomic laboratory at the University of Chicago — that it was wrong to drop the bomb on Japan without giving the country warning and a chance to surrender. This recommendation was made both on immediate humanitarian grounds and in the belief that a system of international control might be jeopardized once the bomb had actually been used against human life. Several schemes for demonstrating the bomb — for example, on an uninhabited Pacific island with neutral observers — were put forward but rejected by high authority in Washington. A demonstration might not work, in which case the United States would stand convicted of a bluff. Even if it did work, there was slight assurance that the Japanese government would be moved to surrender. On the contrary, they might interpret the tactic as a sign of American war-weariness and redouble their resistance in an effort to win a negotiated peace. The only way to use the bomb, the Interim Committee agreed, was against a major industrial city with a high concentration of workers' homes. Stimson wanted to minimize the loss of civilian life, but given the bomb's destructiveness and the proximity of residential and industrial sections in Japanese cities, this was impossible. Stimson did succeed, however, in overcoming the military's taste for bombing Kyoto, Japan's most cherished cultural and religious center.

Closely related to the decision against a prior demonstration of the bomb was the issue of how, if at all, to give further definition to the meaning of unconditional surrender for Japan. Throughout the war American attitudes and policies toward Japan had been curiously divided. The general public, encouraged by government propaganda, adopted a stereotyped and very racist image of the Japanese as cruel, subhuman monsters and of Emperor Hirohito as monster in chief. Even though Hitler's regime was committing far worse atrocities, the most vehement popular wartime hatred was directed against the Japanese. The herding of Japanese-Americans in the United States into concentration camps, in blatant violation of their constitutional rights, was an aspect of this attitude. German- or Italian-Americans were not similarly treated.

Within the American government — where officials were better informed and somewhat less susceptible to comic-book imagery — there were three attitudes. Political leaders feared that any display of moderation would be unacceptable to the public and ultimately might cost votes at an election. James F. Byrnes, who became secretary of state in July 1945, is an example of those in this position. Significantly, Byrnes argued that the public would be wrathful if the atomic bomb were not used. Another group were vengeful toward Japan because they hoped that China under Chiang Kai-shek would play the leading postwar role in Asia. But as Chiang's reputation in the United States declined, so did the influence of his American advocates. The third group, in charge of specific planning and growing in influence, saw postwar Japan as an essential element in Asian stability. They were the Asian equivalent of those who opposed the Morgenthau plan for Germany.

As early as September 1943, Hugh Borton, a member of the third group and a State Department planner, argued that if "the terms of surrender . . . provide for the impoverishment of Japan and its reduction to economic impotency, permanent peace in the Pacific will be seriously threatened. Such a policy will only create an economic vacuum in the north Pacific . . . [and] make Japan the prey of powerful neighbors." Borton and his colleagues believed Japan should lose conquered territory, should accept social and political reform, but should not be enslaved. They also believed that the institution of the emperor should be retained, for, as Borton wrote, "it is likely to be one of the more stable elements of postwar Japan. As such, it may be a valuable factor in the establishment of a stable and moderate postwar government."[6]

The issue of the emperor came to symbolize the internal American conflict over how to treat Japan. Stimson and Grew, who had been American ambassador to Japan from 1931 to 1941, agreed that the emperor should stay. They believed that without an assurance on the emperor, the Japanese might find it psychologically impossible to surrender and would fight on with heavy loss of life. Even with the use of the atomic bomb and Russian entry into the war, it would then prove necessary to undertake the bloody invasion that everyone now hoped to avoid. American military planners strongly supported the proposal to let the

---

[6]Quoted by Akira Iriye, *Power and Culture: The Japanese-American War, 1941–1945* (Cambridge, Mass.: Harvard University Press, 1981) — a brilliant analysis of parallel Japanese and American patterns of thought during the war.

emperor remain. They did not relish the prospect of occupying Japan if the population were rebellious and unstable.

Secretary of State Byrnes and other officials more sensitive to their ideas about American public opinion than knowledgeable about Japan said the emperor should go. They believed that Japanese militarists might continue to exploit the throne, as they had in the past, and that the American people would rebuke any departure from the stern formula of unconditional surrender. Truman followed Byrnes — who was himself influenced by former Secretary of State Hull — on this crucial point.

When a warning, known as the Potsdam Declaration, was issued to Japan by Truman, Churchill, and Chiang Kai-shek on July 26, there was no hint that the Japanese might be allowed to retain the emperor — although they were assured freedom of speech, religion, and thought; controlled economic revival; and eventual participation in world trade. The country would be disarmed and war criminals punished, but on the whole the declaration was a moderate document, reflecting considerable, although not total, victory for those planners who understood Japan best. If Japan rejected the invitation to surrender, it would face "prompt and utter destruction." No hint was given that an atomic bomb existed.[7]

The Potsdam Declaration reached the Japanese government in the midst of an agonizing debate over whether and how to end the war. For over a year, peace sentiments had been growing among influential leaders. Former Prime Minister Fumimaro Konoe, for example, said he feared "a leftist revolution more than defeat in the war, since we can preserve and maintain the imperial household and the emperor system after defeat, but not after a revolution."[8] A cabinet change in April, bringing in Kantaro Suzuki as prime minister, was an important indication of a growing peace sentiment. But the views of diehard military leaders were still powerful in July, notwithstanding the fact that Japan's ability to continue effective resistance was at an end. Reason demanded surrender, but the apparent likelihood that the United States would abolish the monarchy was an insurmountable obstacle for the advocates of peace. Forlornly and indecisively, they

[7]For the final text of this much-revised document, see *Foreign Relations, Potsdam,* vol. 2 (1960), pp. 1474–1476.

[8]Iriye, *Power and Culture,* p. 176.

sought Russian help in bringing about conditional surrender. They received a curt rebuff from Moscow. Truman, informed by the Russians of these overtures, interpreted them as a deceitful attempt to divide Russia from the United States. Similarly, the United States refused to pursue a variety of Japanese hints that they would welcome secret talks directly with American agents.

Japanese Prime Minister Suzuki was inclined to respond favorably to the Potsdam Declaration, but he believed he needed time to strengthen his domestic political position and prepare public opinion. Thus, he told the press that "it would not be necessary to take the declaration seriously." This statement, rendered into English, appeared as meaning something like "we dismiss the declaration with contempt." Truman, therefore, was confirmed in his belief that only the atomic bomb would make Japan face reality. Would the Japanese government have surrendered before the dropping of the bomb if the Potsdam Declaration had contained a clause permitting the retention of the emperor? Probably not, if we assume that the bomb would have fallen on August 6. If we assume a double "if" — an assurance on the emperor and the patience to hold back on the bomb while the Japanese cabinet went through the final agonies of debate — it does seem probable that Japan would have surrendered before many weeks had passed, probably before the November 1 invasion date set by the American military planners.

Meanwhile, Truman at Potsdam had faced the question of how and when to tell Stalin of the new weapon. One alternative was to give the Soviets detailed advance notice of the bomb and — before the bomb was used — to take the initiative in proposing international control. Truman did not even contemplate this course, one already rejected by Roosevelt and Churchill. The other extreme was to keep silent and let the Soviet Union draw its own conclusions by observing what the bomb did to Japan. Truman selected an intermediate approach. On July 24, eight days after the Alamogordo test, he casually remarked to Stalin, after a formal session of the conference had adjourned, that the United States had a new weapon of unprecedented power. Stalin appeared unimpressed and simply replied that he hoped the United States would make good use of it against Japan.

The president's deliberate reticence reflected his rapidly ebbing patience with the Soviets in general and in particular a new distrust of Russian intentions in East Asia. Sino-Soviet treaty negotiations were stalled because Stalin was insisting on concessions going beyond what had been granted at Yalta; in effect, the Russians were demanding control of Manchuria. Truman was reluctant to see the United States become deeply involved in this Sino-Soviet quarrel, but neither was he prepared, as Roosevelt might have been, to seek Russian cooperation in one area by a show of unsolicited generosity in another. Whether or not the president lost an opportunity at Potsdam to lay the foundation of international control over atomic weapons is another of those controversial questions that can never be settled. With the Soviets behaving badly, from the American point of view, on several fronts, the time did not seem ripe for such a gesture. Furthermore, Truman wanted to wind up the conference and get back to the United States.

The Potsdam conference ended on August 2, 1945, and President Truman quickly headed home. The United States Air Force in the Pacific had orders to drop the two available bombs on Japan as soon as they could be readied. While on board ship on August 6, Truman learned of the atomic bombing of Hiroshima. By prearrangement, a short announcement in the president's name was released to the world: a bomb equivalent to more than 20,000 tons of TNT had been dropped. "It is a harnessing of the basic power of the universe." If Japan's leaders do not now surrender, he said, "they may expect a rain of ruin from the air, the like of which has never been seen on earth." The president added that he would soon recommend to Congress the establishment of a "commission to control the production and use of atomic power within the United States." He avoided a direct comment on the issue of international control, but he did promise to "give further consideration and make further recommendations to the Congress as to how atomic power can become a powerful and forceful influence towards the maintenance of world peace."[9]

The bomb set off a string of political decisions in Tokyo and Moscow. The disintegration of Japan's communications prevented the government in Tokyo of learning in detail about Hiro-

[9]Harry S. Truman, *Memoirs*, vol. 1: *Year of Decisions* (Garden City, N.Y.: Doubleday, 1955), pp. 422–423; and Herbert Feis, *Japan Subdued: The Atomic Bomb and the End of the War in the Pacific* (Princeton, N.J.: Princeton University Press, 1961), p. 111.

shima for twenty-four hours. But on August 7, Prime Minister Suzuki advised the emperor to accept the Potsdam Declaration. Military authorities, however, belittled the power of the bomb and sent an investigating team to Hiroshima. On the same day, the Sino-Soviet negotiations, stalled because of Stalin's harsh demands on China, resumed in Moscow. Quickly the Soviets decided it was time to enter the war against Japan, even though China had not yet agreed to Russia's terms. On August 8, the Japanese ambassador in Moscow was told that Russia, allegedly in response to a request from its allies, would consider itself at war on August 9. The Russian declaration of war stunned the diehards in the cabinet, but still the government in Tokyo was unable to reach a decision. The dropping of the second atomic bomb on Nagasaki on August 9 did not break the deadlock. But in the early morning hours of August 10, Emperor Hirohito accepted the unprecedented request of the peace faction that he make the decision personally. Hirohito declared that Japan must surrender, subject only to the preservation of his own sovereignty as emperor. After the cabinet agreed, the Japanese decision was conveyed via neutral Switzerland to the United States.

The Japanese message forced Truman to decide whether Japan should be allowed to retain the emperor. Stimson and Leahy said yes. Byrnes said no. Navy Secretary Forrestal suggested that the emperor be allowed to remain on the throne but that his authority be subject to the supreme commander of Allied powers, a proposal Truman approved, as did Great Britain, China, and Russia (after a short delay). On August 11, Japan was so informed. A minority, led by the war minister, urged the country to hold out for better conditions. But Emperor Hirohito, for the second time making a crucial decision personally, said that Japan would surrender on American terms. On August 14 the emperor's decision was relayed to the Allied governments and shortly thereafter broadcast in the emperor's own voice to the Japanese people. The war was over.

The atomic bombs had hastened the fulfillment of their principal purpose: victory for the United States in the Second World War. Were they also used, as some historians have charged,[10] in

---

[10]The most influential book in this "revisionist" school is Gar Alperovitz, *Atomic Diplomacy: Hiroshima and Potsdam* (New York: Vintage, 1967).

the growing conflict with the Soviet Union? The answer is a very qualified yes. It seems certain that the bombs would have been dropped on Japan even if relations with the Soviet Union were unclouded. On the other hand, the fact that the United States had the new weapon did give President Truman and Secretary of State Byrnes a momentary sense of confidence in facing the Russians. They believed intuitively that possession of the bomb would make negotiations easier, although they were in no way contemplating threatening to use the bomb or even hinting at a threat. Stalin, on his part, does not seem to have been in the least intimidated, although he did order a major development program that produced a Russian bomb in exactly four years. But it is impossible to say that the existence of the bomb caused the Soviet Union to make any concessions to the United States on any issue in the closing months of 1945.

ᢙᡂᡅ

The days following the Japanese surrender were crowded. China and Russia signed (at midnight, August 14) a set of agreements defining Russia's gains in Asia. The Chinese reluctantly gave Stalin what he sought and in return took comfort from the fact that the Russians agreed not to support the Chinese Communists against the Nationalist government. Having achieved their desires in China, the Russians, whose war against Japan had lasted for five days, sought a share equal to that of the United States in the control of occupied Japan. They were rebuffed by President Truman. Occupied Japan was placed under the sole authority of General Douglas MacArthur as commander of Allied forces. There were no zones, as in Germany. The other Allies, including Russia, subsequently enjoyed a nominal right to give advice. This meant nothing in practice. Japan was an American show, and the director was MacArthur.

China presented a greater, indeed an insoluble, problem from the American point of view. All Japanese troops within China, not including Manchuria, were directed to surrender to the Nationalist government of Chiang Kai-shek. Those in Manchuria were directed to surrender to the Russians. But Chiang lacked the transportation to carry his armies into the vast areas of northern and eastern China, where the majority of Japanese forces were located. Meanwhile, the Chinese Communists were advancing rapidly, accepting the surrender of Japanese troops, and building a large supply of captured weapons. Japanese commanders could be and were instructed to surrender only to the Nationalists, but instructions were meaningless if the Chinese Communists were on hand and the Nationalists were immobilized hundreds of miles away. Subsequently some Americans charged that the Chinese Communists would not have become a formidable force if the Soviet Union had not been invited unnecessarily into the war against Japan and were not thus in a position to help. The fact is that the Chinese Communists were already a formidable force and that they received relatively little from the Russians that they could not have achieved by their own efforts.

General Albert C. Wedemeyer, American commander in China, believed it essential for the United States to devote every possible resource in men and equipment to carrying the Nationalist troops north and eastward — ostensibly to take the Japanese surrender but really to be position to block the Chinese Communists. Wedemeyer was allocated some forces, but not enough in his view, and was told to take no action that might involve American troops in action between the Chinese Nationalists and Communists. The official American position was that the United States wanted a peaceful settlement between the Chinese factions. This policy satisfied no one. The Nationalists were unhappy because the United States did not provide more support. The Communists said the United States was not impartial because of the support it was providing to the Nationalists. The recriminating echoes of this predicament would echo for decades into the future.

The future of Korea, to which American planners had devoted almost no thought, was another problem that turned out to have serious long-term consequences. For centuries Korea had been a nominally independent kingdom and a locus of rivalry among China, Japan, and Russia. After its victory in the war with Russia in 1904–05, Japan incorporated Korea into its empire. President Roosevelt's position during the Second World War was that Korea would become independent "in due course." In the interim he would apply his panacea — trusteeship. That is about as far as American thinking went. Syngman Rhee, a right-wing Korean politician in exile, had tried during the war to win an American commitment to support him. Rhee, however, was a premature Cold Warrior who spoke more of the Communist threat than the Japanese enemy. While the war was on, the United States kept him at arm's length.

Japan's sudden surrender required some quick decisions. The United States proposed to the Soviet Union that there be two zones of temporary occupation in Korea, marked by the 38th parallel, which divided the country roughly in half. Japanese troops would surrender to the Russians north of the line and to the Americans south. The Russians agreed. The United States rushed some unprepared forces into its zone and soon found itself enmeshed in both a Korean civil war and an international struggle that prevented unification of the country and which, in 1950, erupted in the Korean War. But in 1945 none of that was anticipated.[11]

---

[11]See Bruce Cumings, ed., *Child of Conflict: Korean-American Relations, 1943–1953* (Seattle: University of Washington Press, 1983), and the essay by Cumings, "American Policy and Korean Liberation," in Frank Baldwin, ed., *Without Parallel: The American-Korean Relationship since 1945* (New York: Pantheon, 1974).

CHAPTER 10

The Legacy of Victory

The United States put first things first throughout the Second World War. No other considerations were ever permitted to interfere with or delay the victory over the Axis. In August 1945 the great achievement was complete. Hitler was dead and Germany lay powerless under Allied occupation. The emperor's wise decision to surrender meant that the landings on Japan were bloodless. Italy, ineffectual minor partner of the Axis, had withdrawn from the war two years before and, having repudiated fascism, was about to acquire a respected place among nations. Americans, virtually unaided, had beaten Japan back across the Pacific while providing the leadership and more than half the men for the attack on Hitler from the West. At the same time they had become the "arsenal of victory" and provided billions of dollars worth of arms for Britain, Russia, China, and dozens of smaller countries. American diplomacy had preserved the great coalition essential for victory, established the United Nations, and laid foundations for peace in Europe and Asia.

Victory had been achieved at an extraordinarily low cost in American lives—292,000 military dead from combat, 115,000 from other causes, virtually no civilians dead. This was a tribute to American industrial power, whereby the profligate use of weapons saved lives, and to Roosevelt's overall strategy. The Soviet Union, in contrast, lost 7 1/2 million soldiers and an estimated 12 1/2 million civilians—almost fifty times more people. Great Britain—with 30 percent of the population of the United States—lost 395,000, of whom 300,000 were in the armed services, 60,000 were civilians, and 35,000 were merchant seamen.

China's losses are impossible to estimate because of the difficulty of separating death from starvation and social disintegration from combat losses, but they ran into the millions. Enemy combat losses totaled about 6 million — more than half of which were inflicted by the Russians.

The public mood in the United States that August was one of exuberant celebration, even euphoria. But no informed American could be optimistic. There was far too much evidence that the legacy of victory was not automatic peace and prosperity for all humanity but, at best, a set of intractable problems that would require years of patient and arduous attention. At worst, the legacy could be continued suffering, unabated hatreds, and war.

The outcome appeared to depend overwhelmingly on the behavior of the two most powerful members of the wartime coalition: the United States and the Soviet Union. American leaders in 1945 were agreed that, a generation before, the United States had made a fateful mistake by repudiating the vision of Woodrow Wilson, refusing membership in the League of Nations, withdrawing from political involvement in European security affairs, following selfish economic policies that provoked retaliation and imitation from other nations, and permitting its armed forces to dwindle away. Now it appeared that the United States had a second chance to do the right things.

The second chance had three aspects. The first and most prominently discussed was the chance to create a workable world security organization in place of the League of Nations. The Charter of the United Nations had been signed at San Francisco on June 26, 1945, and would soon be approved overwhelmingly by the Senate. Perhaps American public enthusiasm for the United Nations was naive and perhaps it diverted attention from the complexity of the world's problems. Perhaps also an excessive faith in the United Nations may have contributed to subsequent disillusionment and denigration of the many useful but limited tasks that the world organization is capable of handling. Public statements by American leaders did contribute to "overselling" the UN, but in private President Truman and his advisers knew that the UN alone was no panacea.

The second aspect of the American opportunity to make amends for past mistakes was economic. The analysis went as follows: high tariff barriers and selfish economic restrictions had stultified world trade between the wars, caused massive unemployment, depressed standards of living, and prepared the way for dictators who promised to bring a better life with radical measures and an aggressive foreign policy. War was the result. Now the United States had a second chance to lead the world toward an open international economy, a sophisticated version of the traditional American belief in the "open door" of equal economic opportunity for all nations. During the war, the United States had used the leverage of lend-lease aid as a means of winning commitment, especially from Great Britain, to open-door principles and abandonment of special trading blocks and preferential tariff arrangements. Correctly anticipating that aviation would soon replace shipping as the vehicle of international passenger transportation, the United States had also insisted (at the Chicago Aviation conference of 1944) on broad access by the American airlines to the routes and airports of the world—as against Britain's preference for tight restrictions that would protect its weak competitive position.

The United States had also convened the Bretton Woods conference, at an estate in New Hampshire in July 1944, where the International Monetary Fund (IMF) and the International Bank for Reconstruction and Development (World Bank) were established. The IMF was designed to stabilize national currencies and thus encourage trade. The International Bank was designed to aid economic growth. The United States, with the largest investment in both organizations, would be able to set policy. Some critics have argued that American economic policy was a form of imperialism whose purpose was American domination and preservation of capitalism. But the Americans who devised the new system sincerely believed they were acting for the welfare of all humanity and for the prevention of future war. They did not deny that they were also acting for the benefit of American economic interests, but they would have been astonished at the suggestion that there was any conflict between what was good for the world and what was good for the United States. Like their English forebears of the mid-nineteenth century, they elevated the concept of reducing trade barriers to something akin to religious dogma and were not moved by complaints from others that a nation with a lion's share of the world's industrial production could jolly well afford to be for free trade.[1]

The final aspect of the perceived opportunity to avoid past mistakes was little discussed in public in 1945. It was the second chance to maintain a military establishment sufficient to deter and defeat aggression. President Truman and his closest advisers believed that the military weakness of the democracies, including the United States, had made possible the rise and early success of the Axis powers and had made the Second World War inevitable. They were determined that such a mistake would not be made again.[2] But in the climate of 1945, when the public and Congress were calling for the boys to come home immediately, it was not politically feasible to call for big military budgets. Some advocates of military strength complained that the United States was in fact committing the mistake of 1919 over again, engaging (in the words of Secretary of the Navy James Forrestal) in the "swift evisceration of our armed strength." But the degree of demobilization never approached previous levels. The United States retained the world's greatest industrial base, biggest navy, largest air force, and the atomic bomb. In the days before intercontinental nuclear missiles, real military power was a question of what a nation could bring to bear in six months or a year after a war began. By that measure the United States was incomparably the military master of the world in 1945 — notwithstanding the larger number of men the Soviet Union retained in uniform.

America behavior was half the story. What of the Soviet Union? Here Americans divided into two points of view, two theories concerning the sources and nature of Soviet conduct.[3] A

[1] Four important books are Lloyd C. Gardner, *Economic Aspects of New Deal Diplomacy* (Madison, Wis.: University of Wisconsin Press, 1964); Richard N. Gardner, *Sterling-Dollar Diplomacy: The Origins and Prospects of Our International Economic Order*, rev. ed. (New York: McGraw-Hill, 1969); A. E. Eckes, Jr., *A Search for Solvency: Bretton Woods and the International Monetary System, 1941 –1971* (Austin, Tex.: University of Texas Press, 1975); and Robert W. Oliver, *International Economic Cooperation and the World Bank* (London: Macmillan, 1975).

[2] This theme is explored by Michael S. Sherry, *Preparing for the Next War: American Plans for Postwar Defense, 1941–1945* (New Haven, Conn.: Yale University Press, 1977).

[3] Daniel Yergin, *Shattered Peace: The Origins of the Cold War and the National Security State* (Boston: Houghton Mifflin, 1977), describes the division between those who adhered to the "Yalta axioms" (cooperation was possible) and those who believed in the "Riga axioms" (confrontation in some form was inevitable). The "Riga axioms" are so designated by Yergin, after the capital of Latvia, where American Foreign Service watches of the Soviet Union were stationed before the opening of the Moscow embassy in 1934.

few disciples of Roosevelt still believed at war's end that the Soviet Union wanted to cooperate in the interests of peace, but was inhibited by memories of past injuries inflicted by the West. But if the United States was generous and sympathetic, the Soviets would respond. The other viewpoint, soon prominently identified with the Soviet specialist and diplomat George F. Kennan, held that the Soviet Union was expansionist by history and ideology, immune to moral appeals, ruthless and realistic in pursuing its aims. According to this view, the United States and the West should not fear bruising Soviet sensibilities but should make its own opposition to Soviet expansion unequivocal, should demand quid pro quos for every concession, and should have the patience and toughness to contend with the Soviet Union over the very long haul.

The optimistic outline dominated American press and movie depictions of the Soviet Union during the war, but it was superficial and easily abandoned once the necessity of working together to defeat Germany had passed. Americans had long feared communism and their fears remained just below the surface, ready to reappear at the first sign of difficulty with the Soviet Union. Much of the internal bureaucratic history of wartime foreign policy involves a struggle by middle-echelon officials against what they saw as Roosevelt's naivete and lack of realism. Roosevelt, however, was a fox. It is probable that he had a less benign view of the Soviet Union than his public posture indicated. His style was to appear optimistic even when he had inner doubts. One should not confuse his public statements with what he really thought — or state confidently what that secretive man really did think.

Harry Truman, in contrast, was an open, contentious leader with a parochial distrust of foreign nations. He did not like the Russians or the pattern of their behavior as he witnessed it upon assuming the presidency. Also, he turned to those middle-echelon advisers who had never accepted Roosevelt's approach and who now felt a sense of liberation and recognition from a new president who would listen to and act on their advice. At war's end, optimism was fading fast, along with its advocates: Roosevelt was dead, Harry Hopkins was dying, Secretary of the Treasury Henry Morgenthau had been purged from Truman's cabinet. The last exponent, Secretary of Commerce Henry Wallace, would linger into 1946 before he too was fired. The hard-line view was in the saddle.

Events in eastern Europe seemed to provide confirmation for the hard-liners. Behind the "iron curtain" (Churchill's phrase) the Russians were ruthlessly suppressing democracy, as it was understood in the West, and were erecting a cordon of Communist satellites: Poland, Hungary, Rumania, Bulgaria. Yugoslavia, although not a subservient satellite, was still closely tied to Moscow and a threat to peace through its territorial claims against Italy at the head of the Adriatic. Czechoslovakia was not yet under Soviet control, although some American observers were dubious of President Eduard Benes's abiliy to conciliate Moscow and remain independent.

Almost daily the United States and Britain complained that Russia was violating the Yalta agreements. Western diplomats and journalists were being denied freedom of movement and inquiry behind the iron curtain. Russia was acting unilaterally without the consultation promised at Yalta. Free elections were not being held; and (a minor complaint) American and British private property within the countries under Russian control was being confiscated. Stalin and Molotov were so unmoved by these complaints that they scarcely bothered to reply.

Germany, under four-power occupation, was already becoming a battleground of the Cold War (although the phrase itself did not emerge in common use until 1947) rather than the symbol of Allied unity that the well-intentioned had hoped it would become. President Truman at the Potsdam conference urged that Germany be treated as a single economic unit, but Anglo-American efforts to work out uniform policies with Russia came to naught. Neither side would accept true economic unification except on its own terms — a free economy or communism. In theory the occupying powers had abandoned their wartime schemes for the dismemberment of Germany, but in practice the boundary dividing the Russian from the western zones had already severed the country.

The most troublesome issue, which occupied thousands of hours of tedious wrangling, concerned reparations to be paid by Germany. The Soviet Union insisted on heavy payments. The United States remembered how disruptive the reparations issue had been after the First World War and wanted payments to be light, and to be made only after the costs of occupation as a "first charge" had been met. In other words the United States did not want to end up, in effect, paying for reparations going to the Soviet Union. The Russians, in turn, accused the United States of hostile insensitivity to Russian needs and suffering. In the end there was no comprehensive agreement on reparations. The Russians were left to do what they wished in their own zone and were denied reparations from the western zones. They also were denied the postwar loans and credits that had been discussed as a possibility while Roosevelt was alive.

There were other German problems. The Soviet Union had turned over a large area of eastern Germany to Poland in defiance of Western protests. Berlin, an enclave in the Russian zone, was divided like Germany as a whole into four zones and was the locus of increasing friction. Austria, which by agreement was to be restored as an independent country after its enforced unification with Germany under Hitler in 1938, was likewise divided into four zones of occupation (Vienna being treated in a manner similar to Berlin) and was a cause of discord rather than cooperation. But Austria's small size and lack of strategic significance left the tension lower than in Germany.

Economically, all of Europe was prostrate. The United States was supplying food for temporary relief through the United Nations Relief and Rehabilitation Administration (UNRRA) and by a variety of stopgap measures. The fact that UNRRA was an international rather than a unilateral American organization, even though the United States was bearing the major cost of its operations, caused resentment among nationalistic congressmen and would soon lead to its demise. Americans had not yet taken full measure of the depth of economic dislocation or devised a systematic response — and would not do so until the Marshall plan of 1947.

The legacy of victory was grim for Americans in Asia — except in Japan. There would be no friction between Russia and the West in Japan because the United States had figuratively told Stalin to go to hell when he asked to share the control of the occupied country. The mutual racial hatred and stereotyping expressed by the Japanese and Americans during the war disappeared almost instantly. The American occupation under the direction of General Douglas MacArthur proceeded with extraordinary good feeling and creativity, in large measure because American planners and the Japanese who were now given responsibility under the occupation shared assumptions about the reforms necessary for

the country and about the constructive role Japan would ultimately play. Japanese-American compatibility during the occupation reinforces the speculation that peace between the two
countries could and should have been achieved sooner — before
the atomic bombs were dropped.

Korea, divided into occupation zones along the 38th parallel,
was an Asian equivalent to Germany. The parallel quickly
became an economic and political barrier. The Russians established a Communist regime to the north and Americans accepted
the rise to power of a right-wing regime under Syngman Rhee to
the south. The stage was being set for civil and international war.

China presented the United States with an insoluble problem.
Few knowledgeable Americans really believed that exhortation
would turn Chiang Kai-shek into a democratic reformer, sensitive
to human rights, or bring about the peaceful unification of
Chinese Nationalists and Communists. But for a nation unwilling
to risk lives and large sums of money (of doubtful utility in any
event), exhortation was the only tactic available. It failed utterly.
In 1949 the Communists won the civil war on the mainland and
proclaimed the People's Republic of China, while Chiang Kai-
shek's Nationalist remnant retreated to Formosa (Taiwan), the
crowded island which, in accordance with the Cairo Declaration
of 1943, had been taken from Japan.

Elsewhere in Asia the Rooseveltian determination to encourage the elimination of European colonialism had faded without
producing a new policy for the colonial areas. The desire of
American military leaders to retain unqualified national control,
for strategic reasons, of islands in the Pacific was a major factor in
this retreat from idealistic anticolonialism. Thus, the United
States emerged from the war with a vast collection of what were,
in effect, Pacific island colonies, Okinawa being the largest and
most important (until it was restored to Japan in the 1970s). On
the other hand, the Philippines gained independence in 1946, in
accord with earlier promises, although the United States retained
major bases on the islands. Hong Kong was returned to British
control, notwithstanding Roosevelt's frequent suggestions that it
should be given to the Chinese. (In 1984 the British and the
People's Republic of China reached agreement on the reversion of
Hong Kong to China, which was to take place in 1997.) The British also regained control of Burma and Malaya, although both

colonies were to acquire independence within the next few years, as were the Netherlands East Indies (Indonesia). After the unsuccessful wartime intervention in British-Indian relations, the United States kept hands off India. The British Labour party moved quickly to grant the independence that had been promised, but their best efforts were unable to prevent a Moslem-Hindu bloodbath or the partition of the country. Indochina, once considered by Roosevelt for trusteeship under Chinese administration, reverted to France. The French offered the different countries of Indochina a specious autonomy within the French Union but could not prevent or win the subsequent colonial war, even with military aid from the United States. In the 1950s the United States assumed the French role — with long and painful consequences for Indochina and America.

In the Middle East the American wartime objectives of liquidating British and French colonialism had been largely achieved. But the end of colonialism did not solve deep-seated conflicts or prevent war in Palestine; anti-Western nationalism in Egypt, Syria, Iraq, and Iran; and generally an increase in Soviet prestige. The most intractable problem was the future of Palestine, including the level of Jewish immigration, the nature of a Jewish national home, and the fate of the Arab population in the area settled by Jews. President Truman supported Zionist political aspirations and a high level of immigration. The British, who still had the responsibility for the Palestine mandate, considered Truman irresponsible, since the United States appeared unwilling to shoulder the burden resulting from the inevitable clash of Zionist and Arab interests. That burden would fall to the United States soon enough, and on a seemingly permanent basis.

Over this conflict-ridden world lay the shadow of annihilation cast by the existence of nuclear weapons. In August 1945 the American government did not know how to deal with this unprecedented fact of technology, which had so suddenly changed all the old conditions in which nations sought through war and diplomacy to gain advantage over one another. Some American leaders believed that safety lay in preserving the American monopoly of nuclear weapons as long as possible — and after that holding unquestioned superiority. They were skeptical of the apocalyptic warning of scientists that there were no atomic secrets, that there was no defense, and that the old system of national rivalries, arms races, and countervailing power could not control this new force.

The existence of the atomic bomb was bonded to the course of Soviet-American relations. Although the bombs had been dropped on Japan primarily to end the war and not to intimidate the Soviet Union, after the surrender of Japan the bombs had little meaning except in relation to the Soviet Union. What should be done? Secretary of War Henry L. Stimson, about to retire after almost a half century of public service, personified American uncertainty and the conflict of views about how to deal with the Soviet Union. He told his associates that one lesson he had learned in a long life was that if you want someone to trust you, you must begin by extending trust. But would that work with the Soviet Union, a closed, totalitarian society animated by an ideology hostile to the West? Stimson thought not. Perhaps, he mused, the bomb could somehow be used to persuade the Russians to change their regime, to become open and democratic and thus a trustworthy partner. But Stimson did not see how this could be done. Actual policy as developed in late 1945 and early 1946 followed a middle course: a proposal known as the Baruch plan to preserve the American monopoly of weapons until an international authority with a capacity for the detection and punishment of violations was established. The international authority, not subject to the veto of any country, would assume control of all weapons as well as nonmilitary uses of atomic energy. The Soviet Union, detecting a scheme to keep it in a permanent position of inferiority and hard at work on its own nuclear research, rejected the Baruch plan. The nuclear arms race was under way.[4]

One of the most somber aspects of the study of history is that it suggests no sure ways by which humanity could have avoided folly. Would the postwar world have been a happier and more secure place for the United States and for all people if Roosevelt had behaved differently during the war? Possibly. It might also have been worse. Russia treated as an adversary rather than a friend might, as people feared at the time, have reached a truce with Hitler. This seems unlikely, but the possibility was there. Or Stalin might have acted with less rather than more restraint in Europe and Asia. Might-have-beens can never be proved.

[4] These events are treated by Gregg Herkin, *The Winning Weapon: The Atomic Bomb in the Cold War, 1945–1950* (New York: Knopf, 1980).

Critics of Roosevelt fall across a spectrum from political right to left. The right appeared first in print, during the early years of the Cold War.[5] They argued that Roosevelt "lost" half of Europe and China to communism. The left were most active during the years of the Vietnam war, when all the established assumptions of American foreign policy were being scrutinized.[6] Their charge was that the United States was insensitive to Russia's needs, opposed to radical movements of the left everywhere in the world, and bent on imposing an American-dominated capitalist order wherever it could. The far right and left share an implicit belief in American omnipotence. The right suggests that had the United States sought to exclude the Soviet Union from eastern Europe and to bring about a victory of Chiang Kai-shek in China, it would have succeeded. The left suggests that a cooperative, humane world would have emerged if the United States had been led by leftists less wedded to capitalism and the preservation of American economic power. Their case is not convincing. Both sets of critics imply that the United States between 1941 and 1945 ought not to have concentrated so hard on military victory but should have been maneuvering either to block the Soviet Union or in some vague way to facilitate the triumph of the forces of leftward movement around the world.

The first edition of this book, in 1965, condemned President Roosevelt for holding to stereotypes about other nations, for thinking that American approaches to political development were applicable everywhere, for assuming that the Soviets used words like "democracy" in the same sense as Americans, and for doubting that the American people would be willing to support significant overseas commitments after the war. Scholarship and documentation appearing since 1965 indicate that Roosevelt was less naive than he once seemed and that he understood the complex nature of the world better than his simplistic comments to others would suggest. He was wrong about whether the United States would undertake postwar commitments, and his indomitable public optimism may have led to some disillusionment and have

---

[5] William H. Chamberlin, *America's Second Crusade* (Chicago: Regnery, 1950), is representative.

[6] The most unrelenting of the left revisionist treatments is Gabriel Kolko, *The Politics of War: The World and United States Foreign Policy, 1943–1945* (New York: Random House, 1968).

added to the pain of learning difficult lessons about the world after 1945. And yet those who expect the worst in international affairs often get it. Was not optimism a risk worth taking?

It was right that the first and overriding American priority was victory over the Axis. Other problems could not be solved until that was achieved. Roosevelt's leadership made possible the great result, and for that he and the United States government, armed services, and people deserve high acclaim. The difficulties the United States has encountered since 1945 cannot be blamed on Roosevelt — on the contrary, they should produce an enhanced appreciation of his achievement.

Suggestions for Additional Reading

Few events in history have produced so much published writing as the Second World War. Twenty years have passed since the first edition of this book, and the number of works on the war in general and American foreign policy in particular has more than tripled. The footnotes of this book are designed to point the way to sources and studies of particular subjects. The "suggestions" offered here are highly selective. They focus on works of exceptional importance, most of which are relevant to more than one aspect of American wartime diplomacy. Additional titles can be located in that indispensable companion to the student of American diplomatic history — prepared under the auspices of the Society of Historians of American Foreign Relations — Richard D. Burns, ed., *Guide to American Foreign Relations Since 1700* (Santa Barbara, Calif.: ABC-Clio, 1983). See also the valuable ten-year bibliographies issued by the Council on Foreign Relations: Henry L. Roberts, *Foreign Affairs Bibliography: A Selected and Annotated List of Books on International Relations, 1942–1952* (New York: Harper, 1955); Henry L. Roberts, *Foreign Affairs Bibliography, 1952–1962* (New York: Harper, 1964); and Janis A. Kreslins, *Foreign Affairs Bibliography, 1962–1972* (New York: Harper, 1976). Useful for military books is Gwyn Bayliss, *Bibliographical Guide to the Two World Wars: An Annotated Survey of English-Language Reference Materials* (London: Bowker, 1977). Frank Freidel, ed., *Harvard Guide to American History*, rev. ed. (Cambridge, Mass.: Harvard University Press, 1974), is the standard bibliography for general American history.

1. GENERAL WORKS

Every student of American diplomacy during the Second World War owes a debt to Herbert Feis, whose massive *Churchill, Roosevelt, Stalin: The War They Waged and the Peace They Sought* (Princeton, N.J.: Princeton University Press, 1957), remains the best account of the interaction of the Big Three from the entry of the United States into the war until the surrender of Germany. Feis's precise narrative, focusing on heads of government, is continued in *Between War and Peace: The Potsdam Conference* (Princeton, N.J.: Princeton University Press, 1960), and *Japan Subdued: The Atomic Bomb and the End of the War in the Pacific* (Princeton, N.J.: Princeton University Press, 1961). In another volume, Feis describes *The China Tangle: The American Effort in China from Pearl Harbor to the Marshall Mission* (Princeton, N.J.: Princeton University Press, 1953). Christopher Thorne, *Allies of a Kind: The United States, Great Britain, and the War Against Japan, 1941-1945* (New York: Oxford University Press, 1978), is the single most impressive book on Second World War diplomacy published in the last twenty years. A detailed and controversial representative of the left "revisionist" studies is Gabriel Kolko, *The Politics of War: The World and United States Foreign Policy, 1943-1945* (New York: Random House, 1968). Kolko's thesis is that the United States fought primarily to uphold forces of order and suppress "forces of movement," i.e., the left. Sir Llewellyn Woodward, *History of the Second World War: British Foreign Policy in the Second World War*, 5 vols. (London: Her Majesty's Stationery Office, 1970-76), is a mine of detail, summarized in the same author's earlier single volume *British Foreign Policy in the Second World War* (London: Her Majesty's Stationery Office, 1962). Also see the superb James R. M. Butler, ed., *Grand Strategy*, 6 vols., in the British official *History of the Second World War: United Kingdom Military Series* (London: Her Majesty's Stationery Office, 1956-76). The best study of Russian foreign policy is Vojtech Mastny, *Russia's Road to the Cold War* (New York: Columbia University Press, 1979). See also Adam Ulam, *Expansion and Coexistence: Soviet Foreign Policy, 1917-1973*, 2nd ed. (New York: Holt, Rinehart & Winston, 1974).

2. SPECIAL STUDIES

Most of the special studies recommended for additional reading are listed only in the footnotes. However, among works already cited, the following deserve special mention: Akira Iriye, *Power and Culture: The Japanese-American War, 1941-45* (Cambridge, Mass.: Harvard University Press, 1981); Wm. Roger Louis, *Impe-*

rialism at Bay: The United States and the Decolonization of the British Empire, 1941–1945 (New York: Oxford University Press, 1978); and Martin J. Sherwin, *A World Destroyed: The Atomic Bomb and the Grand Alliance* (New York: Knopf, 1975). On relations with the Soviet Union, see John Lewis Gaddis, *The United States and the Origins of the Cold War, 1941–1947* (New York: Columbia University Press, 1972) — valuable, among other reasons, for its demonstration of persistent anti-Soviet feeling within the United States during the wartime alliance. Also Lynn Etheridge Davis, *The Cold War Begins: Soviet-American Conflict over Eastern Europe* (Princeton, N.J.: Princeton University Press, 1974); George C. Herring, Jr., *Aid to Russia, 1941–1946: Strategy, Diplomacy, and the Origins of the Cold War* (New York: Columbia University Press, 1977); the dated but still useful Edward J. Rozek, *Allied Wartime Diplomacy: A Pattern in Poland* (New York: Wiley, 1958); and two books by Lisle A. Rose: *After Yalta* (New York: Scribner's, 1973) and *The Coming of the American Age, 1945–1946,* vol. 1: *Dubious Victory: The United States and the End of World War II* (Kent, Ohio: Kent State University Press, 1973). On Germany, see Warren Kimball, *Swords or Plowshares?: The Morgenthau Plan for Defeated Nazi Germany* (New York: Lippincott, 1976), and Daniel J. Nelson, *Wartime Origins of the Berlin Dilemma* (University, Ala.: University of Alabama Press, 1978). On China, Tang Tsou, *America's Failure in China, 1941–1950* (Chicago: University of Chicago Press, 1963), retains value for its study of American attitudes.

3. BIOGRAPHIES, MEMOIRS, DIARIES

Robert Dallek, *Franklin D. Roosevelt and American Foreign Policy, 1932–1945* (New York: Oxford, 1979) is an essential and distinguished work. The last four volumes of Winston S. Churchill's monumental *The Second World War,* 6 vols. (Boston: Houghton Mifflin, 1948–53), cover the period of American belligerency. They are *The Grand Alliance* (1950), *Closing the Ring* (1951), *The Hinge of Fate* (1953), and *Triumph and Tragedy* (1953). Also see Lord Avon [Anthony Eden], *The Memoirs of Anthony Eden: The Reckoning* (Boston: Houghton Mifflin, 1965); David Dilks, ed., *The Diaries of Sir Alexander Cadogan* (London: Cassell, 1971); and Harold Macmillan, *The Blast of War, 1939–45* (New

York: Harper & Row, 1968) and *War Diaries: The Mediterranean, 1943-1945* (New York: St. Martins, 1984). For France see Charles de Gaulle, *War Memoirs*, 3 vols. (New York: Simon & Schuster, 1955-60).

Important books dealing with American leaders (in alphabetical order by subject) include Charles Bohlen, *Witness to History, 1929-1969* (New York: Norton, 1973); Cordell Hull, *The Memoirs of Cordell Hull*, 2 vols. (New York: Macmillan, 1948); John R. Deane, *The Strange Alliance: The Story of Our Efforts at Wartime Cooperation with Russia* (New York: Viking, 1947); Walter Millis, ed., *The Forrestal Diaries* (New York: Viking, 1951); W. Averell Harriman and Elie Abel, *Special Envoy to Churchill and Stalin, 1941-1946* (New York: Random House, 1975); Robert E. Sherwood, *Roosevelt and Hopkins: An Intimate History* (New York: Harper, 1948); George F. Kennan, *Memoirs, 1925-1950* (Boston: Little, Brown, 1967); Admiral William D. Leahy, *I Was There* (New York: Whittlesey House, 1950); Fred L. Israel, ed., *The War Diary of Breckinridge Long: Selections from the Years 1939-1944* (Lincoln, Neb.: University of Nebraska Press, 1966); John M. Blum, ed., *From the Morgenthau Diaries*, vol. 3: *Years of War, 1941-1945* (Boston: Houghton Mifflin, 1967); Robert Murphy, *Diplomat Among Warriors* (Garden City, N.Y.: Doubleday, 1964); Thomas M. Campbell and George C. Herring, Jr., eds., *The Diaries of Edward R. Stettinius, 1943-1946* (New York: New Viewpoints, 1975); Barbara W. Tuchman, *Stilwell and the American Experience in China, 1911-1945* (New York: Macmillan, 1970); Henry L. Stimson and McGeorge Bundy, *On Active Service in Peace and War* (New York: Harper, 1948); Harry S. Truman, *Memoirs*, vol. 1: *Year of Decisions* (Garden City., N.Y.: Doubleday, 1955); Robert H. Ferrell, ed., *Off the Record: The Private Papers of Harry S. Truman* (New York: Harper & Row, 1980); Arthur H. Vandenberg, Jr., ed., *The Private Papers of Senator Vandenberg* (Boston: Houghton Mifflin, 1952); and John M. Blum, ed., *The Price of Vision: The Diary of Henry A. Wallace, 1942-1946* (Boston: Houghton Mifflin, 1973).

4. DOCUMENTS

The indispensable documentary collection is the Department of State's *Foreign Relations of the United States: Diplomatic Papers*

(Washington: U.S. Government Printing Office). For the war years there are an average of six volumes per year divided by region plus special volumes in the conference series: Casablanca, Washington and Quebec, Cairo and Teheran, Malta and Yalta, Potsdam. The volumes for the Second World War have now all been published. They are accurately edited. The selection of documents is good, suffering only from the fact that under President Roosevelt not everything of importance was committed to paper. Also see Warren F. Kimball, ed., *Churchill and Roosevelt: The Complete Correspondence, 1939–1945* (Princeton, N.J.: Princeton University Press, 1984), skillfully edited and containing some material not published before.

Index

195

About the Author

Gaddis Smith is Larned Professor of History at Yale University, where he earned his B.A. and Ph.D. degrees and has taught American diplomatic and maritime history since 1961. He has also taught at Duke University, the George Washington University program at the Naval War College, and the Munson Institute of maritime history at Mystic Seaport Museum. He is the author of *Britain's Clandestine Submarines, 1914–1915* (Yale University Press), *The Aims of American Foreign Policy* (McGraw-Hill), *Dean Acheson* (Cooper Square), and of a forthcoming study of foreign policy during the presidency of Jimmy Carter (Hill and Wang). His articles and reviews have appeared in *The American Historical Review, American Heritage, The American Neptune, Foreign Affairs, The New York Times Magazine*, and other journals. He was Master of Pierson College at Yale (1972–81) and chairman of the Department of History (1979–83).

A Note on the Type

The text of this book was set on the Editwriter 7500 in a typeface called California. It belongs to the family of printing types called "modern face" by printers—a term used to mark the change in style of type letters that occurred about 1800. California borders on the general design of Scotch Modern but is more freely drawn.

Composed by Dianne Rooney Enterprises, Inc., Staten Island, New York. Printed and bound by R.R. Donnelley & Sons Company, Harrisonburg, Virginia.